Authentic Art with Children
Second Edition

Margaret Brooks

Published by Margaret Brooks

Design by BookCreate
BookCreate.com

ISBN 978-0-6454044-8-7

Printed in USA

Authentic Art
with Children

Second Edition

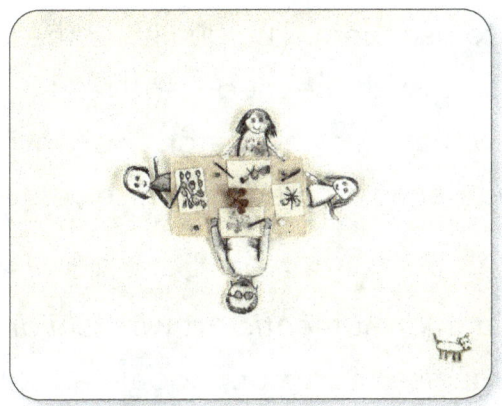

Margaret Brooks

When you give children fat brushes and thick splodgy paint you get splodgy paintings. If this is the only media children are given for art making, how can they express the delicacy of a butterfly wing or a detail of the flower on which it sits?

Young children deserve authentic, quality art media to work with. Artists choose media especially for their expressive qualities. It takes time and practice to learn how to use them. The quality of the representation rest upon the artist's familiarity with the media and repertoire of skills in their use. However, we know that many educators, not having had experience with art making and authentic art media themselves, do not feel confident doing art with children.

This is the second edition of *Authentic Art with Children*. The book has been revised and reorganised to accommodate an extra chapter and QR code access to some instructional videos. This beautifully illustrated book is a 'hands on' practical guide that aims to fill those gaps in an educator's experiences with art making. As studio practices are unpacked and demonstrated the reader is invited to join in a journey through the same kinds of exploration, experimentation, practice and processes that artists engage in.

The author is both artist and educator with over thirty years of experience and research in the arts and early childhood. She takes the reader into the studio and explains and demonstrates how many artists think and work. The reader gets to 'try on being artist'. Studio practices are then braided with socio, cultural, historical theories to develop and rich set of pedagogical practices for working with young children in the visual arts.

This companion to *Drawing to Learn* brings the theory developed there alive. It illustrates and demonstrates how the theoretical framework outlined in *Drawing to Learn* can be applied to support young children's thinking, development and meaning making. Together these two books comprise a resource for students, practitioners and researchers in early childhood that is both inspirational and practical.

About the author

Dr Margaret Brooks is an adjunct Associate Professor at the University of New England, Australia. She has been researching drawing and art for almost thirty years. Her research focuses on young children's drawing processes and the relationships between drawing and meaning making from socio cultural perspectives. She uses arts-based and visual ethnographic methods to examine the drawing processes of both children and adults. She is also a practising artist. Her most recent art work involves collaborations with artists, young children, and art museums around environmental, cultural and social issues. Her studio work focuses on drawing and installation. She believes in the power of art to facilitate 'trans-actions' between people, issues and places.

Margaret has a strong global audience and is owner and editor for the International Art and Early Childhood website and the International Art in Early Childhood Research Journal. See https://artinearlychildhood.org/. The International Art in Early Childhood Association supports a biennial conference, and more recently a virtual symposium from which is emerging a beautiful set of eBooks.

About this book

For the past years many of my early childhood student teachers have struggled with the visual arts. There is a deeply ingrained belief that they cannot draw and are no good at art. This lack of self-efficacy is compounded by the lack of a strong contemporary theoretical framework for the visual arts in early childhood. The roles and rules for doing art with young children are not congruent with current practice. In confusion and frustration teachers turn to superficial and catchy activities that often have little to with art. This book tries to address both issues, first by providing practical guides that demonstrate how to use authentic art materials and provide real artistic experiences for children. Then by threading contemporary theory throughout with a strong focus on the role of the teacher. There is even a section that teaches you how to draw.

Foreword

I am honoured to have the opportunity to write a foreword for the second edition of the book, Authentic Art with Children, by Dr Margaret Brooks. This edition of the book retains the wealth of helpful detail for teachers supporting young children's efforts in the visual arts that was noteworthy in the first edition. In addition to the first edition, Margaret has added some features that will be most helpful to teachers. The book has been revised and reorganized to accommodate an extra chapter and QR code access to some instructional videos. There are many teachers who lack confidence in their own ability as artists. In this second edition of her book Margaret has added ideas to further help teachers who need support in understanding artists' studio practices. There are practical suggestions encouraging teachers to further develop their own art and explore with the children the practices and experimentation at the heart of artistic activity.

Margaret has developed her ideas through her own experience as a classroom teacher, extensive research and many years of providing practical advice to early childhood classes and their teachers. Her book mixes personal and professional artistic anecdotes with detailed suggestions on the use of authentic art materials for both teachers and children.

This is the first book in a pair. In her second book, Drawing to Learn, Margaret presents a strong socio cultural framework for the visual arts in early childhood. This is particularly important at this time as the field is lacking a theoretical foundation that is compatible with current practices.

Margaret and I first met at the University of Alberta Child Study Centre, Canada, and have enjoyed almost thirty years of collegial collaboration around the Project Approach. Working alongside Margaret I watched the development of her ideas on the topic of 'Art with Young Children' with considerable interest. These books draw on her many years of outstanding work with children and teachers in classrooms in Canada, Australia, Bali and Bhutan. Margaret has a PhD in both Education and Fine Arts and regularly exhibits, not only solo exhibitions of her own work but also a number that incorporated art produced by children. She began her career in Scotland and then moved to Canada. She took up her current position at the University of New England, in Armidale, Australia in 2002, and subsequently developed and expanded the International Association for Art in Early Childhood. It was then that she came to realise that teachers in many countries did not understand how to effectively teach art to young children and, more importantly, were not aware of the theories that underpin modern practices.

It is exciting and timely to see such helpful and insightful books available in a second edition. Teachers will certainly appreciate the additional support in the second edition of the books Margaret Brooks has provided here to further promote progressive, thoughtful and positive art education in early childhood classrooms. It is with great pleasure and admiration that I recommend unreservedly the second edition of this book to teachers of young children everywhere.

Professor Sylvia Chard

Professor Chard is an author of the best-selling book, Engaging Children's Minds: the Project Approach. Now in its third edition.

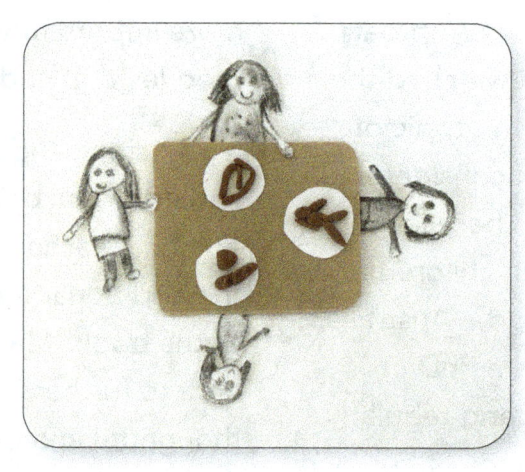

Authentic art media: practical guides

In addition to regular preschool art media, like play dough and finger paint, young children deserve to experience authentic art media like clay and charcoal and enjoy their expressive qualities. However, not all educators have experience with these unfamiliar media, and often feel ill-equipped to work with them. This book is a set of practical guides for early childhood students, student educators, educators and other adults who would like to know more about providing and supporting the use of authentic art media with young children.

Authentic art media are important because that is what real artists use, and consequently are finely tuned to their expressive qualities. Age old art media includes material like charcoal, clay and graphite. They are authentic because they offer immediate and direct feedback about the actions taken. The subtleties that are possible with these media provide for a wider range of more satisfying marks and representations. A responsive dialogue between the child and the material used is possible so that the child is supported in the pursuit of an ever increasing complexity of ideas and techniques.

Some background information about these media is provided. Basic techniques are demonstrated for the adults to try for themselves before working with children. The practicalities of how best to provide, present and support young children's exploration in each case is suggested. Examples of young children working with specific media will give you many ideas for engaging arts-based activities with children. The children's learning experience is demonstrated and the important role of the adult is discussed throughout.

Table of contents

Chapter 1

~

Drawing

I believe it is important to have some personal and embodied experience of doing art to refer to. This chapter provides you with a personal drawing experience that will give you a broader lens with which to look at children drawing.

Art practices are built upon a set of skills we need to learn and feel comfortable with. We need a certain fluency with media and techniques so that they become tools we have at our fingertips rather than barriers to overcome. We need to be aware of certain conventions and possibilities so that we have good grasp of the grammar of drawing. Drawing is a language that we need to learn and practice. Like writing, it has sets of rules we need to be aware of, even if we choose to ignore them. Drawing is simultaneously practical, cultural, cognitive, physical, investigative, and creative. It is something that can be taught.

Adults often avoid drawing. We believe we cannot draw, so we don't. So we never practice drawing and of course our drawing never improves. This confirms our belief that we cannot draw. Sometimes, even if we practice, we are confronted by the fact that our drawing looks different from the thing we are drawing or different from someone else's drawing. Of course it does! We cannot replicate reality with a pencil. Each person has a different way of seeing the world and making marks. Just because it is different does not mean it is wrong.

A closer look at the processes and thinking of artists helps us understand that art is not just about replication but rather about big ideas. It has been well documented that those who engage with the arts, and in art making, develop skills, knowledge, and dispositions that set them up for future success in all aspects of life. Elements of the practice of artists can also support many early childhood practices. Drawing is too important to ignore. It is as important as reading and writing.

There are significant cognitive benefits to drawing. When we draw what we see, we engage with the subject in a very rich way. When we engage with drawing in a meaning-making manner, we pull together our visual knowledge of the image, our kinesthetic understanding of our hand drawing the image, and our memory. In combination, this greatly increases the likelihood of a deeper understanding of that concept being drawn and allows for clearer recall later.

It has been demonstrated that drawing improves memory by promoting the integration of elaborative, pictorial, and motor codes—that is, when we are drawing, we elaborate on a word's meaning so we understand it better, we create an image rich in detail that can aid recall later, and we form the body's physical memory of making the drawing. Together these create a context-rich representation. Importantly, the simplicity of drawing to improve memory means it can be used by people with cognitive impairments to enhance memory. Preliminary findings suggest that there are measurable gains in performance in both normally aging individuals and patients with dementia (Fernandes, Wammes, and Meade 2018).

Try on "Being Artist": Drawing with Graphite

One of the best ways to get to know what artists do, and discover which elements of their practices might be relevant to early childhood today, is to do as they do and draw regularly and often. It is important to experience the arts from the inside, to try on "being artist."

I'm sure a few of you are thinking that you can't draw. You are not alone. The good news is that it is possible to learn how to draw. This section is especially designed for you. Drawing is so important for developing thinking that it is worth spending time on it. Join me in a fun, self-directed course about drawing with graphite. Graphite is a simple and core drawing media. I will guide you through a series of drawing exercises that will gradually extend your drawing skills. At the end, your knowledge, drawing skills and confidence will have greatly improved to the point where you will have the confidence to use drawing with children in all aspects of their program.

Please note that this self-directed course is only meant for adults. It is NOT suitable for children.

Working with graphite pencils

Drawing is foundational to all other visual art forms. Most children will draw before they can write. Like handwriting, each person's drawing style is unique. Young children usually love to draw and will happily spend hours drawing the world as they know it. However, school soon demands that they write instead of draw, and their fluency with drawing disappears. Soon many of them claim that they cannot draw. But really, like anything else, drawing involves practice. We learn to draw by drawing and if we draw very little then there will be no progress. No progress is disheartening, so the motivation and inclination to draw disappears and the downward spiral goes. Drawing is a very useful skill to have for everyday life. We use it to make plans, give instructions, show directions, and problem solve. To lose such a useful and important skill is quite a hindrance.

Drawing is a universal language and one that young children understand. We as educators need to be comfortable with, and knowledgeable about, drawing. Let us see what happens when you practice your drawing every day for eight weeks.

Your materials

First you need to gather your materials. You will need:

- One visual diary (A4 size); it should have a spiral binding so you can fold the pages back easily as shown here to create a flat working surface.

- A set of eight graphite pencils (2H, HB, B, B2, B3, B4, B5, B6) and a container to protect them.

- A white eraser for graphite; if the eraser is not white it will leave a mark on your page.

- A pencil sharpener; I like the two-hole, double blades, shavings-catcher kind.

Now let's explore your drawing equipment and get to know what it can do. We will begin with pencils. First, let's look at how we hold our pencil to draw. Our pencil grip needs to be

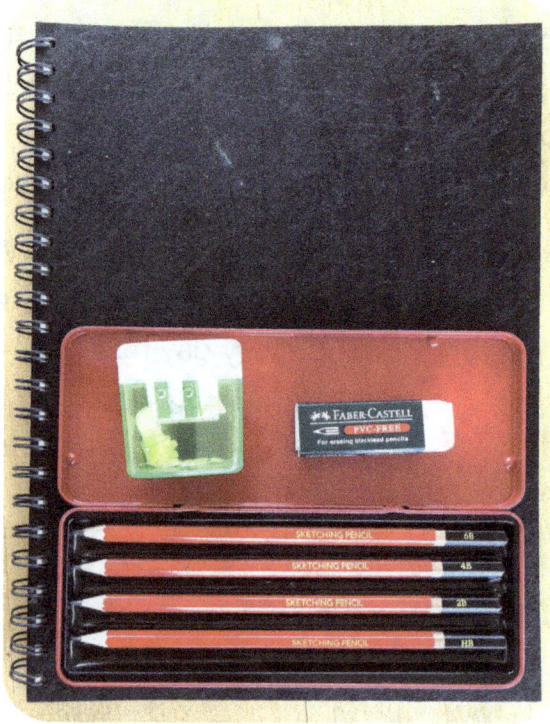
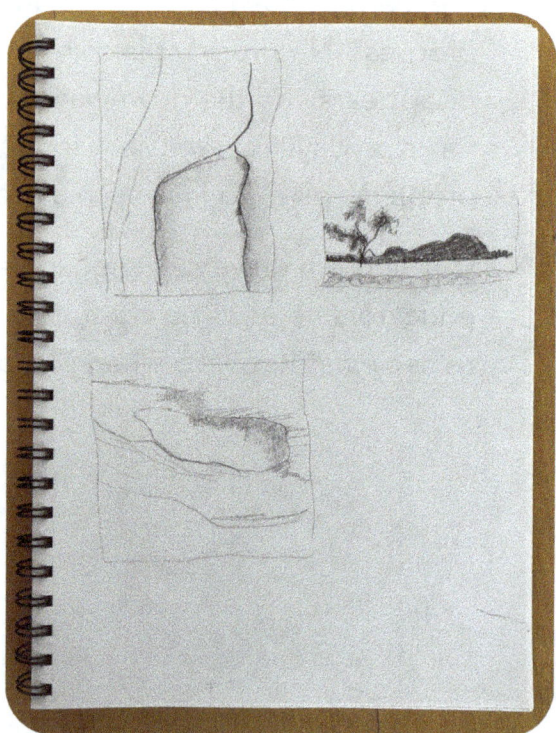

looser for drawing, so we don't usually grasp the pencil in the same tight tripod grip we use for writing. Rather our pencil grip looks like one of these holds. They allow for a wider range of movement.

Let's begin by exploring some pencil scales. The numbers on your pencils denote how hard or soft the graphite is. Your 6B is the softest and the 2H is the hardest. Soft graphite makes a thicker and darker line than hard graphite.

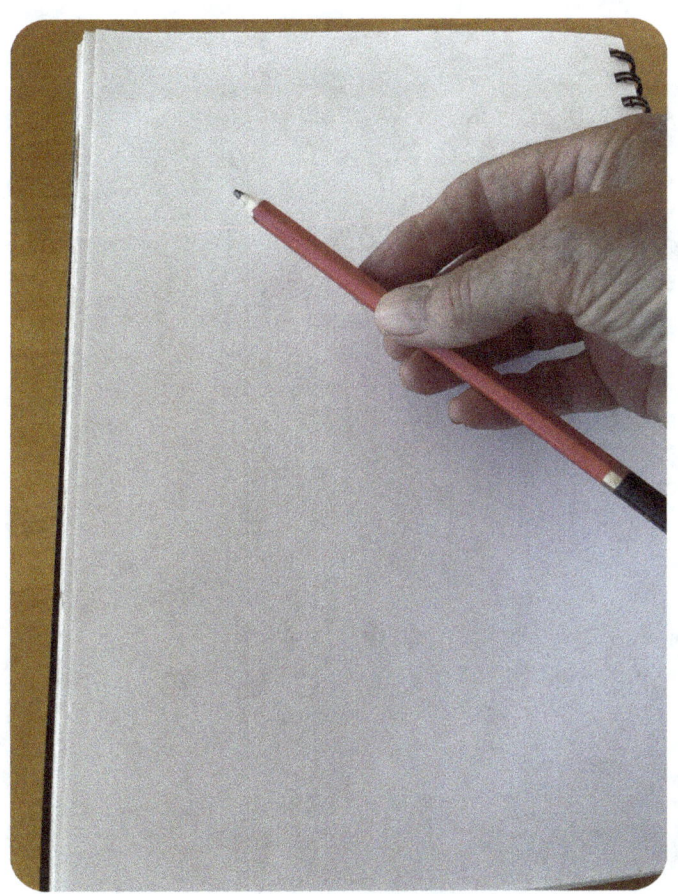
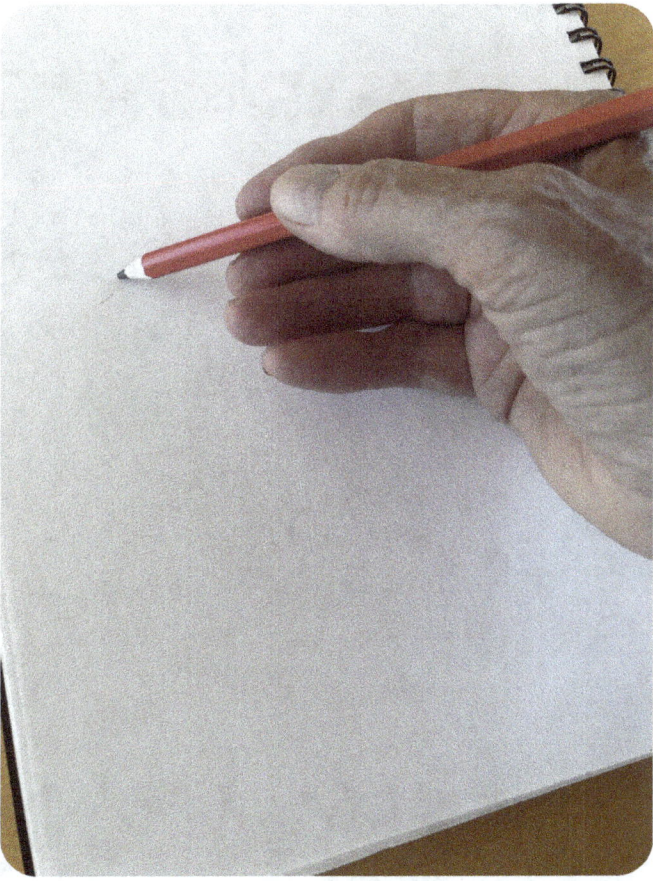

Draw eight squares in your sketch book, about 2x2 cm each. Don't use a ruler. Now shade each square with a different pencil as illustrated. What do you notice?

Next, you need to practice getting a tonal range with just one pencil. Begin by drawing eight

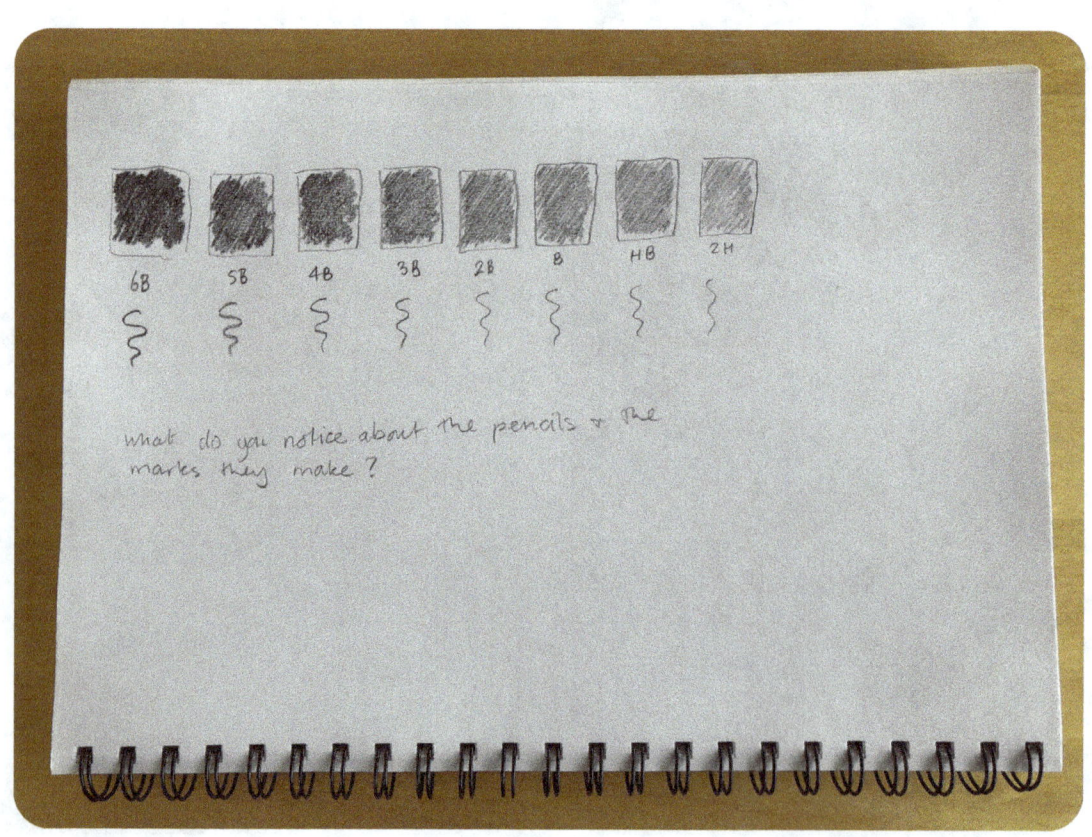

rectangles. Again, don't use a ruler. That is one rectangle for each grade of pencil. Then carefully shade each rectangle starting with the hardest pencil and moving incrementally through to the softest. Use just one pencil per rectangle. See if you can get an even gradation from light to dark. Grade each rectangle from light to dark.

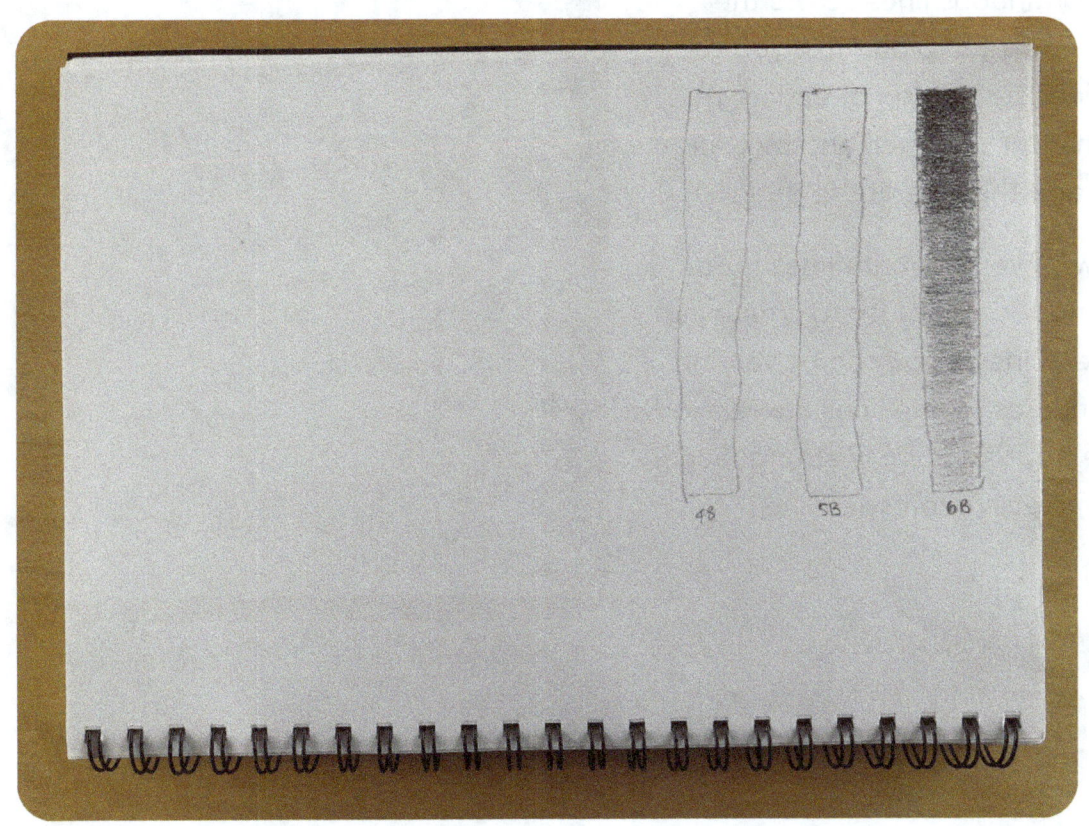

Lines

Every drawing is made up of lines.
Even shading is just lines that are close
together. Drawings become more or
less interesting according to the quality
and expressiveness of the lines used.
Using all your eight pencils in turn, draw
as many continuous lines across the
page as you can. Explore how you can
vary the lines by shifting direction, by
pressing harder or softer, and by using
the point and the side of the pencil.

Take a few of your favorite lines for a
walk around the page. Try to create as
expressive a line as you can by varying
your techniques. Some lines are relaxed
and some tight and highly strung. See if
you can make an expressive line.

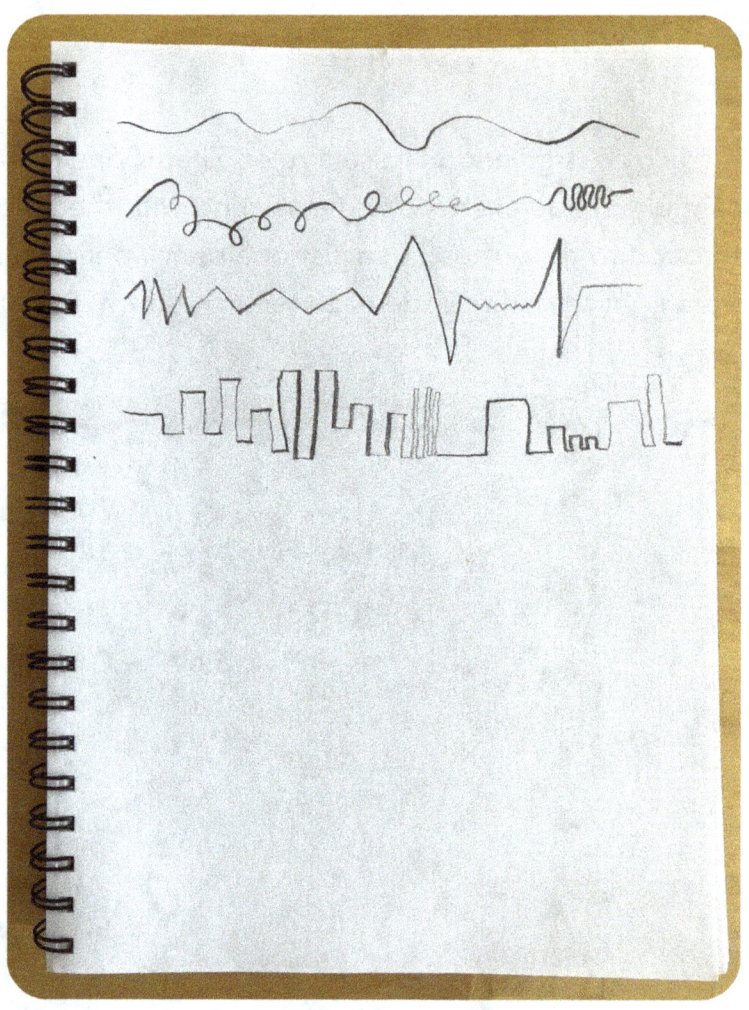

Here is a set of different kinds of lines that express texture and volume. Draw squares on your page and copy these examples. Make up some of your own. Artists often borrow techniques and ideas from each other, and copying and imitation is part of learning to become an artist. Traditionally, artists learned through an apprenticeship to a more established artist. This way of learning continues today but in a more informal way.

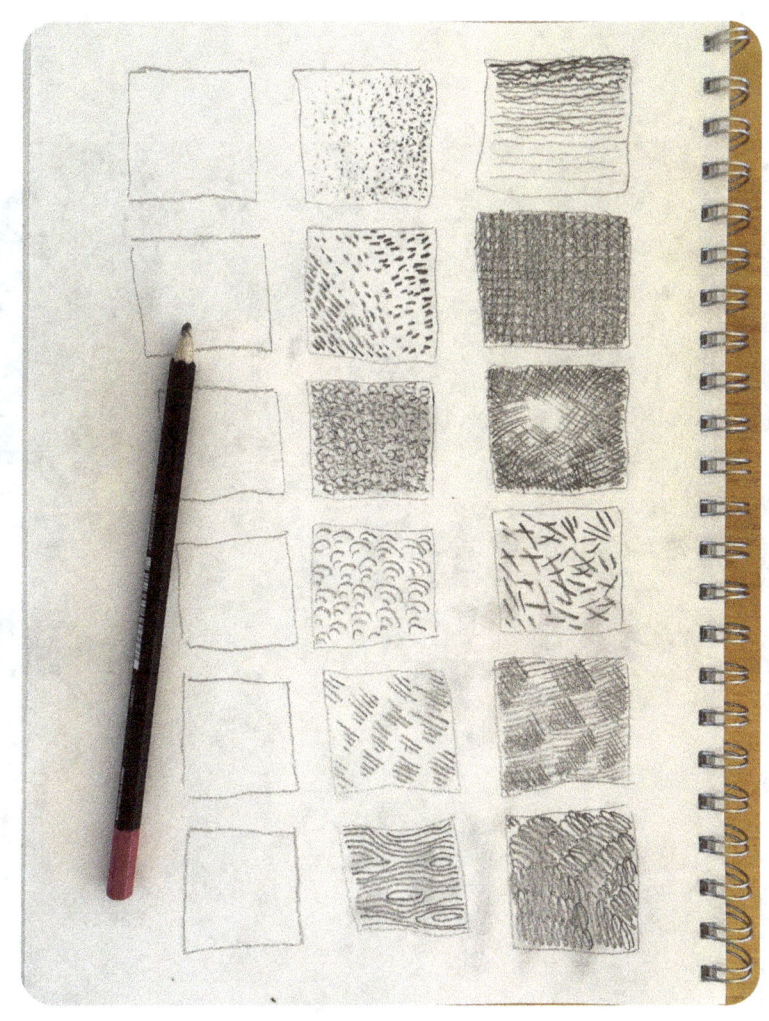

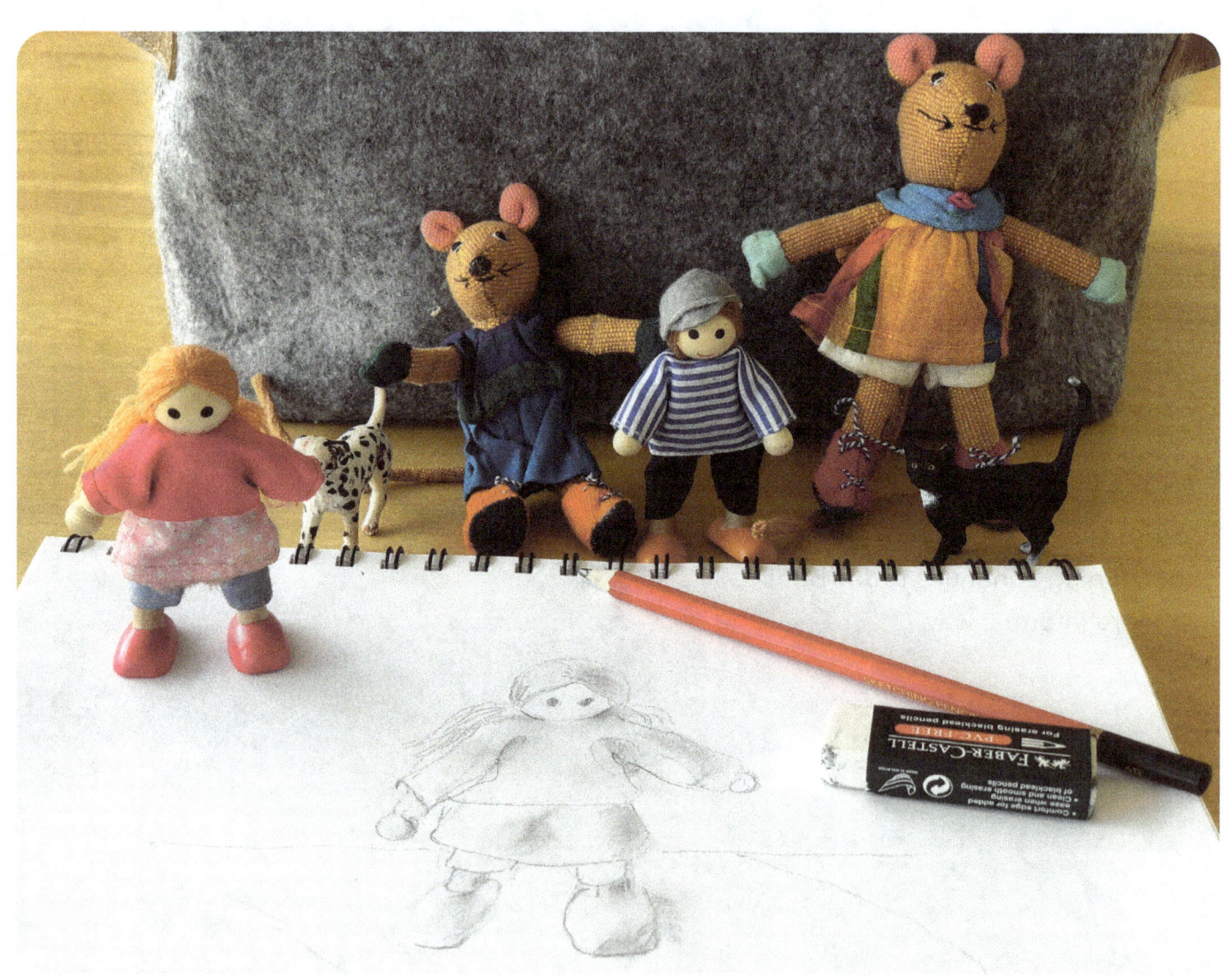

Drawing from Observation

What is observational drawing? It is carefully and intensely looking at a real life object and then rendering it as accurately as possible. Close attention is required in order to get information and record the fine details. We usually begin by either drawing in the air or laying down a few light guidelines until we feel we have a believable line. Observational drawing requires us to first approximate and then refine. Drawing trains our minds to work with our mistakes and use the approximations as a stepping stone towards something more satisfying. The tug and pull of risk taking in this process is fundamental to any art project. Working with mistakes is also an essential life skill.

Drawing from observation is not an easy thing to do and requires much practice to become confident and competent. Artists will get to know their subjects by doing many observational drawings. Drawing brings together imagination, memory, and observation. These three things engage the emotions, the mind, and the body. Using these three essential elements simultaneously makes drawing a powerful learning tool.

Observational drawing slows us down. It makes us take our time and moves us beyond the superficial. When we are drawing from observation we are also learning how to really see. We are noticing details. We are analyzing what we are drawing. We gain confidence to try new ideas and approaches. Drawing is a tool to tap into our imagination and draw out ideas to be further developed. Drawing puts us in a space where we can access the creative parts of our brain.

But First a Little Experiment...

Task 1

Before we begin doing an observational drawing I want you to draw something from memory. You will need to choose something familiar that you use everyday, like your set of keys. Please do not look at them before you draw them or while you are drawing them.

Task 2

When you have finished drawing your keys from memory, take a new page and put your keys in front of you where you can easily see them. Now I want you to look very carefully at them and draw as much detail as you can.

Task 3

Now compare the two drawings and note what the differences are. Which drawing did you prefer doing? Why?

It is difficult to remember what something looks like. Remember this when we work with children.

How to Do an Observational Drawing

For the next few exercises you will need to get a couple of small figures or soft toys and a couple of small plastic animals. Like you see below:

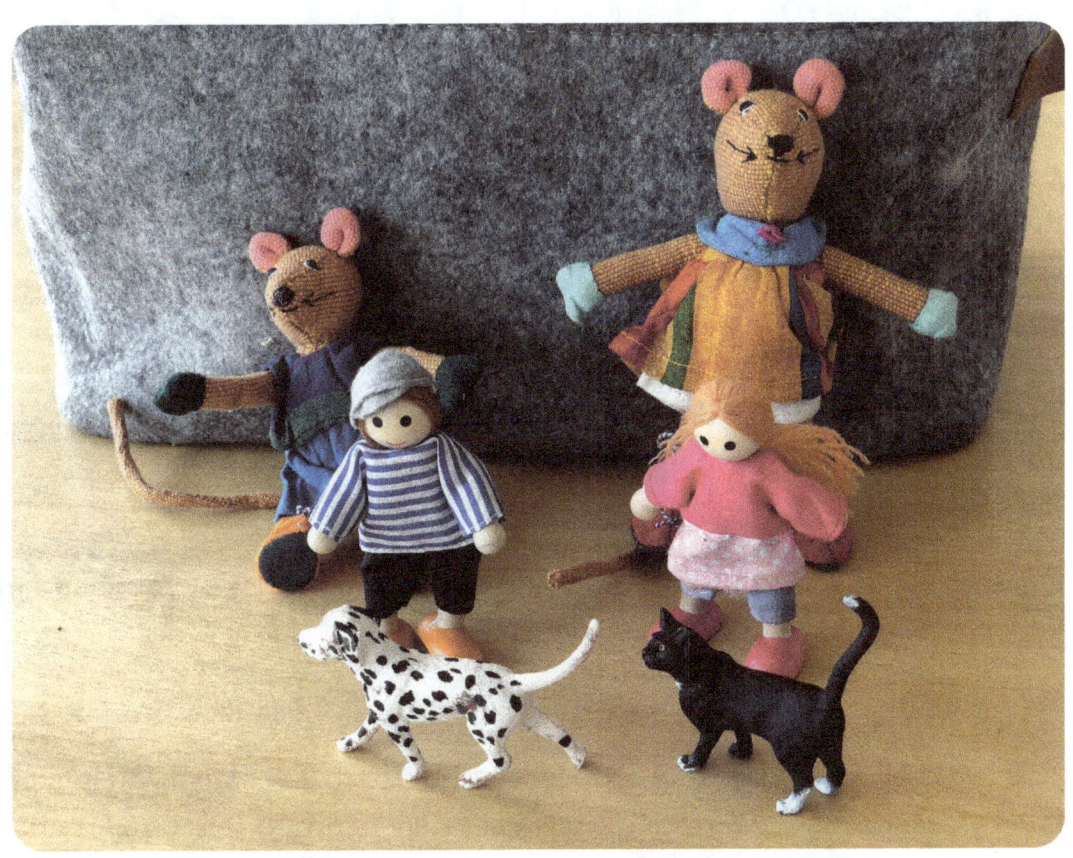

Arrange just one of your figures in front of you so you can easily see it. Arrange your sketch book and eraser so that you are comfortable. I sometimes prop my sketch book up against the edge of the table.

Spend some time just looking at the figure and getting to know it. Observational drawing is an exercise in seeing. Try to find the basic shapes of the underlying form. Look for strong lines created by shadows. Don't look for detail yet.

Lightly put some rough guide marks on your paper. I find that if I close one eye the object flattens out and it is easier to see the basic shapes. Keep looking back and forth between the figure and your drawing. Check that this light underdrawing is proportionally as good as you can get it. Do not outline the objects in your drawing, as this will give the drawing a cookie-cutter look. Parts of the drawing should have no outline drawn at all, leaving room for the eye to fill in the gaps.

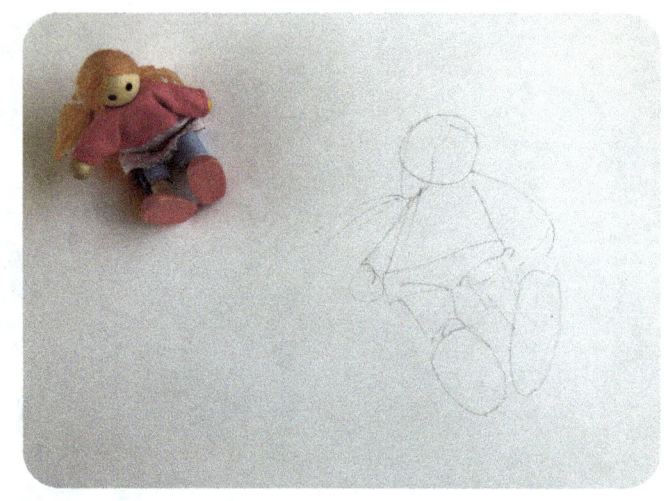

Draw as big as you can. Small drawings restrict the fluency of your hand movements. Keep looking up at the object at least half of the time.

Set up a different pose to draw each day for a week, to make seven drawings.

This is a challenging but very supportive exercise that will give you lots of ideas for making later drawings more interesting. How the figure is posed tells us a lot about the figure and its disposition.

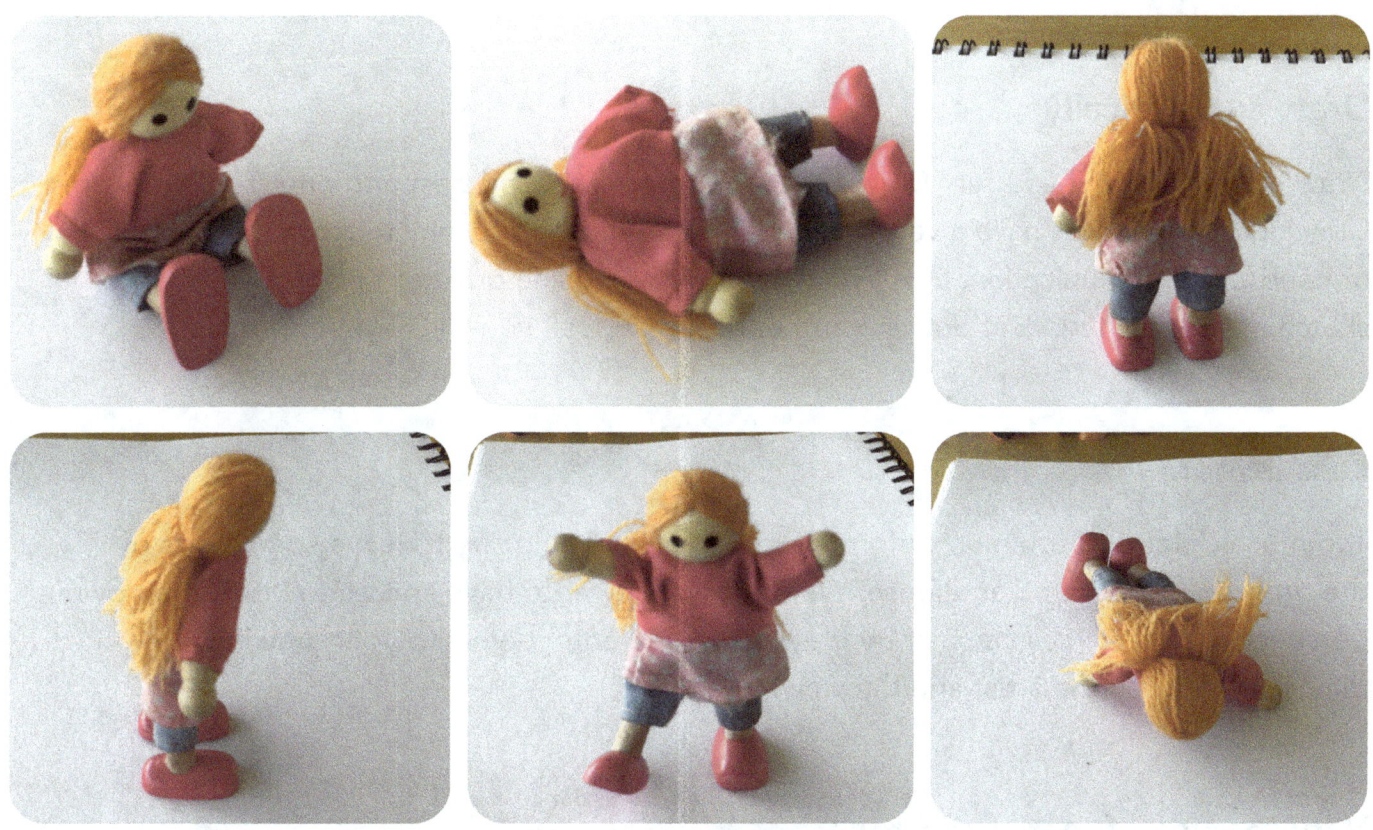

More tips for observational drawing

Keep observing, keep looking

Get into a position where you can easily see what you are drawing. Ideally your drawing paper should be lined up so you only have to glance up and see what you are drawing. Remember that you need to glance very often; more than 50 percent of your time should be spent looking at what you are drawing so that you draw what you see and not what you think you see and not what you remember.

Draw authentically

Draw the real thing if you can. Drawing from photos is second best and one step removed. Drawings from photos have a very static feel to them. Don't try any tricks that get in the way of hand/eye communication. Don't draw around the outline or trace or borrow from another sketch. If you don't work at drawing authentically yourself you will never improve

Less is more

Too much detail and too much information is overwhelming. Try to leave some parts of the drawing understated and loose. We want the viewer to have spaces to insert their own perspective, where they can rest their eyes and find entry points to your drawing. Viewing is a dialogue between the artist and the viewer.

Vary the use of marks and tones

The marks we make need to be interesting and varied to engage the viewer. Lines need to be able to express the essence of the subject. Likewise a wide range of tones gives the image some depth and atmosphere. Try to use the full range of tone. But do not invent what you think should be there—observe closely.

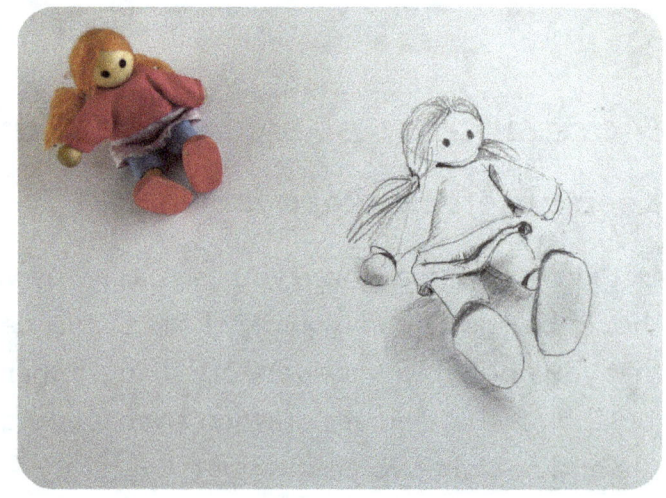

Perspective Drawing Exercise

I'm going to use the figures below to demonstrate a series of drawings with different perspectives. You are going to use your own figures and do a series of perspective drawings in this fun exercise.

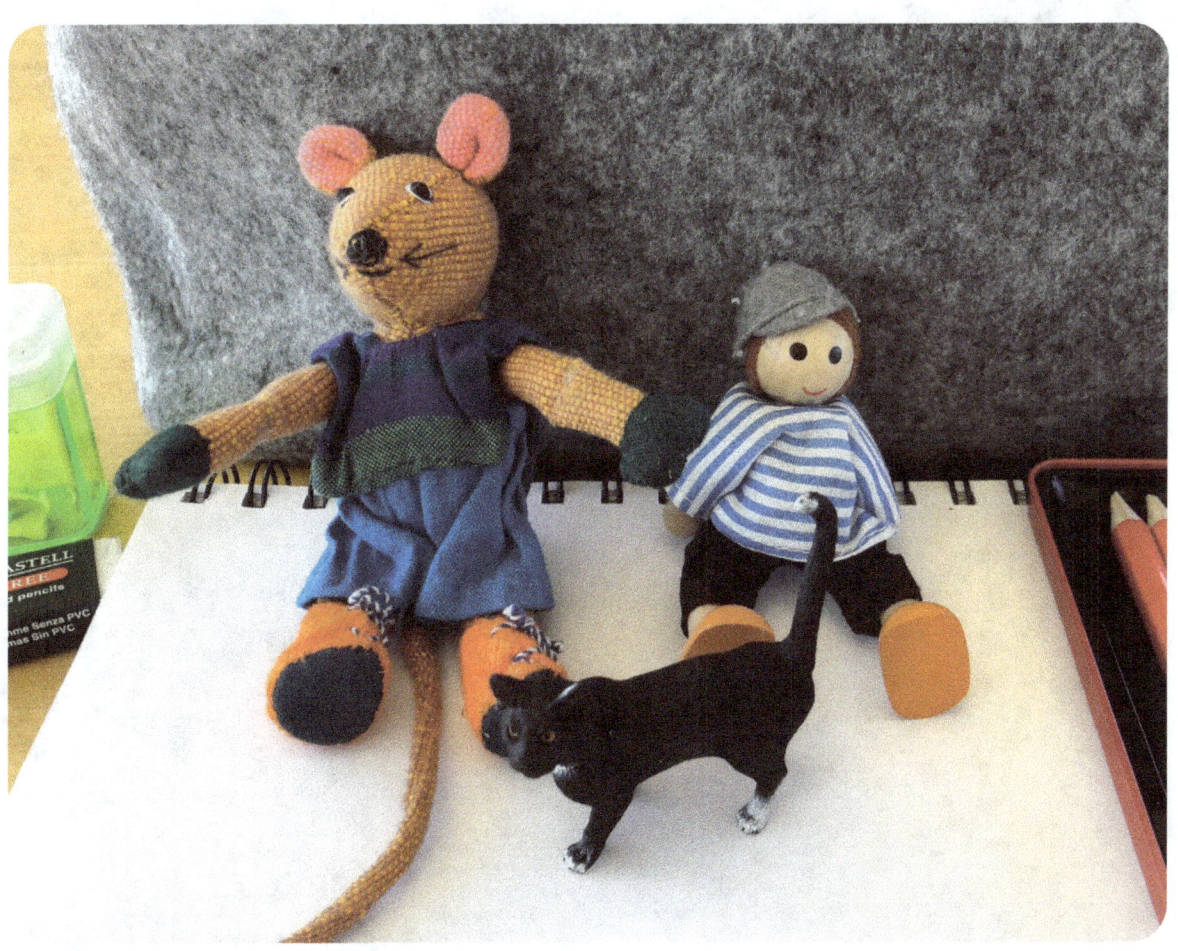

For the first drawing, place one figure close to you and one far away. Try and draw just what you see. It is quite tricky to get the sense of distance.

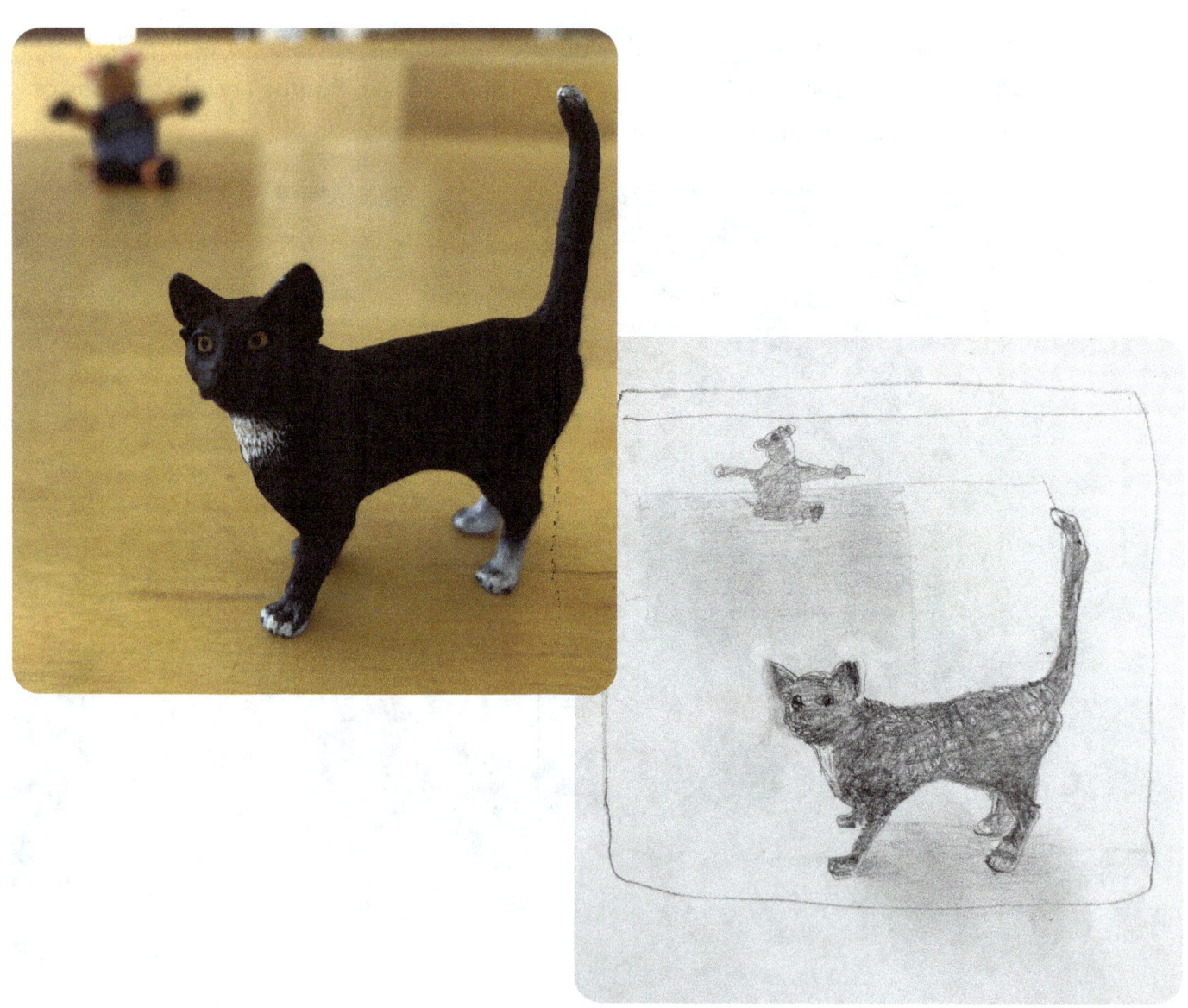

For this next drawing, place both figures far away. Now draw what you see and not what you know. Keep plenty of foreground.

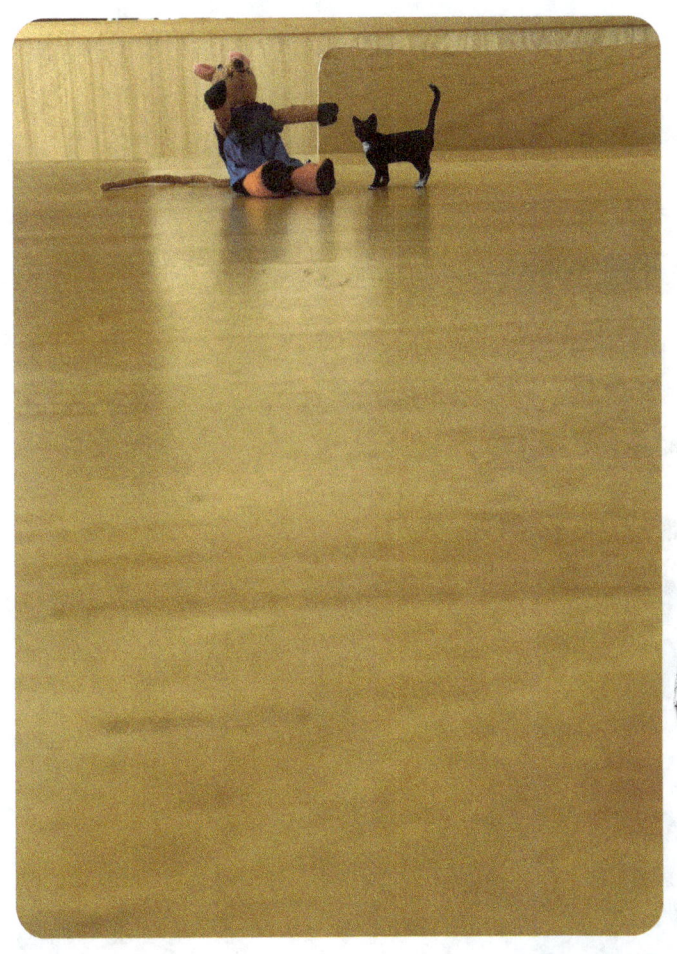

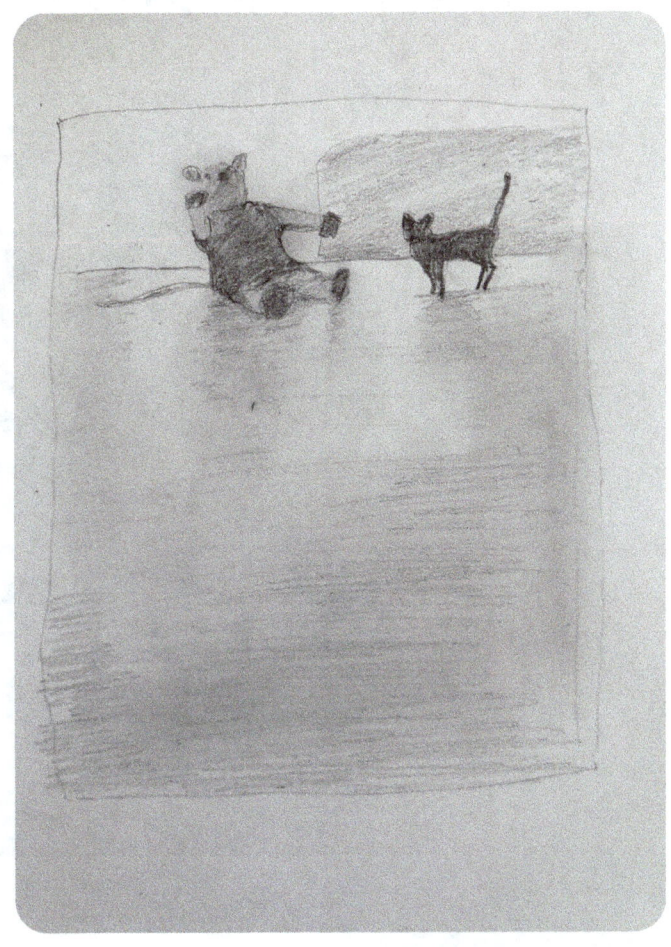

Move a figure very close to you. It has to be so close that the whole figure will not fit on the page and parts cannot be seen. Again draw just what you see, looking carefully and often.

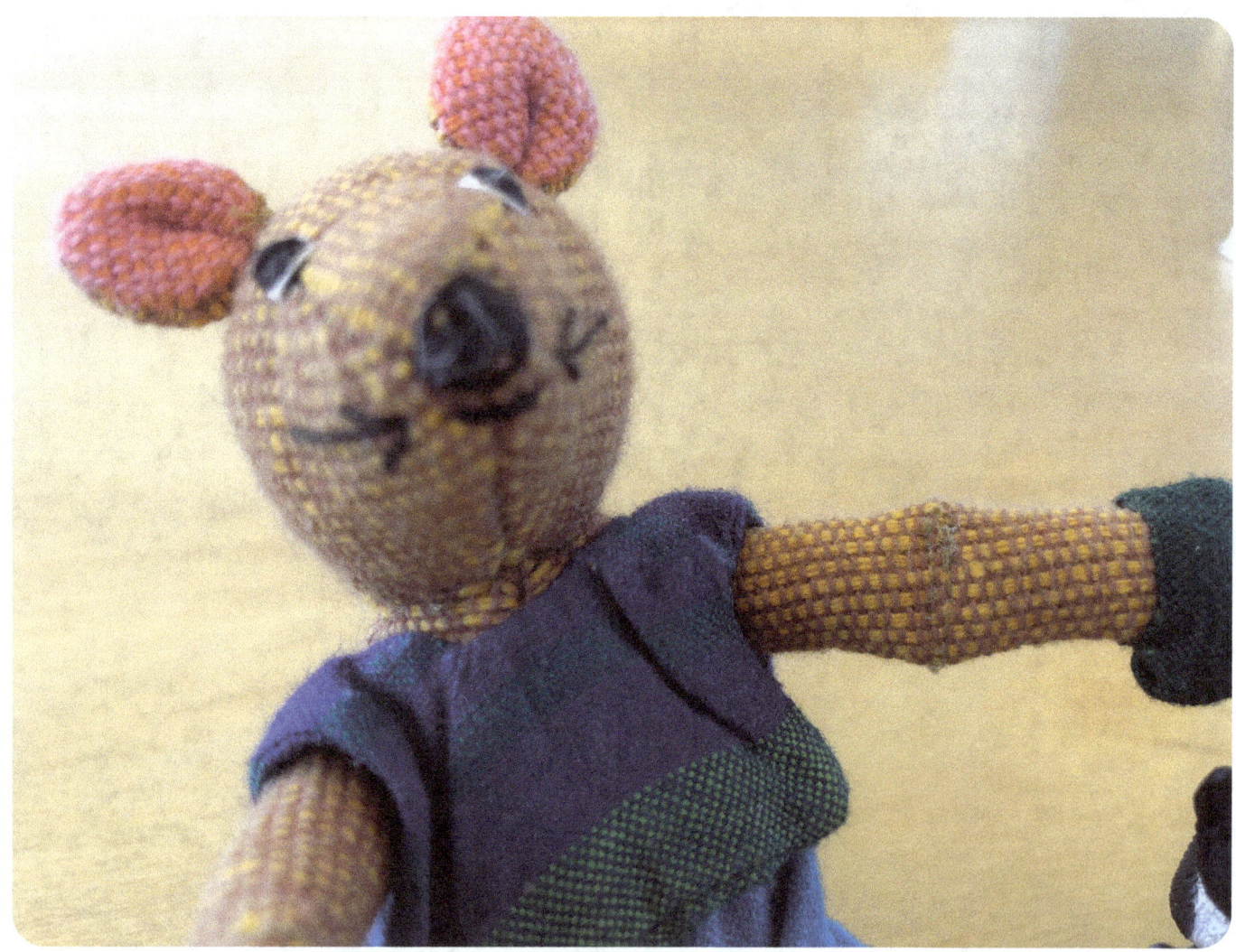

Place two figures on the floor and draw them from above. This is a bird's eye view. This is a very challenging perspective to draw.

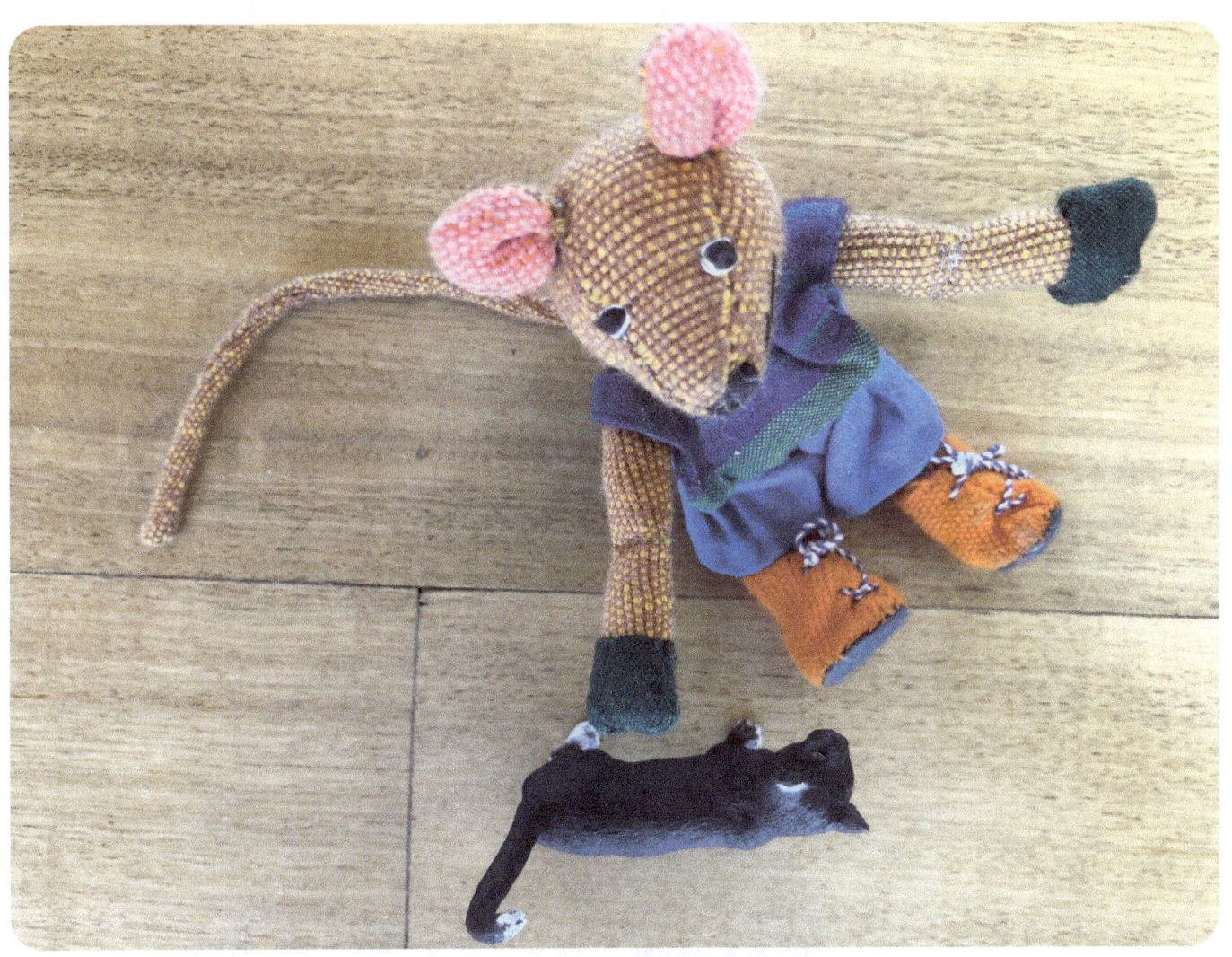

Occlusion, where the one of the figures hides part or all of the figure behind it, is something usually not understood by young children. They tend to show an x-ray image through the object in front.

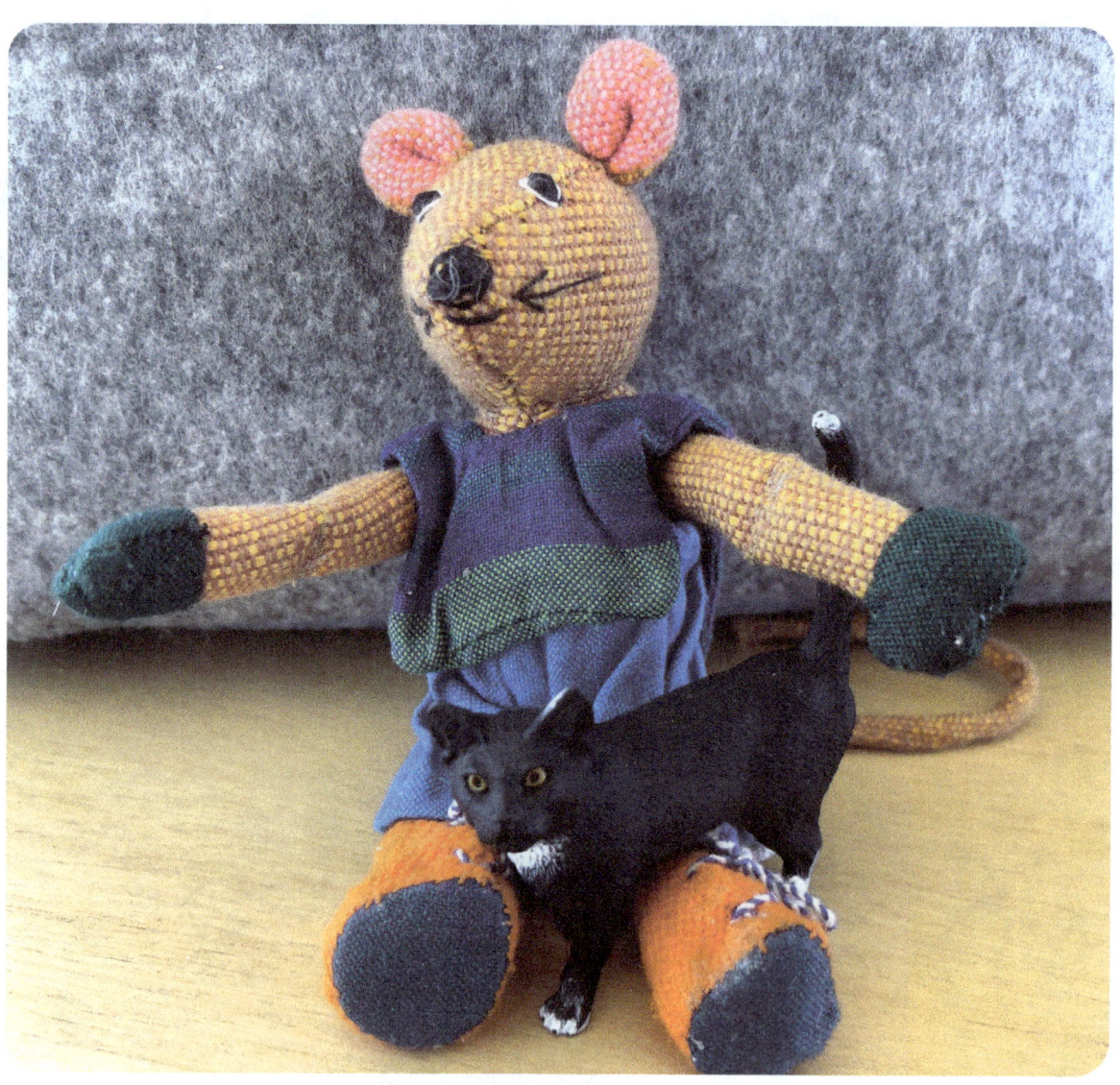

Now you can have some fun with your figures. Find different places to position them and add funny captions to your drawings.

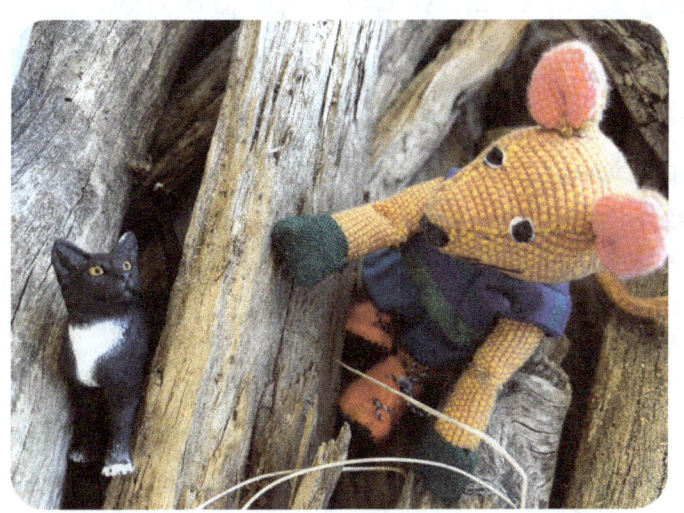

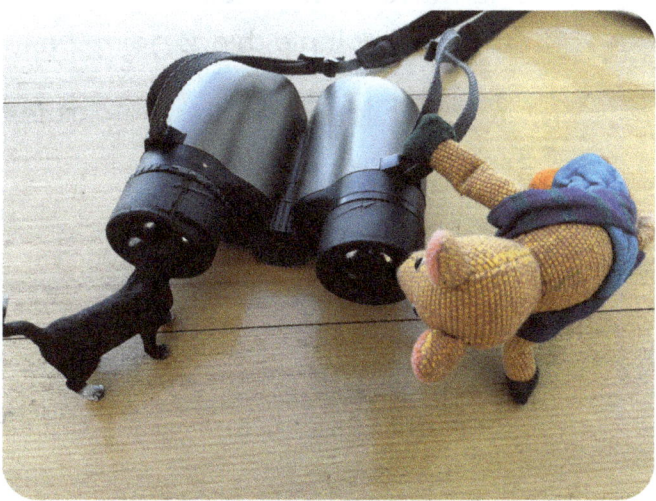

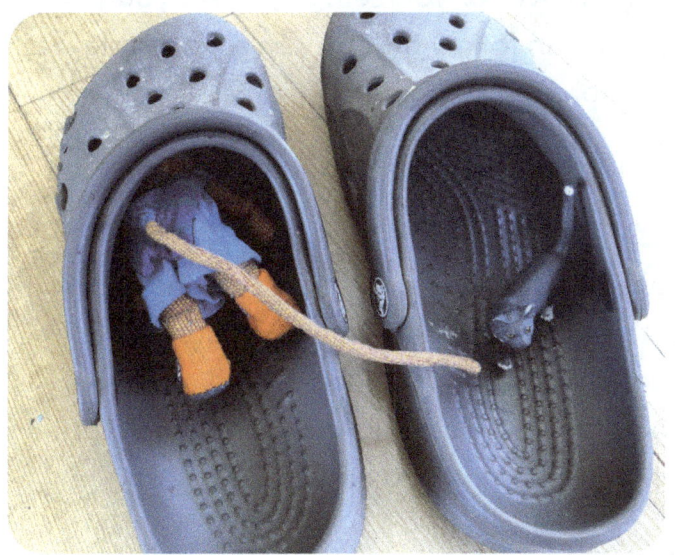

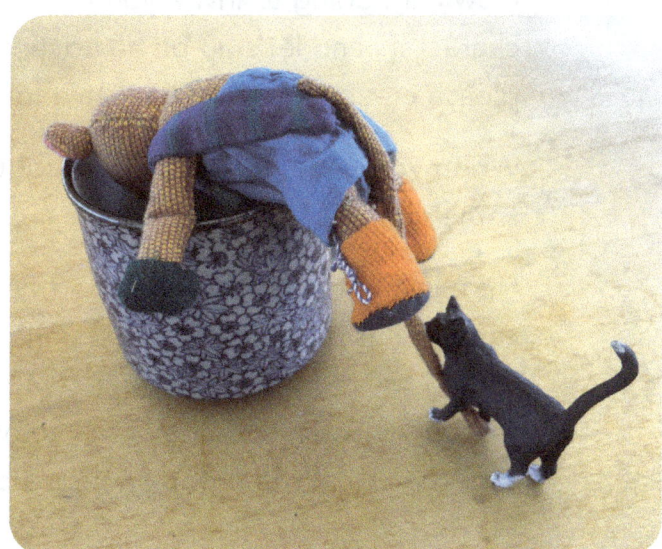

Drawing as Narrative and Planning Tool

Narrative drawing tells a story. It can be a series of drawings or a page of drawings that has multiple things going on in it.

Young children love to take part in the process of developing a narrative. I have spent many hours with my grandchildren developing adventures of Oliver mouse and Ink the cat. One of us begins the drawing and the other helps add details and actions to the story. We draw over several pages, adding bits of text here and there.

I have also done this with groups of preschool children. We plan first on a storyboard (an example of drawing as a planning tool) and then children work on individual pages either alone or with a friend. We end up with many class books that we have made ourselves and can read.

Now I am going to invite you to create a narrative for yourself. So, select your characters and let's go on an adventure. You can follow my story as an example but please create your own narrative for your story.

When you have finished, you might like to read your illustrated narrative to some children.

Here is my storyboard for a short narrative about Oliver mouse and Ink the cat. You can see it is roughly done but manages to capture the action and the story line. Next, I will draw each page with more detail and care. I will also create a polished text for it. Then I will add some color and place the pages in order and staple them together. Finally, the book needs a cover with the title and author.

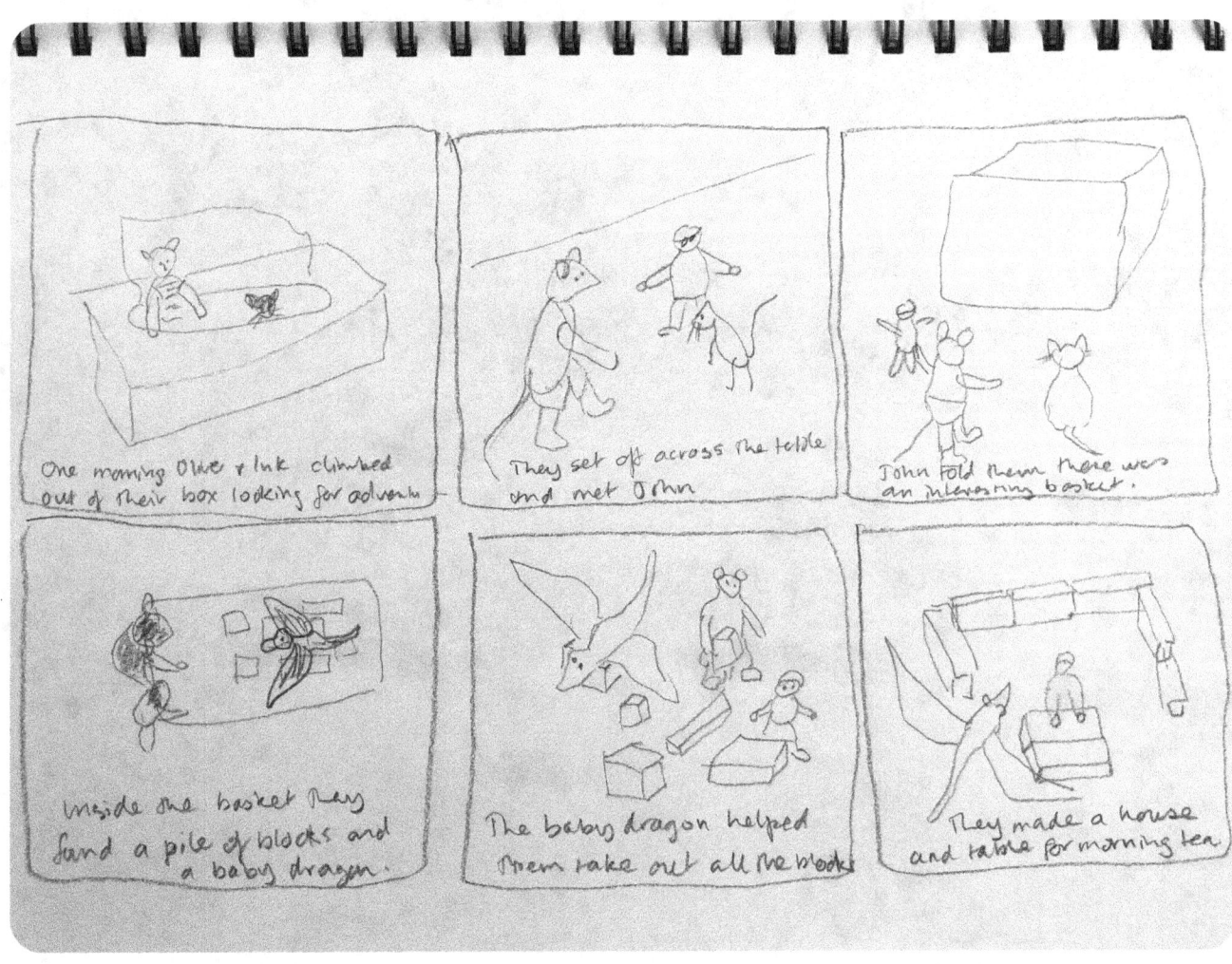

One morning Olive + Ink climbed out of their box looking for adventure.

They set off across the table and met John

John told them there was an interesting basket.

Inside the basket they found a pile of blocks and a baby dragon.

The baby dragon helped them take out all the blocks

They made a house and table for morning tea

I used my observational drawing and mark making skills to create the first page of the narrative. I will use computer text to do the writing so that it is clear and even.

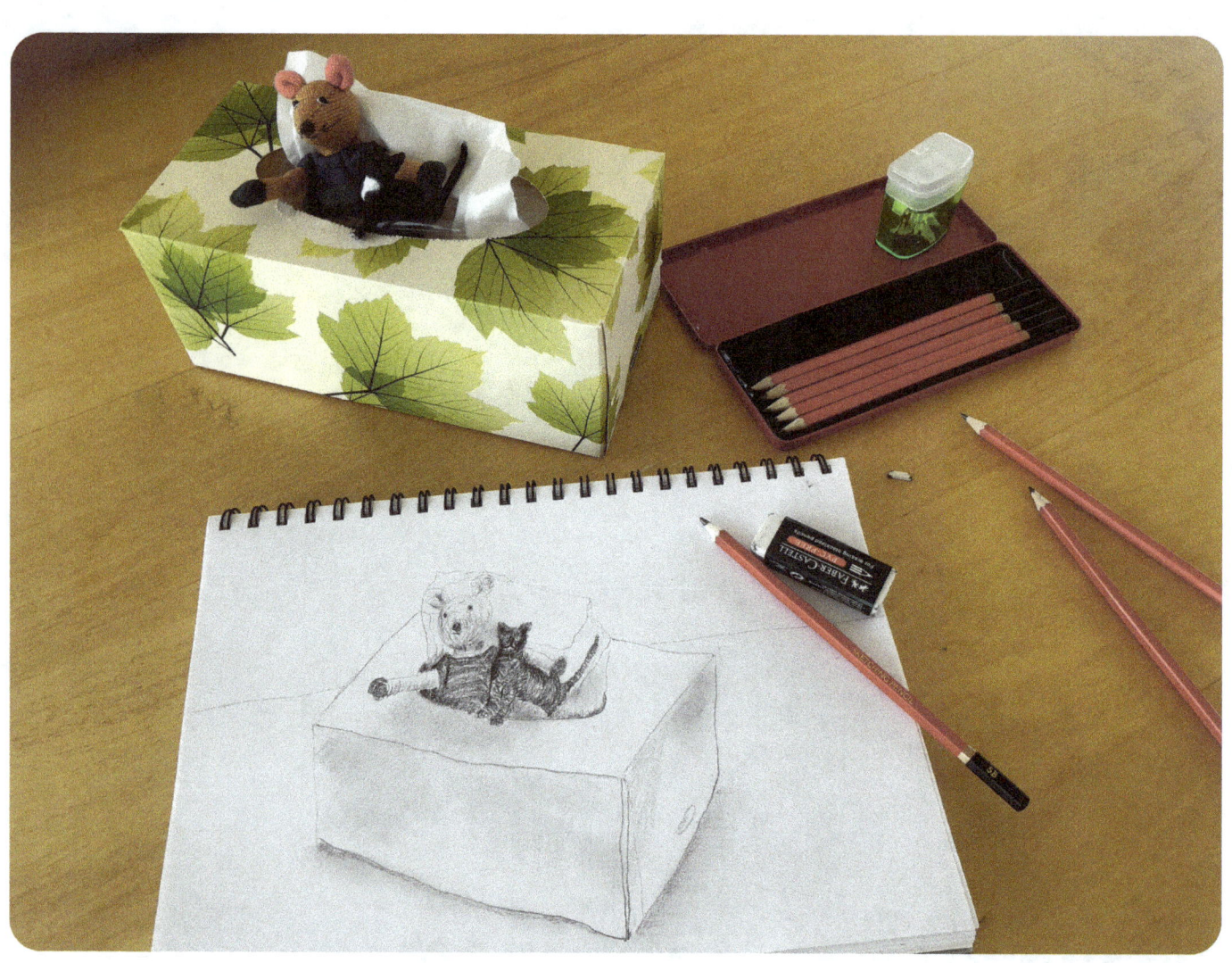

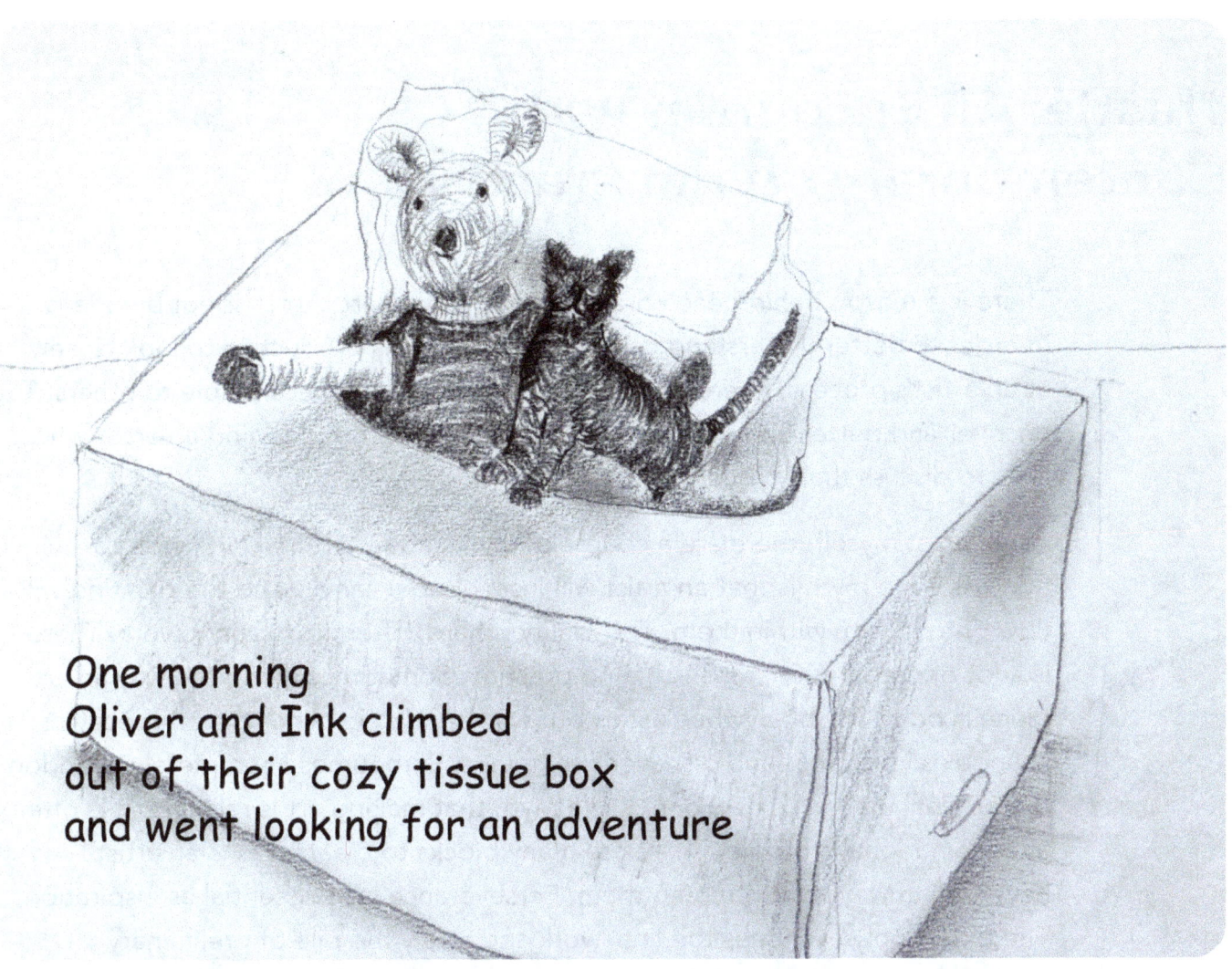

One morning
Oliver and Ink climbed
out of their cozy tissue box
and went looking for an adventure

Now you can do the same for the pages of your narrative, and then compile them into a small book. Then find some children to read it to. You are about halfway through the drawing tutorial.

Thistle: An Encounter with Contemporary Studio Practice

There is a reason behind each drawing and work of art. Art is about big ideas. In order to better understand contemporary art, it is productive to look closely at an artist's process. There are things artists do that are not visible to others. To uncover and better understand these processes, we need to find an artist who likes to discuss their process.

As an artist myself, there are a couple of myths about art making I wish to address. One myth is that an artist will just set up a canvas and the painting will flow onto it from within them. The reality is hard, often frustrating, work. There is a lot of preparation, research, and practice. Sometimes along the way an art piece is born. But even when I start out with an idea in mind, the art piece can change as I progress and discover new things. Sometimes I completely abandon the original idea for a new one. It is a myth that making art is relaxing. It is often a real emotional struggle. There are many blocks to creativity. As an artist I have to find ways to overcome them. Perseverance is as essential as inspiration. The public only ever sees the final work and rarely the pile of preliminary explorations.

In this section I unpack bits of my art process to provide some examples of the kinds of things artist do. I will use some work I did for an art festival, Cementa17. This festival had an underlying environmental theme to it, and I was asked to work with weeds. I chose the nodding thistle, a weed I am always fighting on my twenty-five-- acre block in New South Wales. I also chose the nodding thistle because I was born and brought up in Scotland and it has many special memories for me. It is part of my identity.

Two of the initial big ideas underlying my thistle work are migration and identity. In Scotland, my sense of identity is tied to my national flower, the revered nodding thistle. Yet when I migrate to Australia I find I am classified as a noxious weed to be eradicated. With my identity bruised, I am determined to create something beautiful with the thistle in the hope of some kind of reconciliation.

When a migrant begins a new life in a new country they usually work very hard to contribute all they have to their new place. But while they strive to be accepted they also carry with them all of their previous experiences. Migrants cannot forget where they came from. Everything in the new place is overlaid with memories of the place of origin.

Getting to know my thistle

I began my art project by getting to know my thistle. I picked a fine specimen and took it into my studio to draw. It was a huge plant so I cut parts off and focused on one part at a time. While drawing I also looked at old botanical drawings to see how they were typically done.

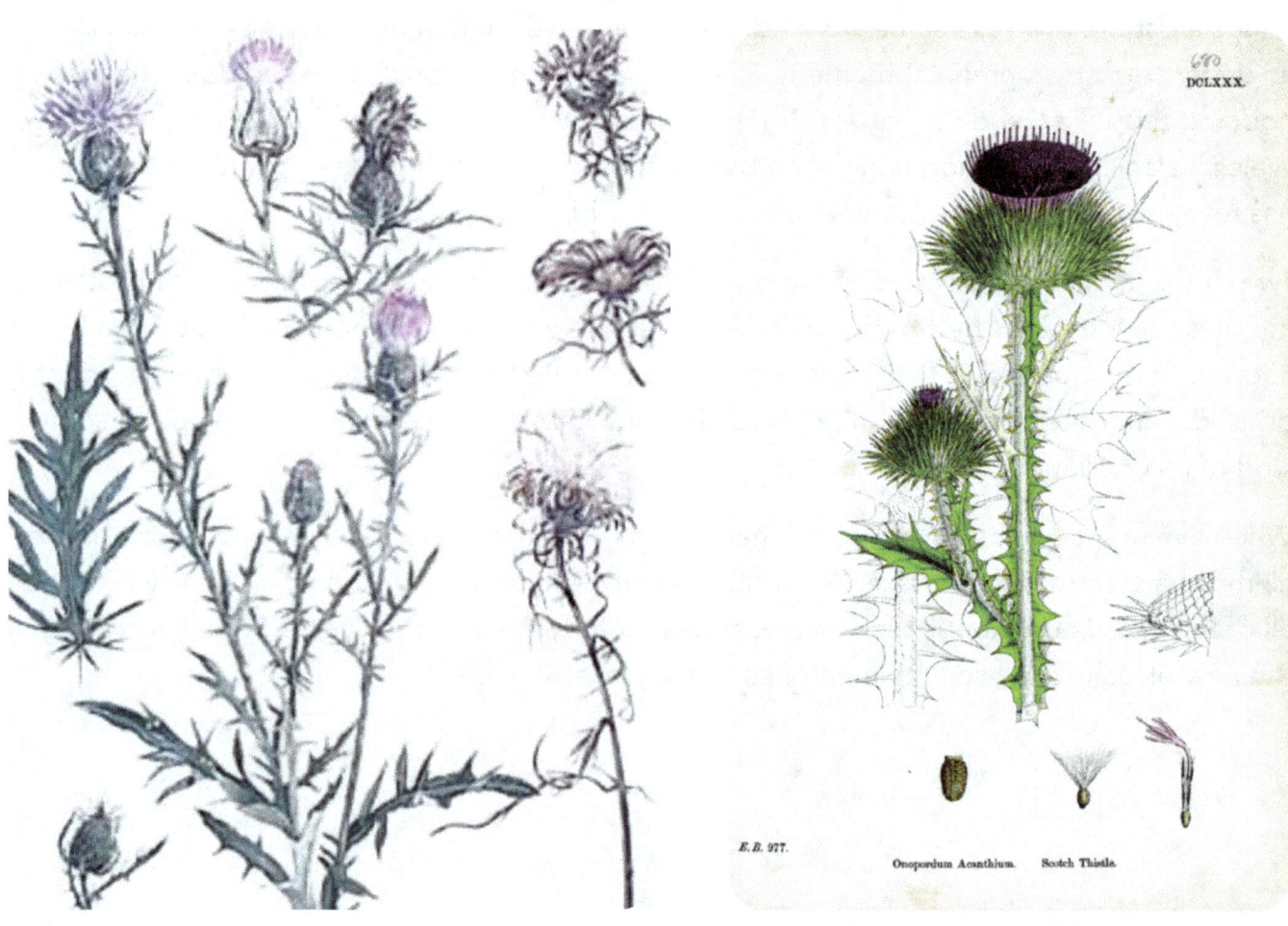

Some of my observational drawings of different parts of a thistle, at different stages.

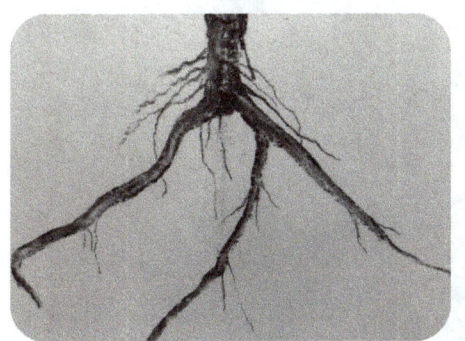
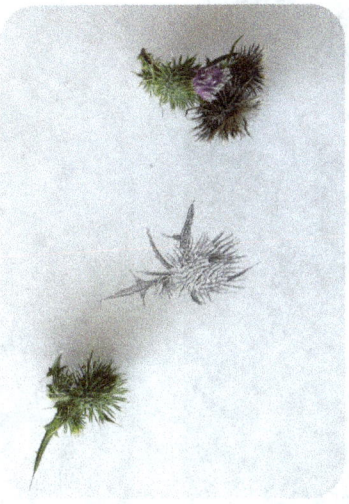
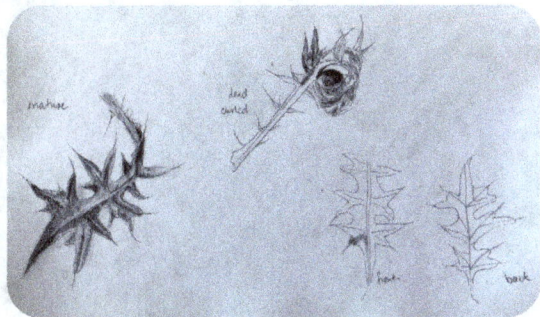

Please choose a plant that is meaningful to you (something that is local to your region and easily accessible) and work along beside me for the rest of this section. How you draw it and look at it will determine your outcome. Begin by doing a few quick studies of different parts of the plant.

Choose two details that you are drawn to and do two more sustained drawings.

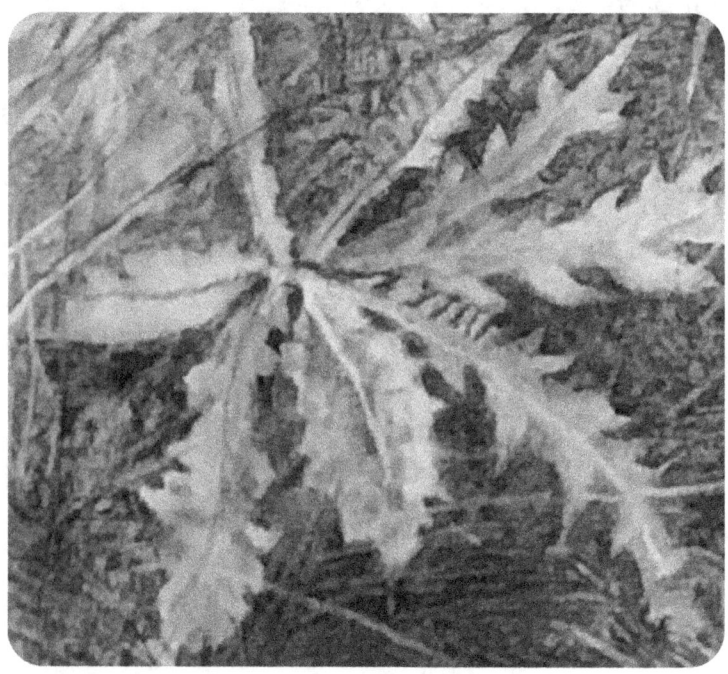

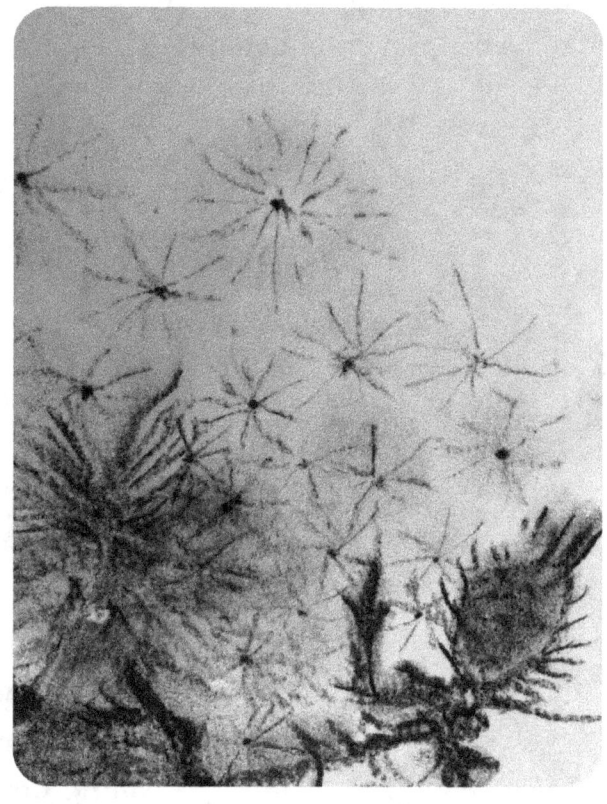

*Drawing
a Plant*

Art as research

As I continue to examine and draw parts of the thistle, I am also researching. I get to know a landowner who buys land that has been degraded through misuse and restores it. As we walk around his property, he shows me how all plants have a use, even weeds. I learn that the thistle is known as a colonizer because it takes root in land that has poor nutrition. It is a bit like a warning system to let the farmer know that the balance of nutrients in the soil is off. Its big tap root pulls nutrients and moisture to the surface to create a microclimate around itself, which also allows native plants to return. These plants stabilize the soil and don't allow water to run off.

Spend some time researching your plant. What can you find out about it? Where did the name come from? Is it used for any special purpose, such as medicine? Does it have significance for anyone? Are there any experts studying this plant? Is it edible? Can you make anything with it?

Making connections and growing ideas

I begin to see a link between the migration of thistles and the migration of people. Scots have been colonizers and often have contributed to places they migrate to. But like thistles they are not always appreciated and do not always do good. However, I am still keen to present the thistle as beautiful and useful, and in a way that might make people rethink their prejudices about them and migrants. But I don't yet know how. Hopefully as I draw something will emerge. I share this thinking with you to demonstrate that drawing and painting are not usually just mimetic of what we see. There are bigger ideas involved, which emerge from deconstruction, reconstruction, and playing with the materials. As I work I evaluate the pros and cons of each idea. I think about the narratives I am creating, the accessibility of my metaphors and meanings, and the anticipated response of the viewer.

Letting the subject/object speak to you

As I draw different parts of the thistle I become more familiar with the patterns and structure of the plant. I notice spirals and symmetry and a logical order to things. I extend my looking to the context of the plant and the life cycle. Each part of the plant has an important role to play. As I draw I also play with the parts to see how pliable they are. I cut the stem down into the thinnest strips I can and try to weave with it. I take the large prickles and arrange them in patterns. I collect fistfuls of soft down and play with it to see how it behaves. Maybe I can contain it in large quantities as a reminder of how many seeds come from each plant. I dig some plants up and examine the roots. There are so many possibilities the plant is throwing at me now.

Review, evaluate and reposition

With so many possibilities, the process of evaluation becomes critical. Review and evaluation requires higher-order thinking skills. We have to weigh all the pros and cons and then decide which path to take. I have to think about the kinds of messages the artifacts hold and how to present them. I am constantly re-positioning and re-presenting. Each drawing and artifact is an investment in time and effort. I have to factor in the practical elements too.

Botanical drawing—Drawing for Information

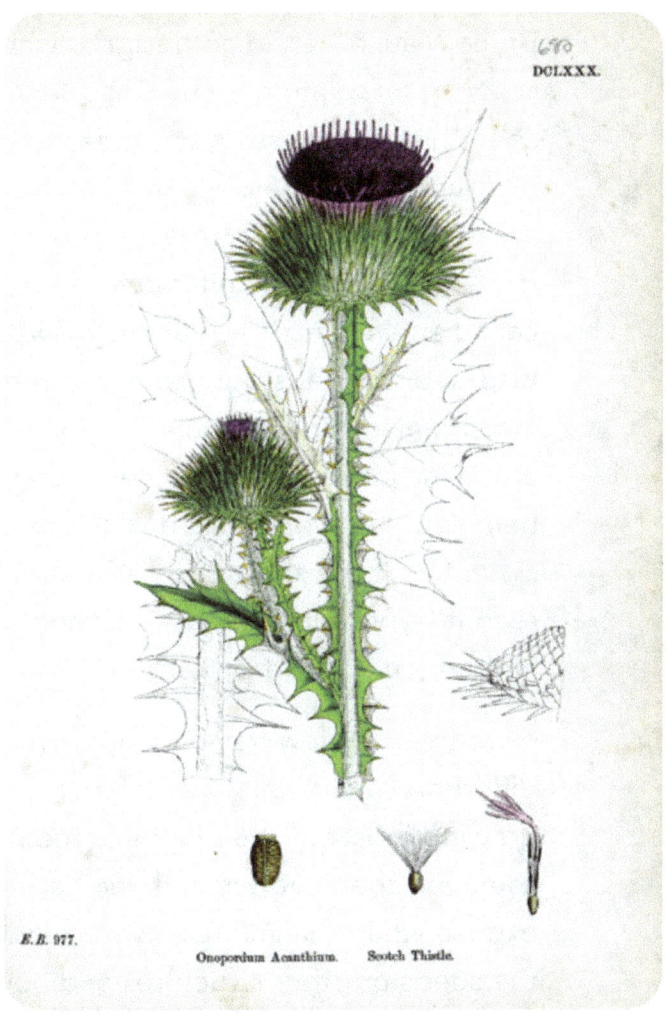

Drawing for information has a long history. Before cameras were invented, detailed drawings were made of many species. These were often labeled and annotated too. While I find these drawings aesthetic they were actually never created with that goal in mind. Rather, these illustrations documenting details of species help us more easily identify plants we find.

This is an old print of a thistle. It shows important parts of the plant like the seed and parts of the seed.

A Few Drawing Exercises for You...

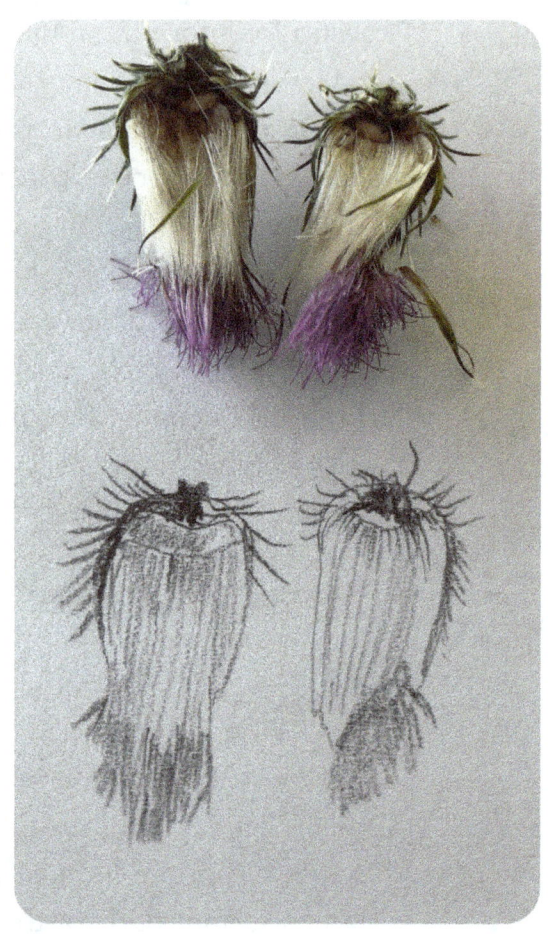

Bruce Mau, a Canadian designer who grew up in isolation in the Canadian bush, spent his days messing around with things he found. This "messing around" is an important part of the creative process. Later in life, he wrote a manifesto for growth, called an 'Incomplete Manifesto for Growth. https://brucemaustudio.com/projects/an-incomplete-manifesto-for-growth/ There are many ideas in this manifesto that can help you get over blockages and reach your potential. It is a short and easy read. Please read it—you will find it useful when you embark on your art project.

Over the next few days, try out some different ways of messing around. First, try drawing a part of the plant like the bud or seed and then cut it in half and carefully expose what is inside. Can you clearly see the seeds or other structures and how they might work? What patterns did you reveal?

Event maps

Make a pictorial map to show the location of your plant. Look up 'event maps' to see how you can make a pictorial map.

When I looked at where the thistles were on my block I found they tended to cluster in one area. The old dead thistle would still be there and all the new plants were in close proximity. When I mapped the thistles on my block I used a drawing of a thistle flower head to show where the thistle was and its size in relation to the others around it. This gave me the inspiration for a drawing in my exhibition.

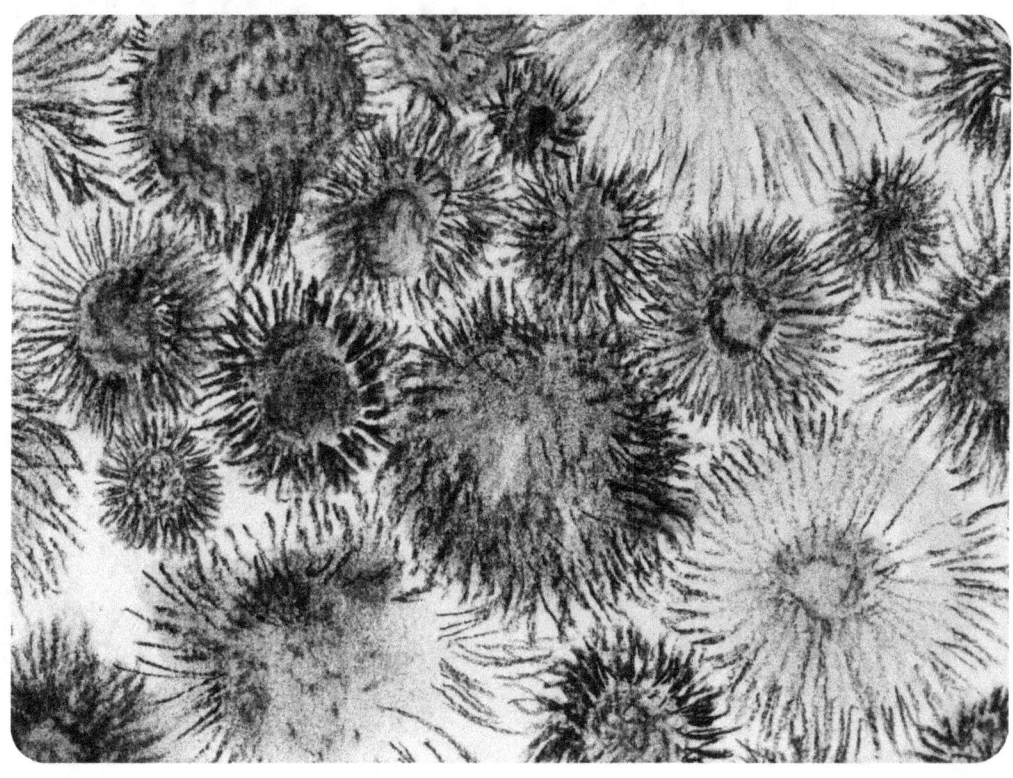

Compare

Collect one part of the plant in a range of sizes, such as flower heads from small to large, leaves from small to large, or stems from thick to thin. Now draw them.

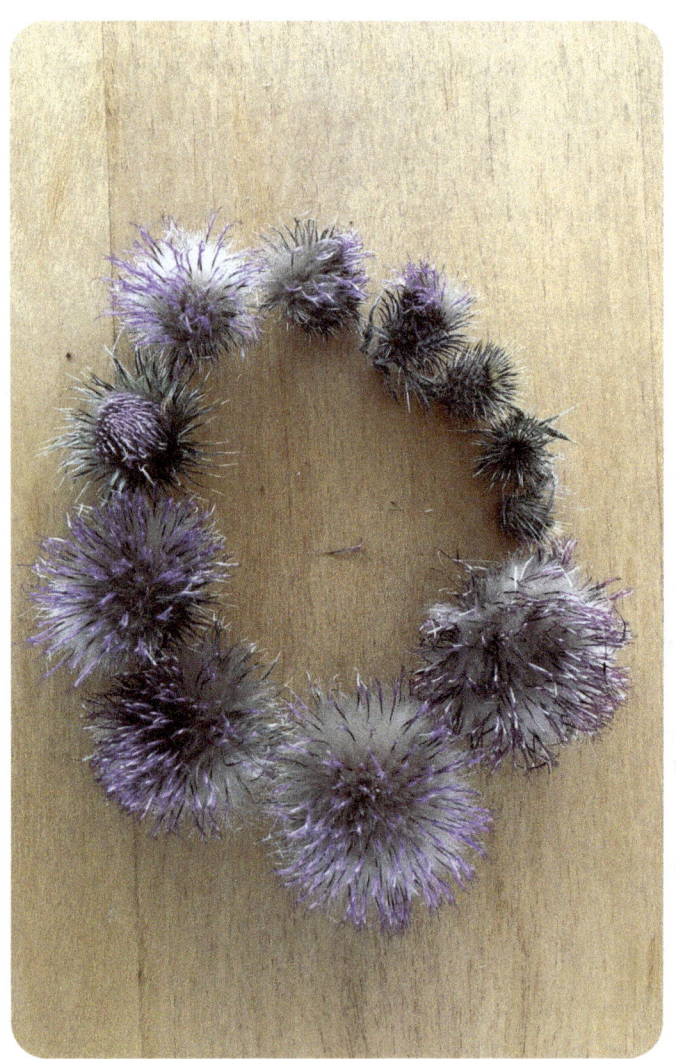 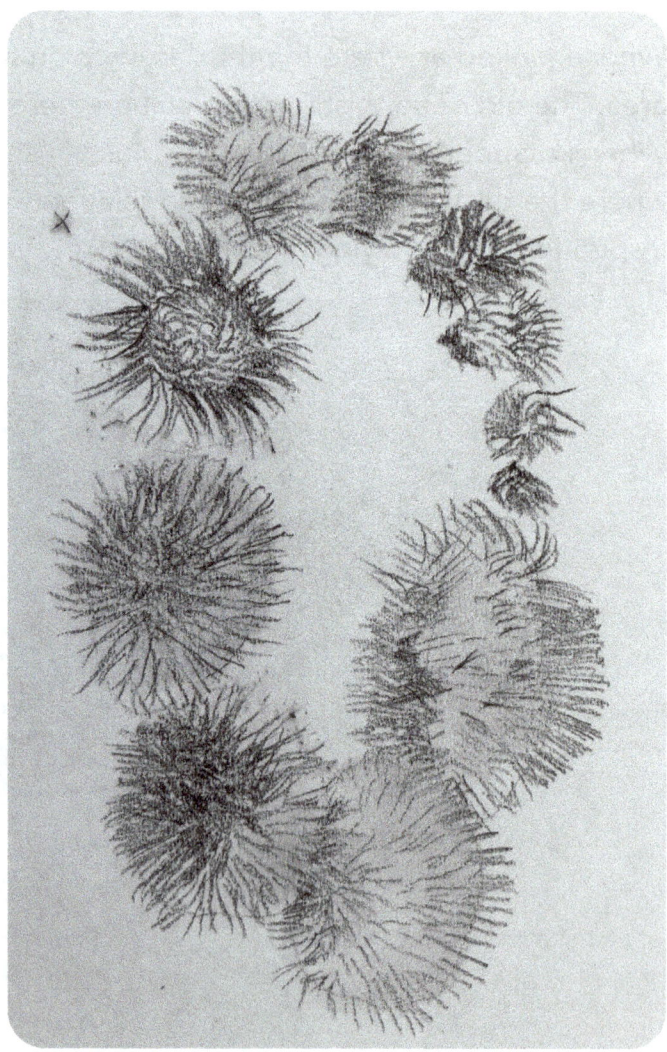

I compared the Scotch nodding thistle with the soft thistle or milk thistle because I always wondered why this plant was called a milk thistle. I guess it is because it has seeds like the thistle and it bleeds a milky substance when picked. Find a second plant to compare with yours.

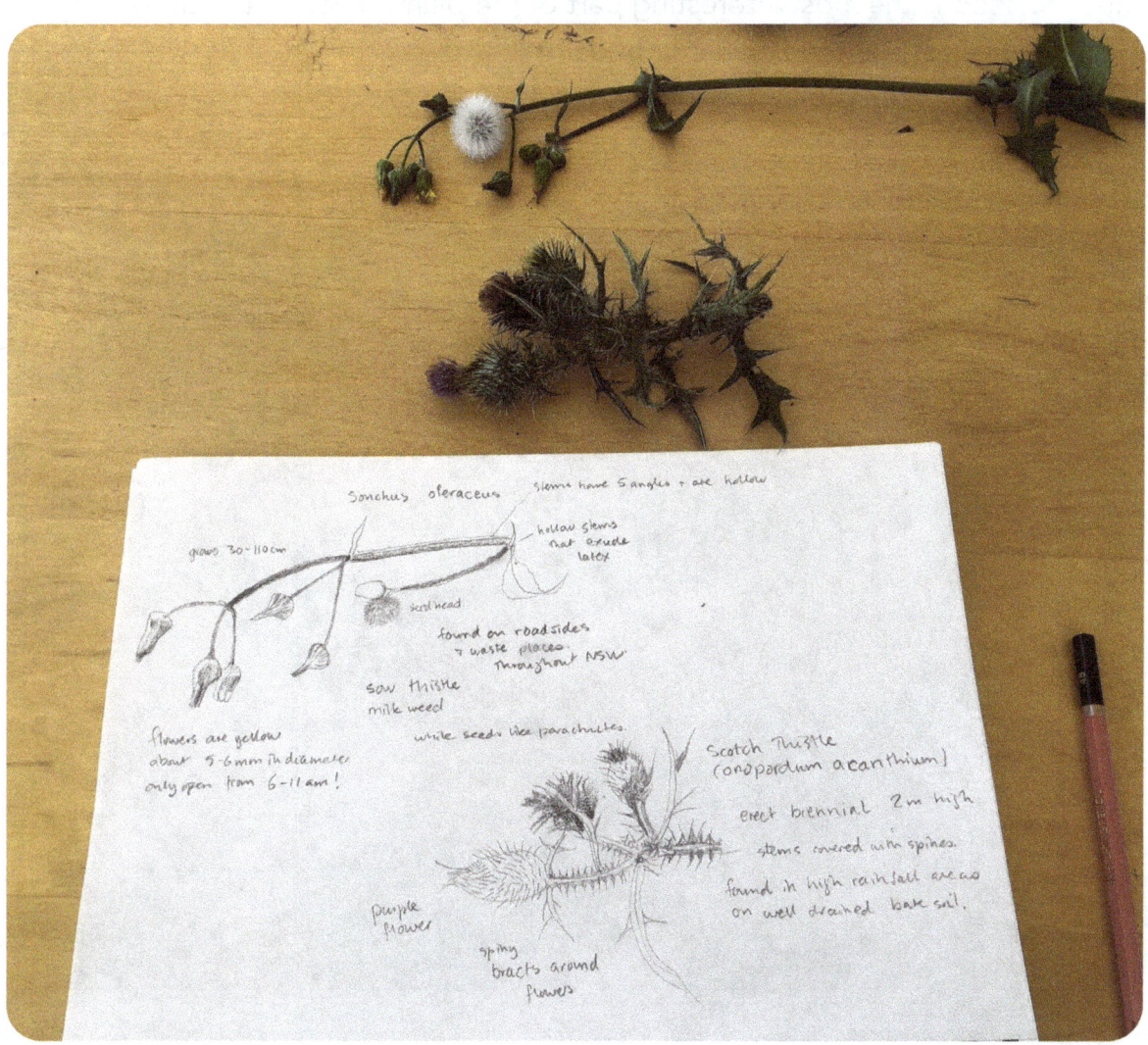

Sometimes the seed is the most interesting part of the plant. If your plant does not yet have a seed, don't worry—just use the flowers or buds.

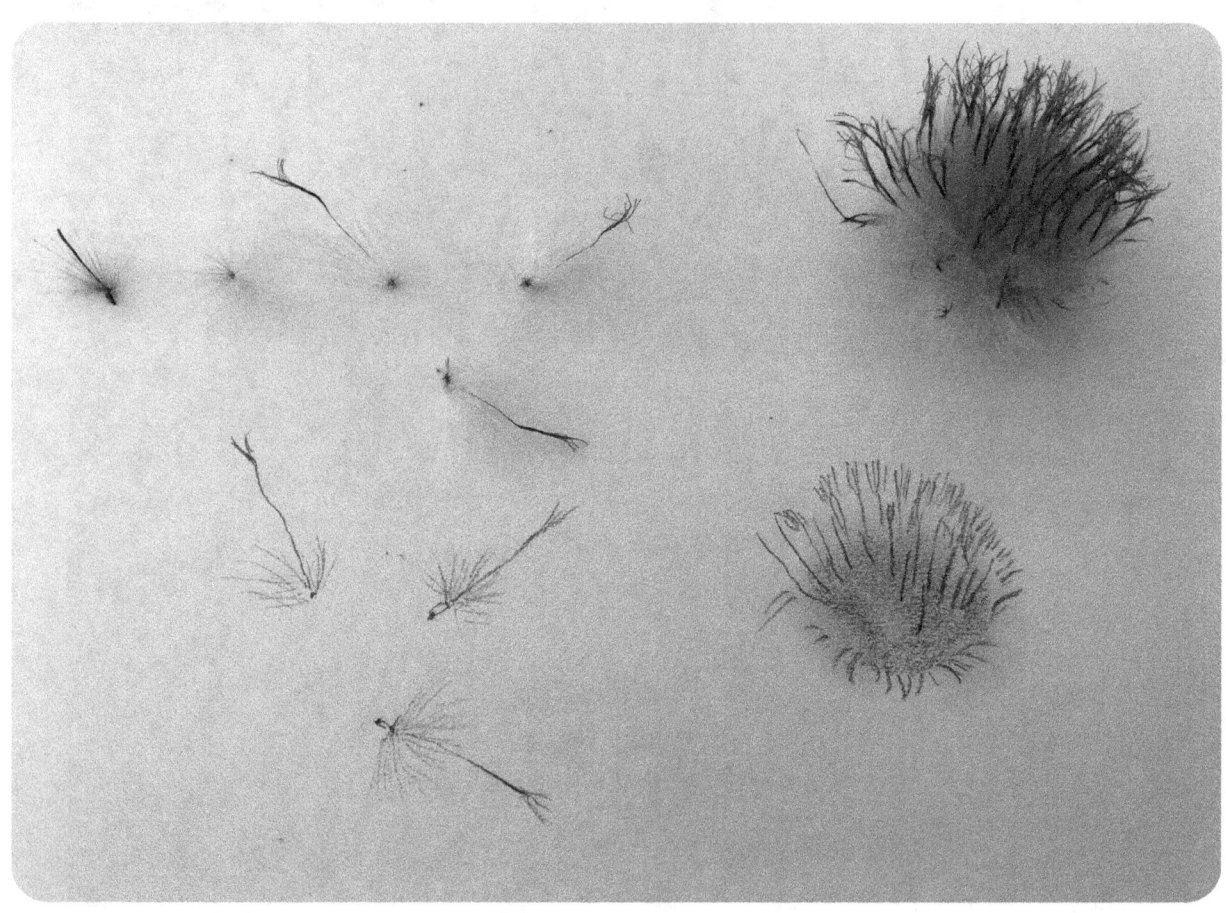

Close up

You can learn so much when you magnify a part of the plant. I chose the tiny seed and parachute because I wanted to use my hard pencils. This was drawn with a 6H and 4H pencil. The shadow was done with a 2B pencil. I should have put just a tiny shadow under the parachute.

It was difficult to look through a magnifying glass and draw.

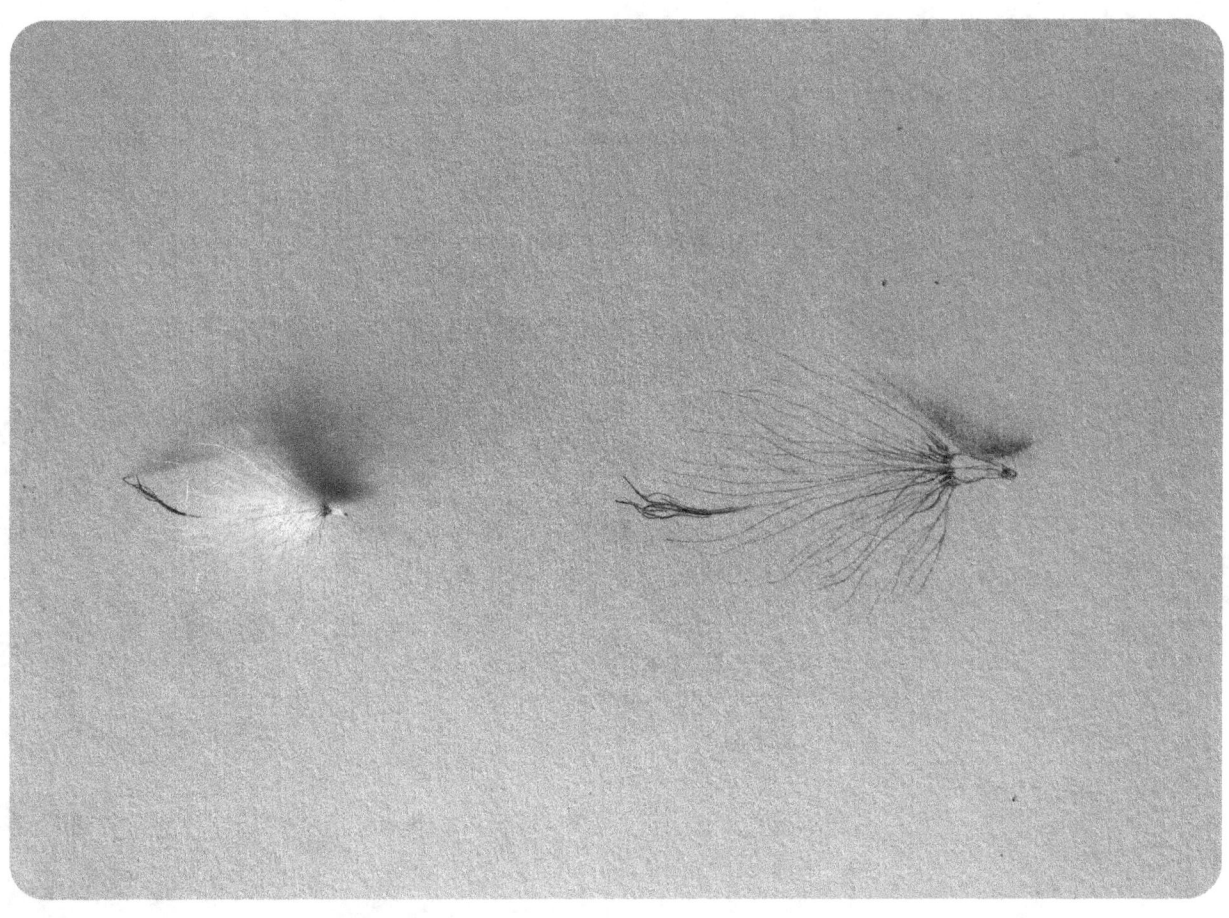

Working with Metaphors

I use metaphors a lot in my art. They help me move away from a too literal representation of the topic. They bring a depth and subtlety to the work.

Metaphor for migration: Coracle

A small, round, traditional Scottish boat made of wickerwork or interwoven laths covered with a waterproof layer of animal skin, canvas, tarred or oiled cloth, or the like. It was used to migrate from one island to the next. I could borrow this structure and see if I can make something like it out of thistle parts. It would represent my own and my ancestors' migrations.

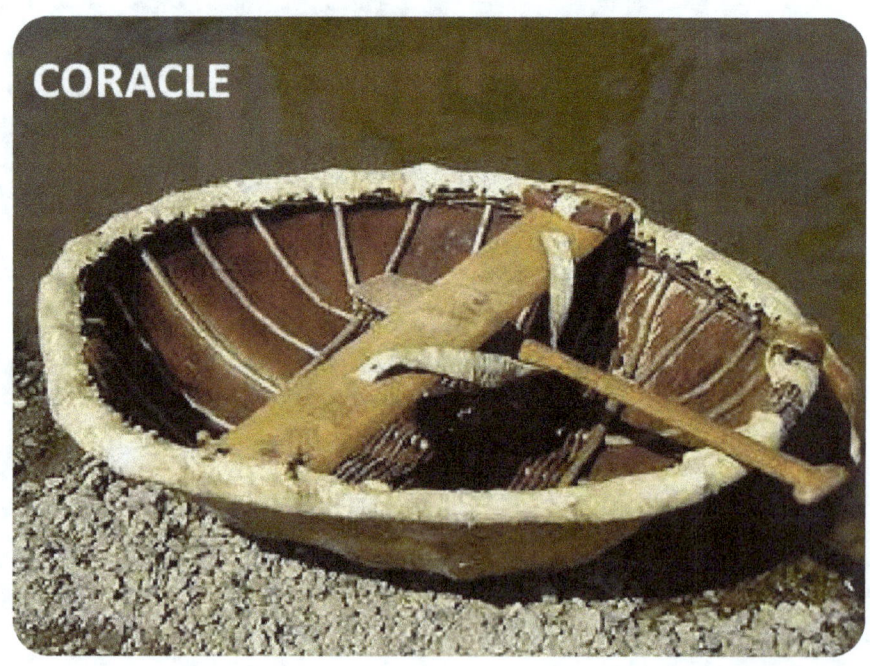

Metaphor for identity: The Order of the Thistle

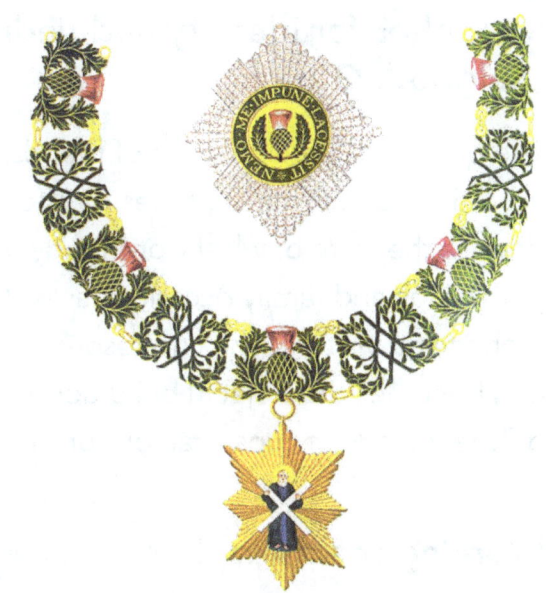

The Order of the Thistle is Scotland's greatest order of chivalry. The knights have the motto Nemo me impune lacessit, which translates as "No one assails me with impunity," but is more commonly read as "Wha daur meddle wi' me." This motto is also used by Scotland as a nation and, thinking of the spiny prickles of the thistle, could hardly be bettered.

Metaphor for identity and migration: Thistle

The thistle is the national flower of Scotland. Delicately beautiful flower heads. Viciously sharp thorns. Stubborn and tenacious grip on the land. Defiant ability to flourish in spite of efforts to remove it. .

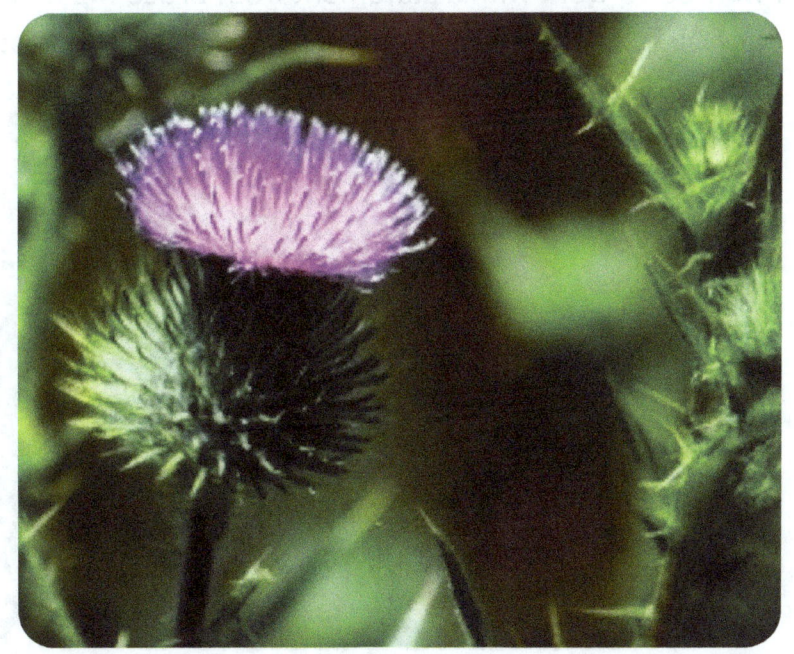

Metaphor for identity and finding the good: Quaich

The quaich is Scotland's cup of friendship. It has been used throughout the centuries to offer a welcoming drink in the form of whisky or brandy at clan gatherings and family occasions as well as to greet friends and visitors. The cup resonates most with me and becomes the object I build upon. I create all the different kinds of cups I can out of thistle parts.

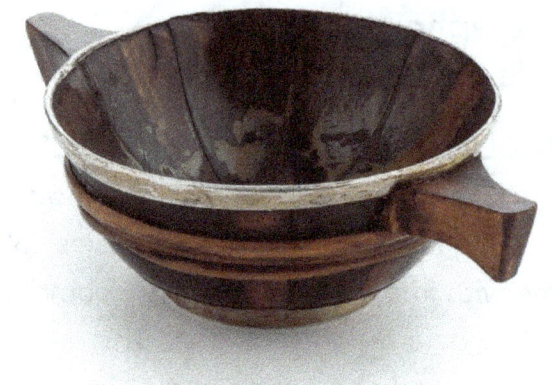

Working the metaphor

I wanted to work with a statement from Bruce Mau: "#37. Break it, stretch it, bend it, crush it, crack it, fold it." So I began to take parts of the thistle to do just that. I played around with them and started to see a pattern in what I was doing. I was revealing links to the metaphors. Using the cleaned split stems of the thistle I created a sort of coracle boat.

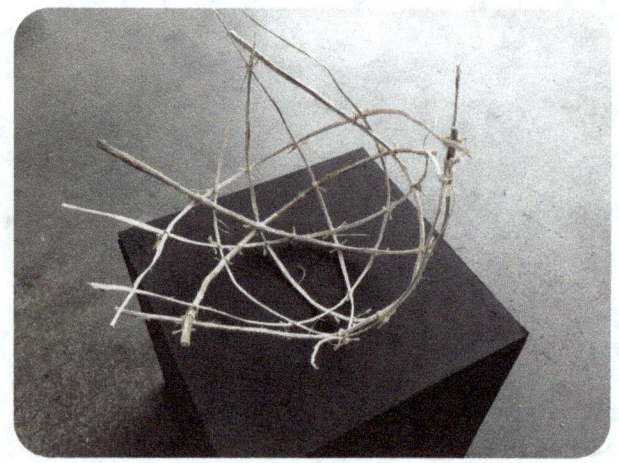 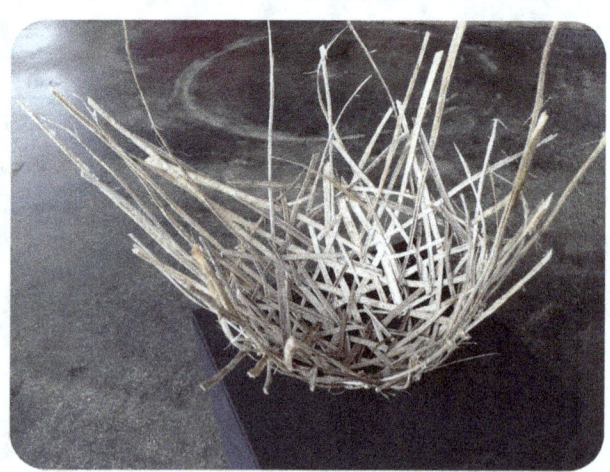

I was faced with the problem of how to cover the skeleton of the boat. Drawing on what I had learned about making Washi paper in Japan the previous year, I decided to use parts of the thistle to make some paper. Thistle paper was a very forgiving material to work with. So I went on to make more vessels with different parts of the thistle and with thistle paper. These structures held everything together quite well. I knew that for the festival I would be exhibiting in an old shop front. So I made black plinths and displayed the vessels as if for sale.

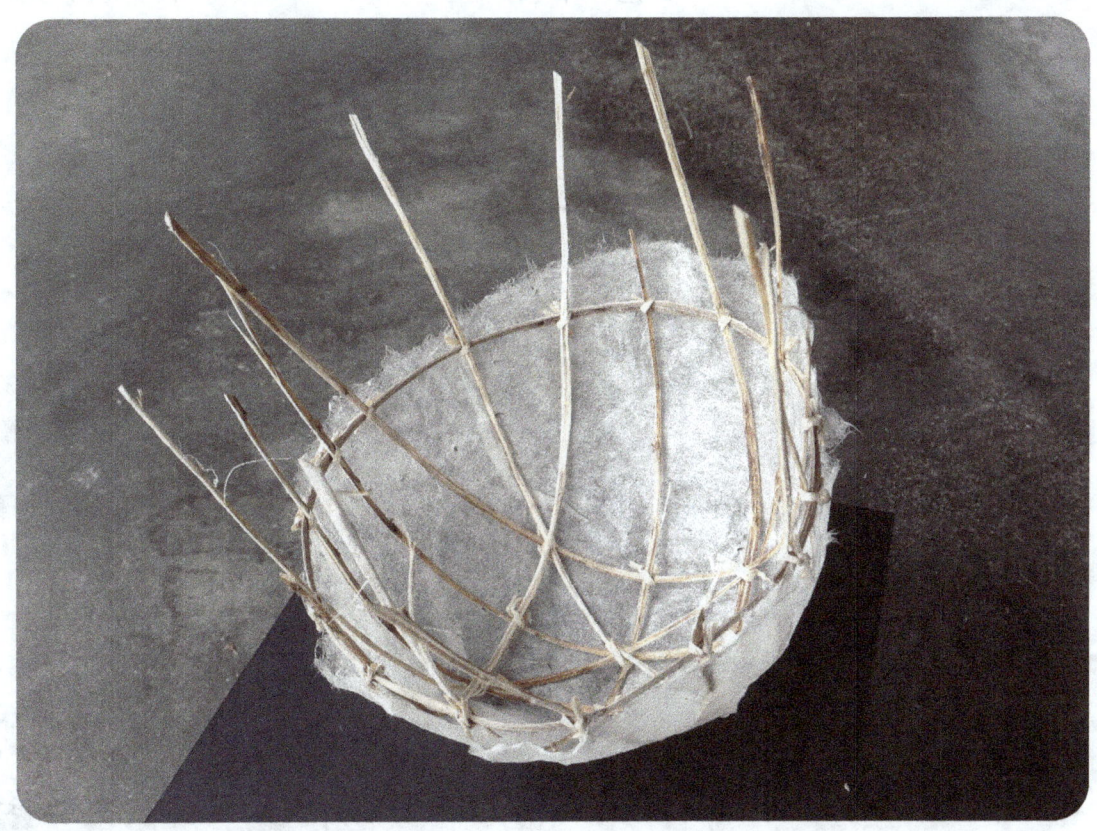

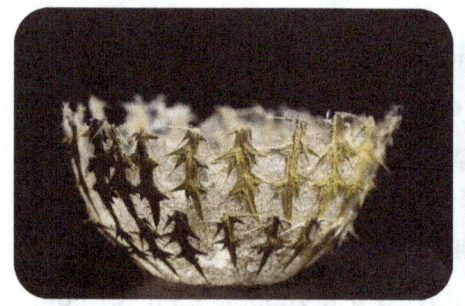

Leaf bowl

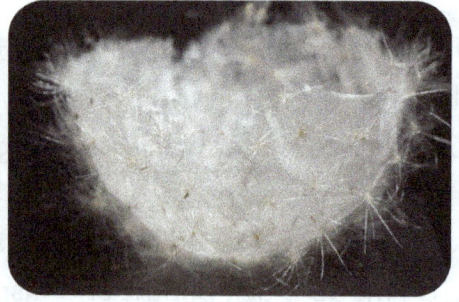

Down bowl

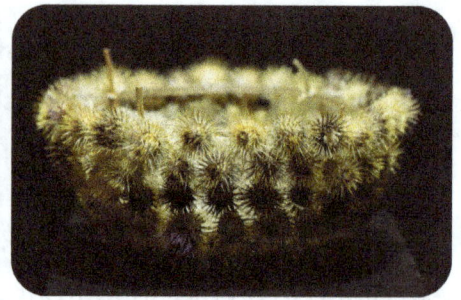

Flower bowl

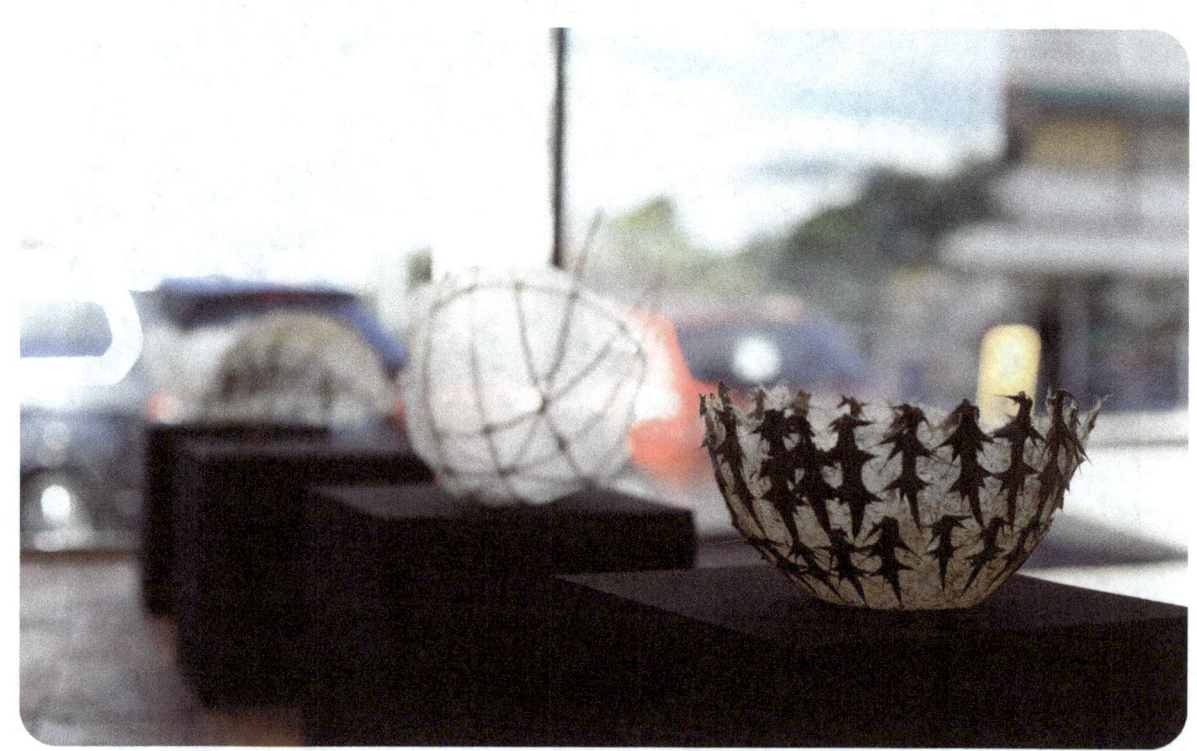

I used an event mapping process similar to the lesson above to create a large charcoal drawing of flower heads. I began the drawing with some mapping. Then I spread the idea of mapping over a very large piece of paper. I used my drawing of thistle heads to represent where some of the thistles were and then gathered a wide variety of flower heads.

The charcoal drawing is 180 x 70 cm and is drawn on heavy art paper.

By following my journey through the Thistle Project you have been able to experience some of the processes that an artist engages in the making of art. I still have many things I can do with this topic. Indeed, my collection of artifacts grew and subsequent exhibitions in different galleries were quite different.

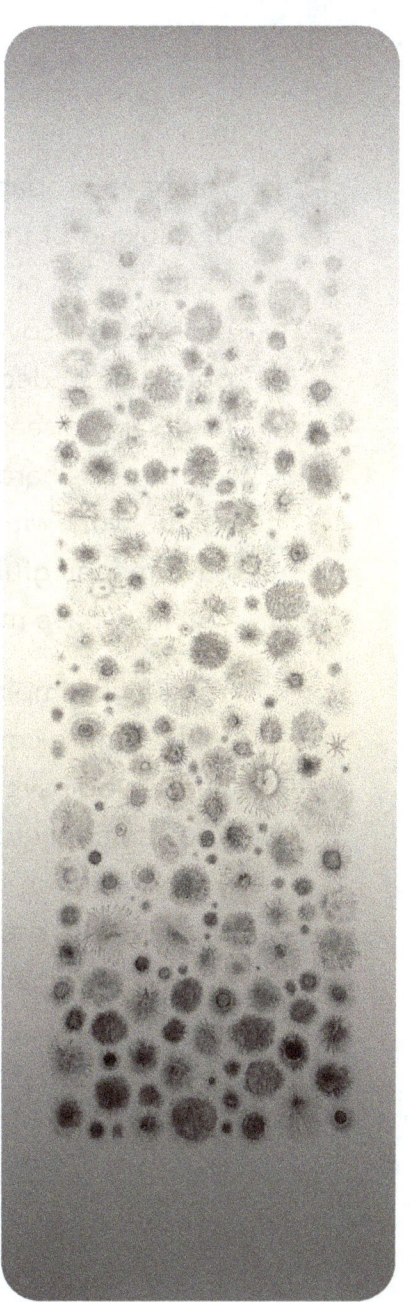

You have probably begun to realize that making art takes quite a lot of thinking of the kind that cannot be hurried. Often being given a blank canvas or open-ended task to work with is daunting. You have probably discovered that it is hard work to make art. It takes a lot of persistence, decision making, problem solving, organizing, trial and error, and research. It is quite a journey. If you have not been on that journey it is hard to imagine. I hope that you remember your journey as you work with children and that you become more involved and can have meaningful discussions with them about their big ideas. Hopefully you now have more possibilities to suggest and techniques to model.

You have completed your brief course in drawing and I hope you are feeling more confident and capable. You have tried on "being artist." I hope you have a wider repertoire of skills, techniques, and ideas that you can apply to your own art while feeling better able to support young children's art making. I hope you have engaged with both the text and the drawing. Below is a list of some of the competencies you should have gained.

Contemporary Art Practices

As an artist who practices some of the contemporary genres, I have analysed my own and other artists' approaches to art making today. I have identified a set of practices that I believe to be core for contemporary art creation and important for early childhood. This list is not comprehensive. All the elements are not utilized at the same time, but rather accessed as needed. Artists develop their own repertoire of competencies for each project they undertake. These core practices are not necessarily new but they may be new to this particular context. I would like to suggest these studio practices have a place in early childhood pedagogy and practice, not as a checklist to be worked through but rather as repertoire that we can pick and choose from as needed.

This is my incomplete list:

- Gaining technical skills. In the visual arts there has been a revival of drawing. Traditional drawing exercises have been extended and a high level of technical competency is sought.

- Learning fluency with media. Fluency is important because if you have fluency you are free to concentrate on ideas and get into the flow.

- Working across media. Traditionally media were not mixed. Now innovation in the uses of different media is encouraged, as seen for example in the combination of drawing and video in the work of William Kentridge.

- Problem finding/problem solving. There is a saying, "It is in the unravelling of the knot that the most learning occurs." So looking for the knots is valued in visual art. Finding gaps, uncovering taken-for-granted practices, pushing the boundaries, and experimenting are all part of the process.

- Polishing. Polishing up an art piece will often reveal the flaws. Sometimes it will surprise you!

- aking apart. Deconstruction can be as informative as construction. As we take things apart we see them from a different perspective.

- Borrowing. Look at what other artists are doing and shamelessly borrow from them (with credit to the artist of course!). We need to try on different practices to see how they feel.

- Playing with symbols. More than ever before, our world is full of symbols. We need to embrace them and learn how to use them.

- Playing with metaphors. This is my favorite. Metaphors are powerful and can lift your work into a more abstract and philosophical realm.

- Making connections. Art is all about making new and interesting connections. Art can also connect the viewer with facets of life previously unnoticed.

- Looking for possibilities. Art making is a generative process. We are always looking for possibilities.

- Looking for essences. This is about exploring the big idea and clarifying the focus for the art.

- Abstracting. Sometimes, when we abstract elements of an image (as I did in the large drawing of thistle heads or the thistle seeds) we can rearrange the abstraction(s) in ways that lift the concept to a higher level of thinking.

- Re-positioning. Re-framing. Re-presenting. I have clustered these actions because they probably do similar things. When we take a subject or object and give it a different spin then these actions are helpful.

- Persisting. Persistence is critical. It is frustrating and disheartening when things don't turn out the way you expect. It is important not to give up. We have to learn to love our mistakes.

- Reflecting. It is good to look back and consider how we got to where we are. Reflection happens on a minute scale and a wide scale. We reflect on each mark we make and at the same time mull over every big idea. If we don't reflect like this we will never move forward or come to terms with the direction we have taken.

- Re-contextualizing. When we take an object or idea out of its comfortable and often taken for granted context, we see it in a new way.

Chapter 2

~

Integrating the visual arts:
A project about faces

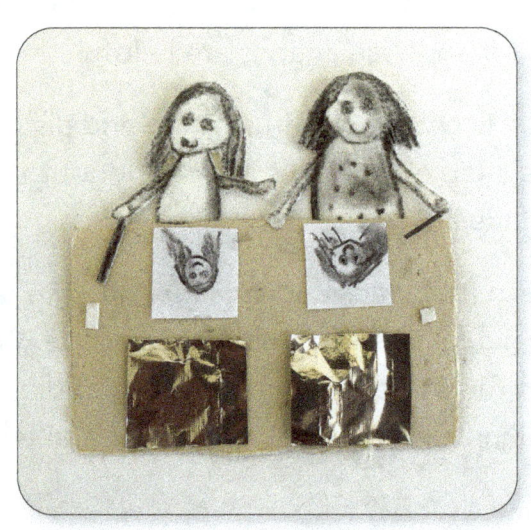

You have just experienced an art lesson that aimed to give you some of the technical skills and insights into the thinking behind art making. These are necessary elements of drawing. However, it is important to remember that drawing is about a bigger picture. It is about 'something'. It is integrated into other aspects of our lives.

This is the story of a project about faces, during which a group of four- to five-year-old children made a study of different aspects of the face. A project is an in-depth study of a topic that is of interest to most of the children and has the potential to be of educational value. As well as supporting children's questions and investigations, good projects support elements of the curriculum and contemporary issues in early childhood. This chapter demonstrates how drawing can support learning, especially making friends and becoming socially competent, through project work.

When children are doing focused art work, they are working at higher levels of mental cognition. The process of drawing involves visual, kinesthetic, and linguistic dimensions. Information is processed three ways, creating more connections in the brain than just hearing or seeing. When children draw something they learn much more and remember much more than if they had just looked at it or were told about it. In order to draw a convincing copy of the object, you have to get to know it very well. Drawing increases the level of engagement, which in turn increases the level of understanding. This project is documented to demonstrate some ways in which the visual arts can be integrated into regular programming and how this enriches the program. It will also demonstrate how a socio cultural framework for the visual arts can engage children in in-depth learning over extended periods of time.

This project was specific to this group of children, in one specific time and place. So, while you might find ideas and elements from it relevant to your situation, it would need to be adapted to support the questions and ideas your children have. For more information about projects visit http://projectapproach.org/.

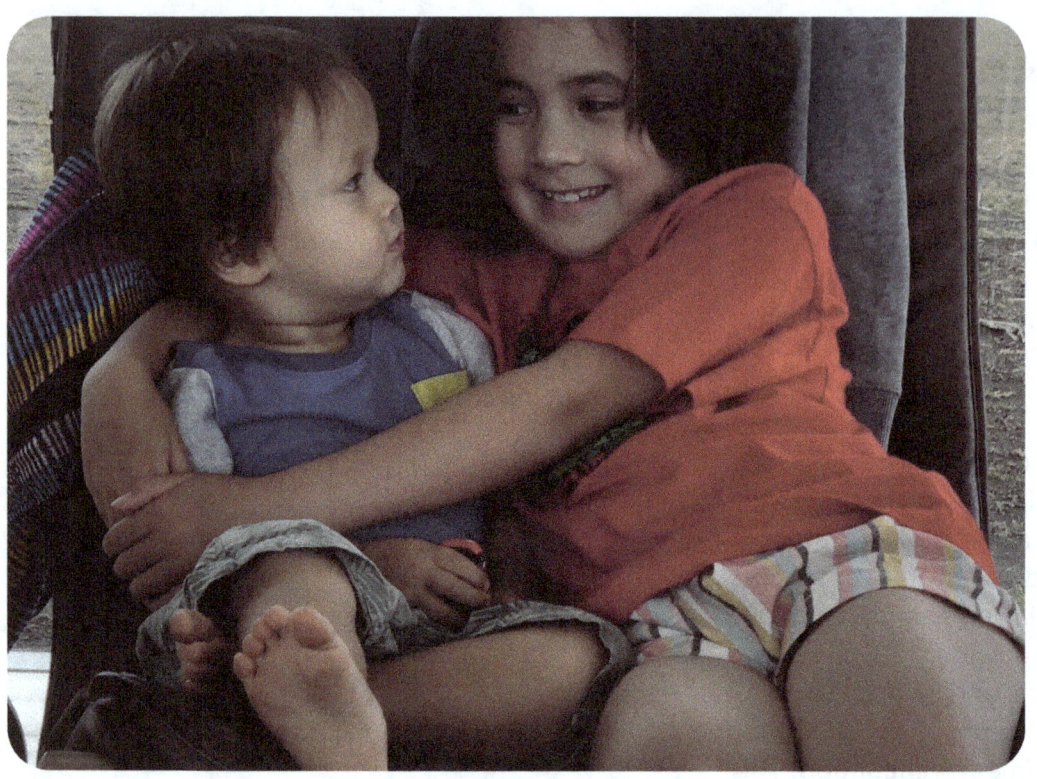

Reading and Drawing Faces

As young children develop more awareness of others in their lives and move into more social settings like preschool, they need to develop skills that will allow them to become successful members of social groups. Social competence depends heavily upon how accurately we can learn to read another's facial expression and respond appropriately. The clues to how another person is feeling are visual clues. The messages sent are often through subtle changes in the shape, lines, and orientation of the face. We have to look carefully at faces in order to read all the messages. It is important for children to pay attention to another's facial expressions so they learn to read the visual clues that a person's face can give us. We know that our facial and body language is a more accurate representation of our true feelings than the words we use to describe our feelings. What we see is often more accurate than what we hear.

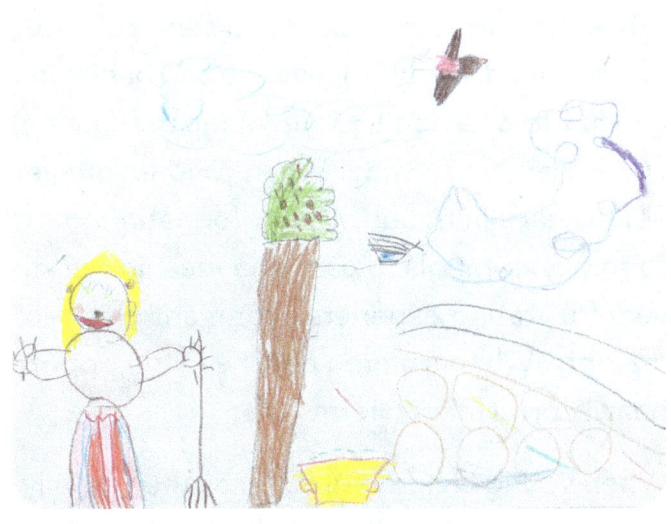

Unfortunately, many of the images used to depict different moods and expressions are oversimplified, as in emojis. In emojis, the feelings have been pared back to the most simplistic of symbols. Symbols contain very basic information and are quickly and easily read. Children often use them in a shorthand and narrative manner. For example, the cloud symbols in this drawing let us know the state of the weather. The canonical view of the person marks her place in the drawing while the brush symbol indicates her intention. The sparse amount of visual information in the drawing gives us some indication that the subject has been observed and that this is what the child can remember.

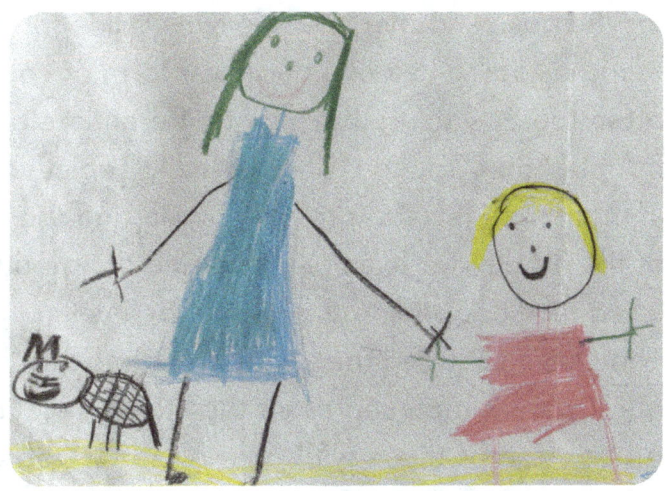

While the narrative is clear and serves the purpose for this child's story, constantly relying on simplified symbols leaves strong habits in a child's drawing memory so that it is often difficult to override the automatic use of a symbol when they are doing a more considered and observed drawing. When children are asked to draw from memory they are not usually able to recall enough visual information to make a representational drawing, so they have to rely on symbols to carry the meaning or mark the place. Drawing from memory can be a very frustrating experience for many children, yet they are often asked to draw things from memory. When children only have the opportunity to draw from memory they tend to rely heavily on symbolic forms.

When young children draw faces they usually draw a circle for the face, two circles for the eyes, a dot for the nose and then a single curved line for the mouth. Adding hair of a particular form or color is often the only thing that might differentiate one face from another. Young children usually depict changes in mood and facial expression by altering the line of the mouth, for example, inverting the mouth for a sad face or opening the mouth for a yelling face. They have acquired the symbols our society uses to quickly and simply represent the human face. Like rubber stamps these symbols are used to represent the generic and the general. In this project we took the children further and found more complex and representational ways to draw faces. The children were challenged to dig deeper and aim higher.

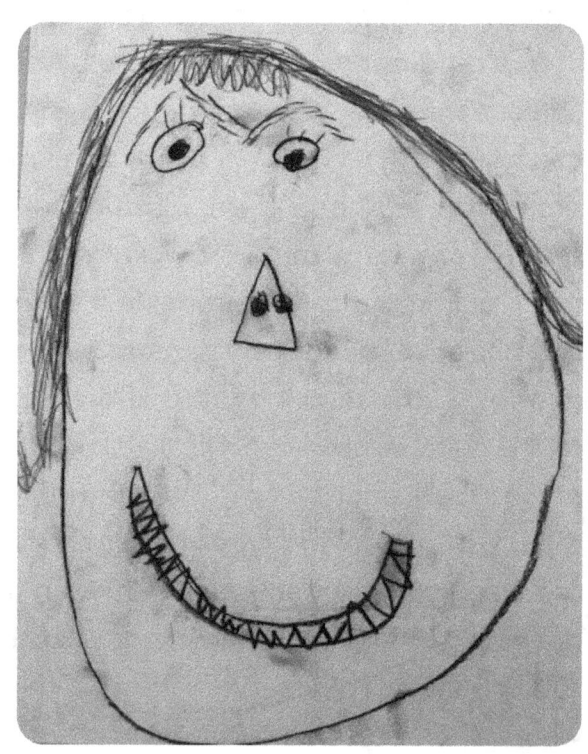

Drawing their theories

We began the project with a closer look at eyes. How our eyes work is a difficult question. The children had many different ideas. In the discussion we found we needed to draw diagrams to explain our theories better. Often words were not only inadequate but they also carried so many different personal interpretations that the discussion was confusing. We modelled three diagrammatic forms for them on the white board: front view, side view, and plan view. We also showed how you can label diagrams, name the different parts, and write short explanations.

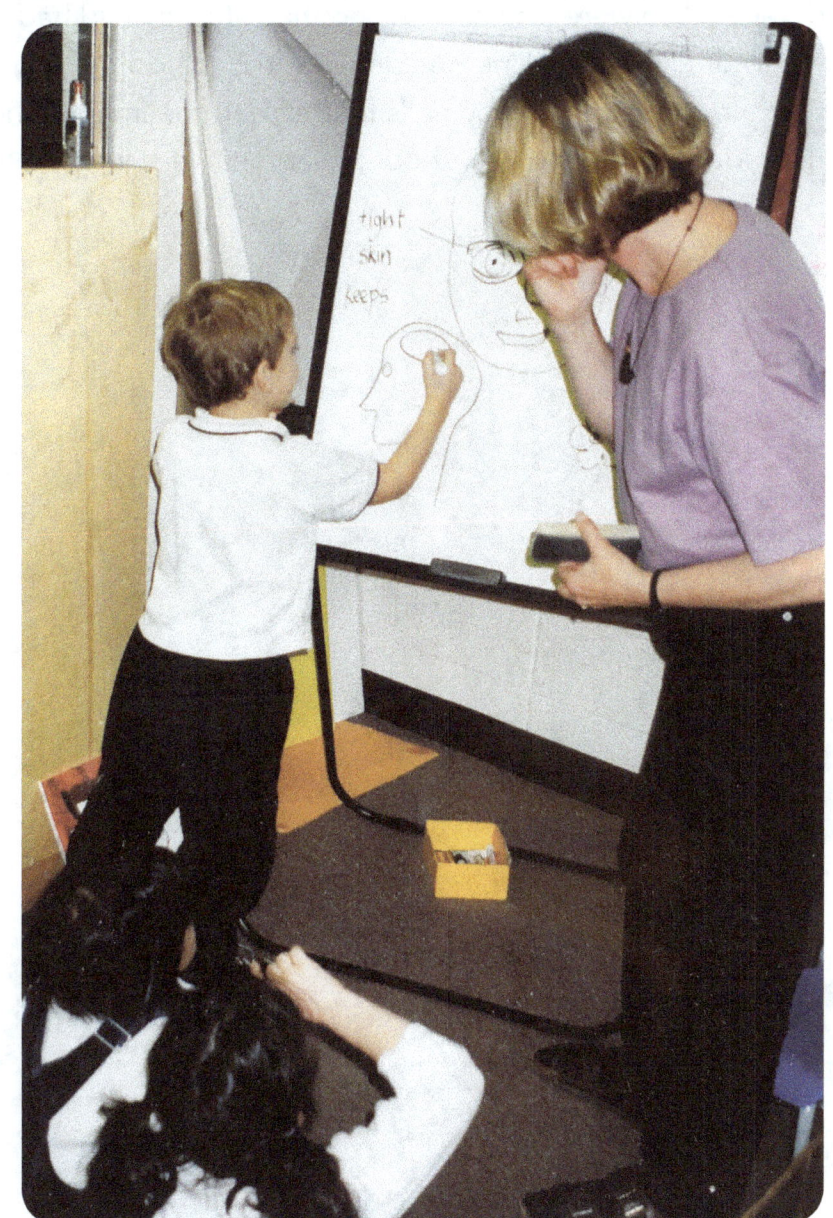

Once the children grasped the concept of diagrams, their explanations became much more detailed. We were also able to see that while a child had talked about a tube from the eye to the brain, in fact the line was drawn with little dots along it. When asked, the child explained that the dots represented cells that carried the image. The diagram helped the child explain their ideas more easily. Without a diagram we struggled to understand what the child meant.

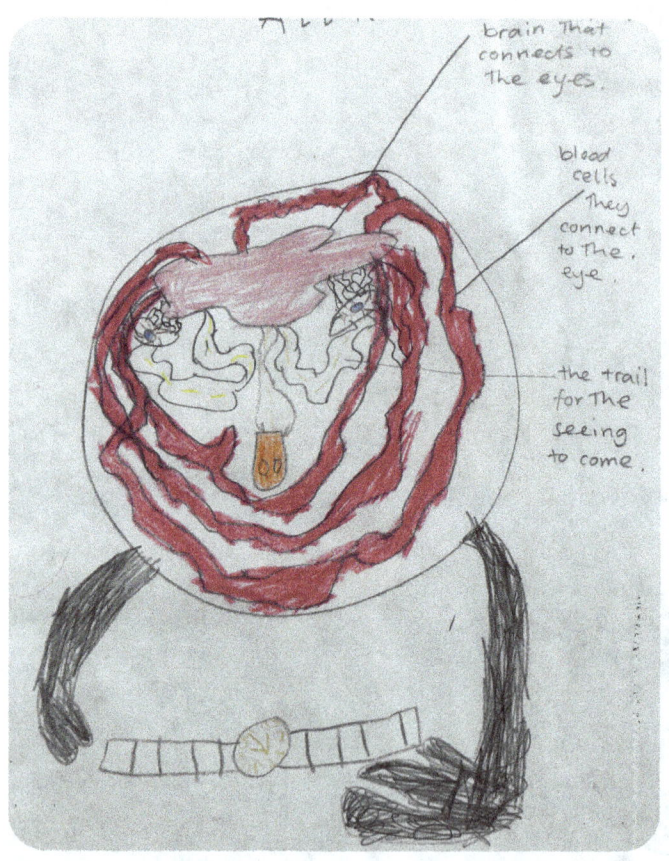

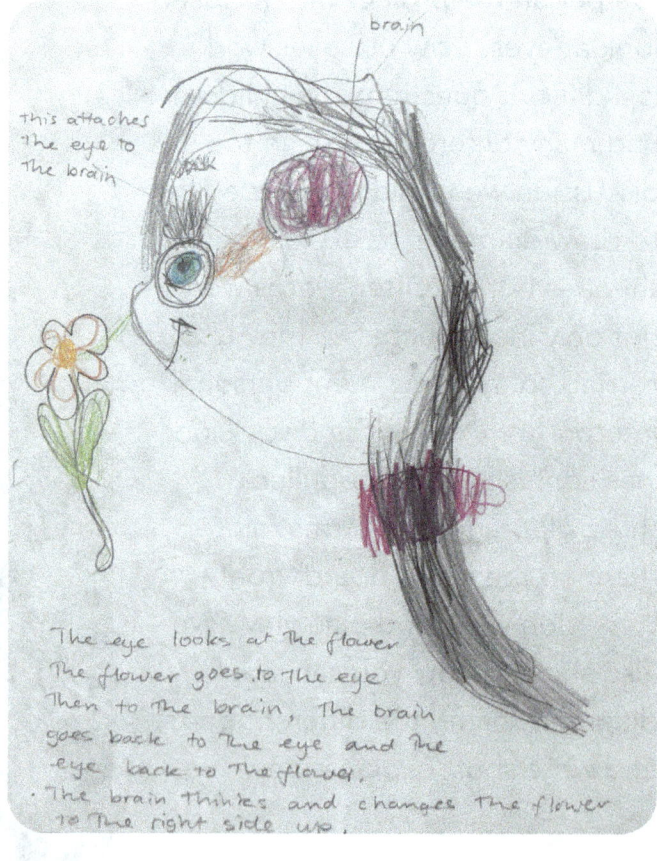

Drawing field notes from life experiences

Project work involves visits to the field. We go out to experience things first hand for ourselves. On field visits each child carries a clipboard and pencil. Their task is to gather as much information as they can, much as an anthropologist might do. Drawing what happens when someone gets their eyes tested gave the children a huge amount of information to be processed. The children noted the sequences of events so they could incorporate them into their dramatic play.

Drawings can remind children about the details of certain events and artifacts and allow them to be recreated back in the classroom. Children quickly learn that they need lots of details in order to re-construct and re-enact certain events and practices. The more real-life experiences children have to pull from, the richer the play scripts and the drawings can be. Public scripts, like drawings, allow for recognition of what is idiosyncratic to the artist and what is held common. This kind of public representation allows children to exchange information about shared events. The children raised many questions and challenged assumptions about the way things worked. Shared events and discussions build a strong community of learners.

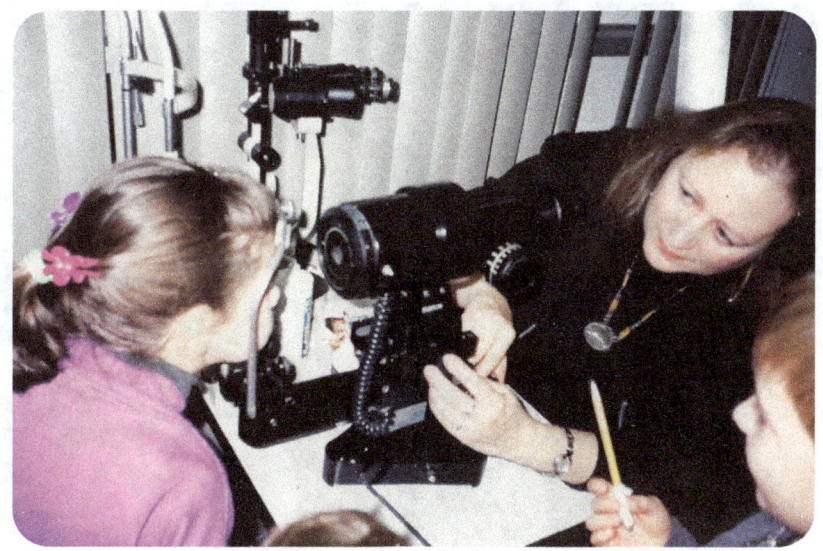

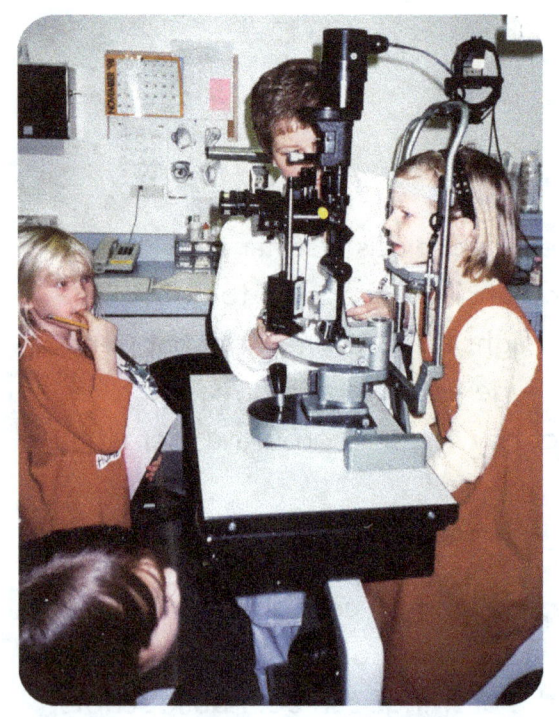
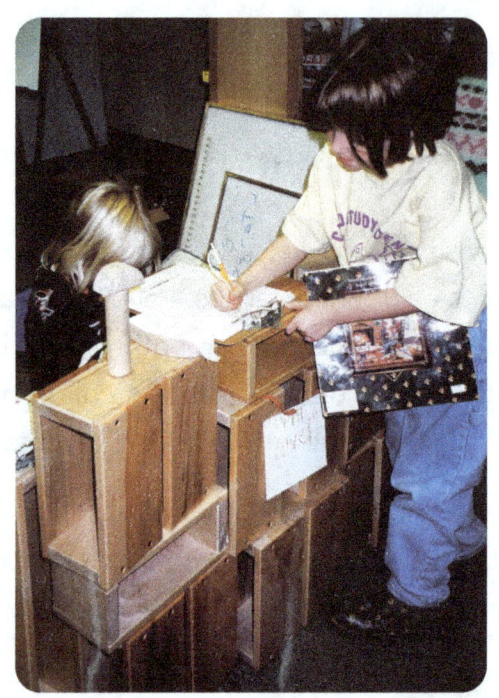
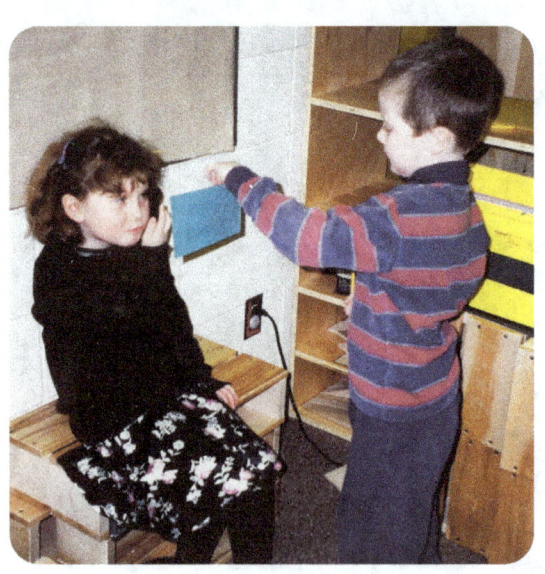
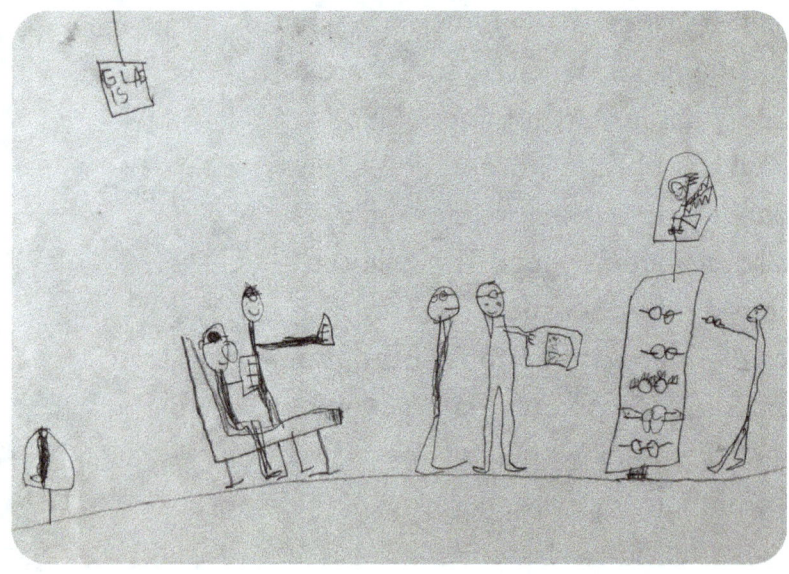

Extending the investigation, we invited nursing students to dissect cows' eyes for us. The children kept a record of these events, drawing each stage of the dissection. This gave them an important job to do—recording scientific information. It also encouraged them to pay very close attention to what was happening. The diagrams were carefully labelled and then used to discuss the working of the eye more thoroughly.

As children drew their individual diagrams they pulled together all they knew into one context. In this visible and accessible format they were able to share information and ideas with their peers and teachers. We observed children altering their diagrams as they acquired new information that seemed relevant to them.

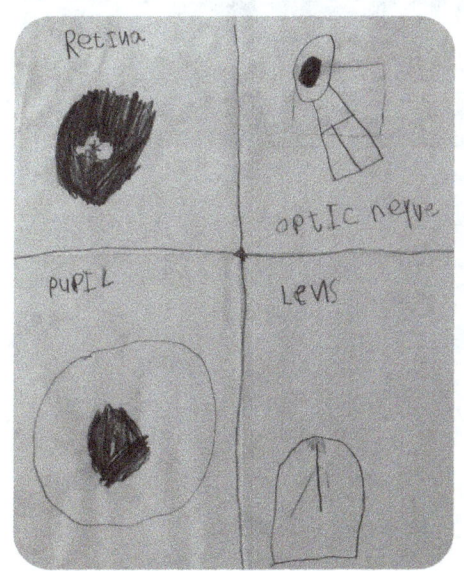
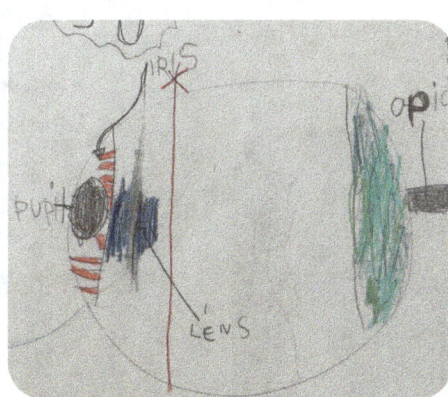
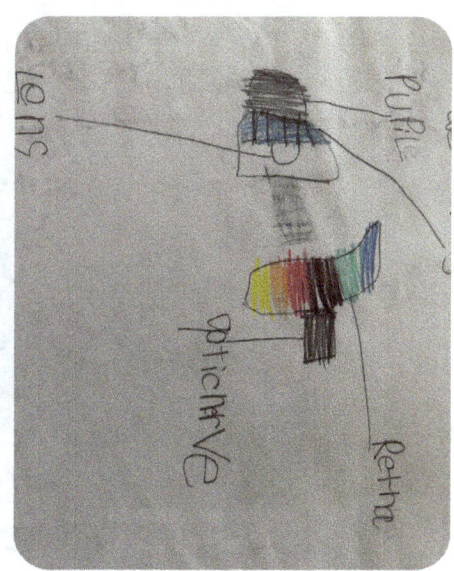

How do eyes work: Drawing the dissecting of cows eyes.

Trying on another's eyes

What is it like to have someone else's eyes? How does this change the way we see and are seen? The children cut their eyes out of a photo copy of themselves and placed them over the eyes of a similar photo of one of their peers. The transformations that took place were fascinating and led to many comments and questions. The eyes that had been cut out were still recognizable even without the rest of the face. We only need eyes to recognize someone we know.

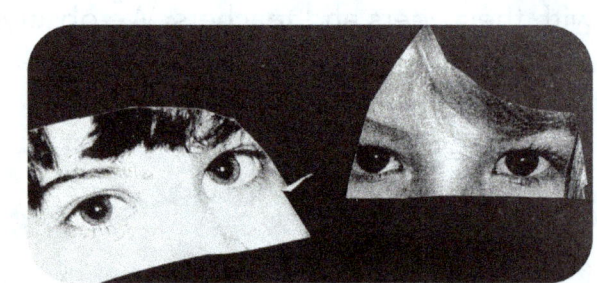

We noticed that people in self-portraits usually had a serious and concentrating expression. The eyes were looking hard at us. Eyes can tell us much about how another person is feeling. The children looked at themselves in a mirror and made many different expressions, like sad, angry, excited, and shy. They looked in particular at their eyes. They noticed how the

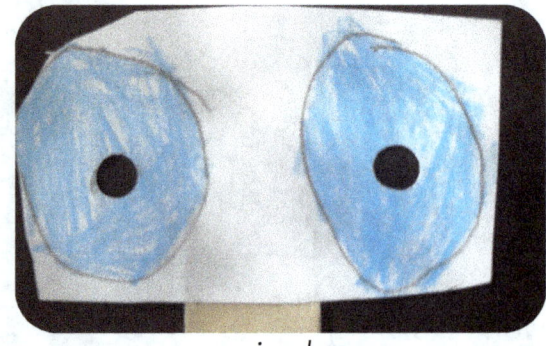

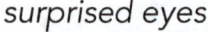
surprised eyes

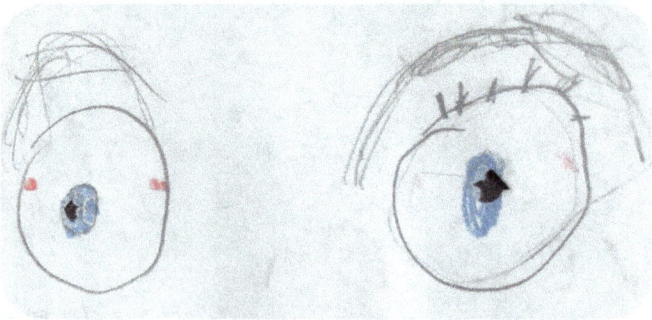
shy eyes

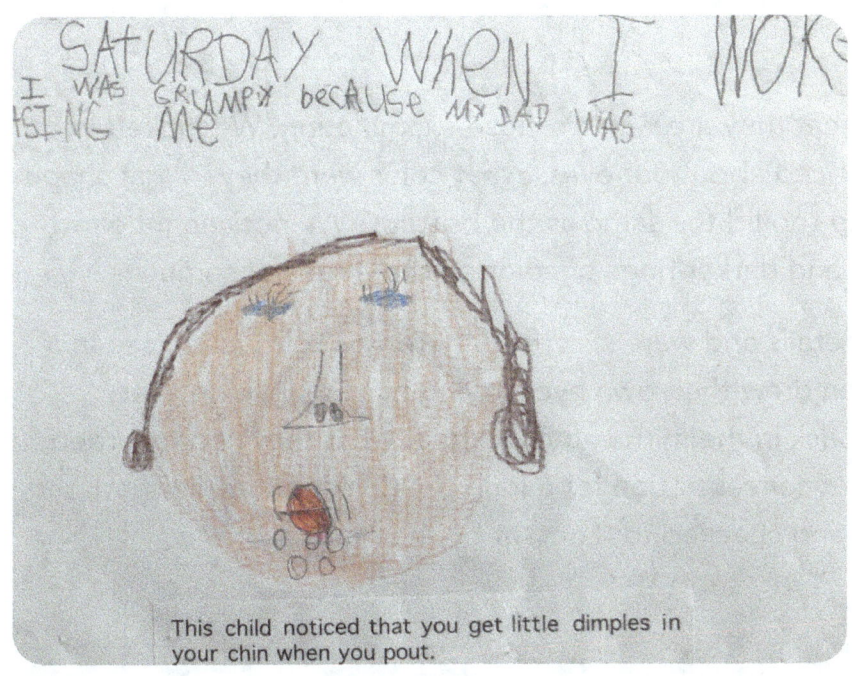

This child noticed that you get little dimples in your chin when you pout.

shape and size of the eye changes as moods change. They acted out different emotions and expressions in the mirror. They drew these expressive eyes and cut them out so they could try them on themselves and others.

We took the combined information from the children's discoveries and made a big book about all kinds of eyes.

In another exercise, we drew our own eyes and then we drew our partner's eyes. It was in doing this that we really noticed how different other peoples' eyes are. Drawing another's eyes gives us permission to look at them in a way that is different from our normal social glances. Often it is considered rude to stare at someone too intently, yet we need to do this if we are to understand what we are looking at. We need to look closely if we are to gather enough visual information for an observational drawing.

Eyes tell us so much about a person that they are worth a close examination. We looked in mirrors and talked about what we noticed about our eyes. What color were they? What shape were they? Were the eyelashes on the top lid the same as the bottom? We noticed little red blood vessels in the white of the eye and darker rings of color on the edges of some iris.

The children kept finding more tiny details and were surprised there was so much to see in the eye. With this awareness they then drew their own eyes, trying hard to include every detail accurately. They kept looking back in the mirror to check that what they had recorded was authentic. They worked with great concentration for a long time. When they finished, the drawing was matched to the subject and checked for content by their peers.

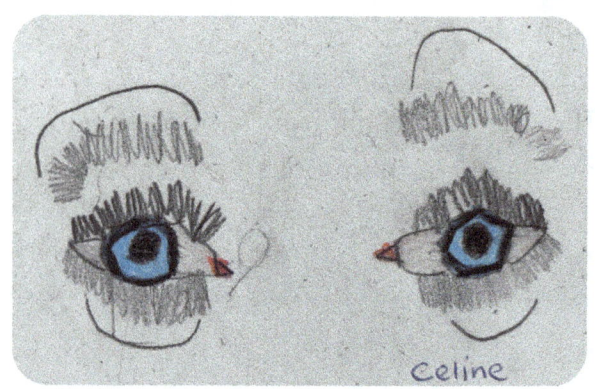

Celine

self portraits

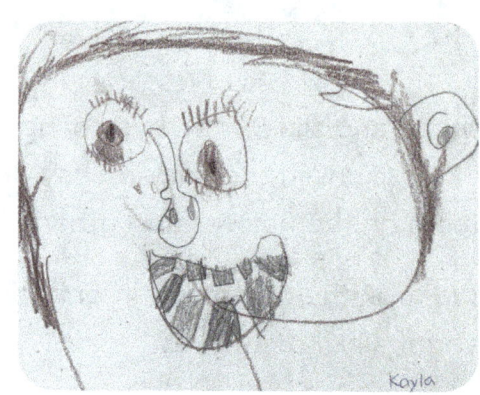

Kayla

CELINES EYES BY KAYLr

*drawing your
partner's eyes*

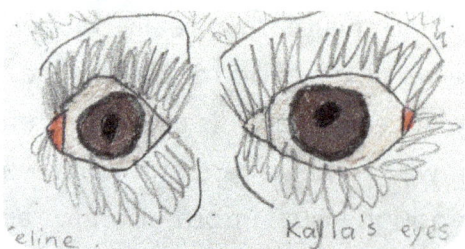

'eline   Kayla's eyes

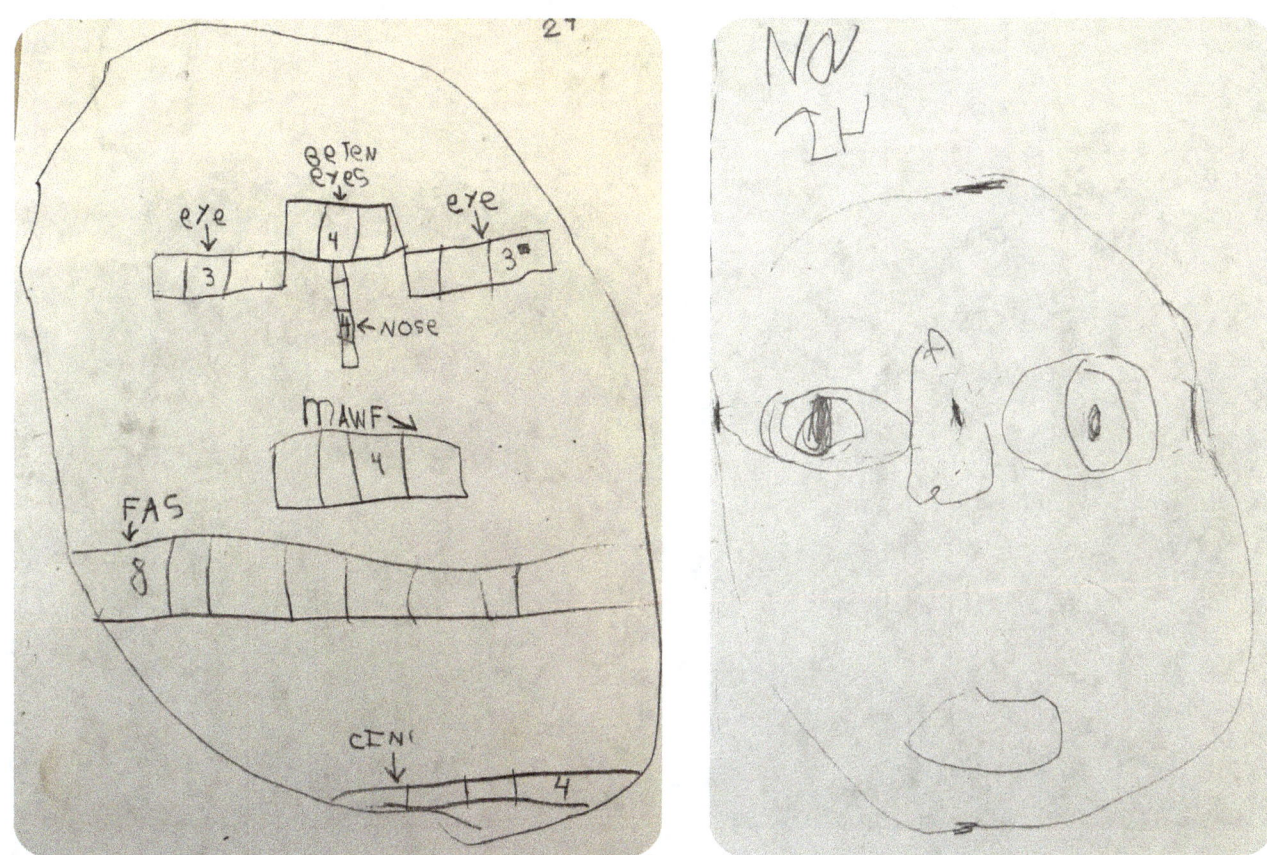

Solving Problems

When we draw a face it is important to get the proportions as accurate as possible so that the face becomes believable. Faces are particularly difficult because even tiny misalignments can distort its representation. We have a tendency to place the eyes too high and this leaves us the problem of too large a space for the nose and mouth. To bring awareness to this problem we used centi cubes to measure as many parts of the face as possible.

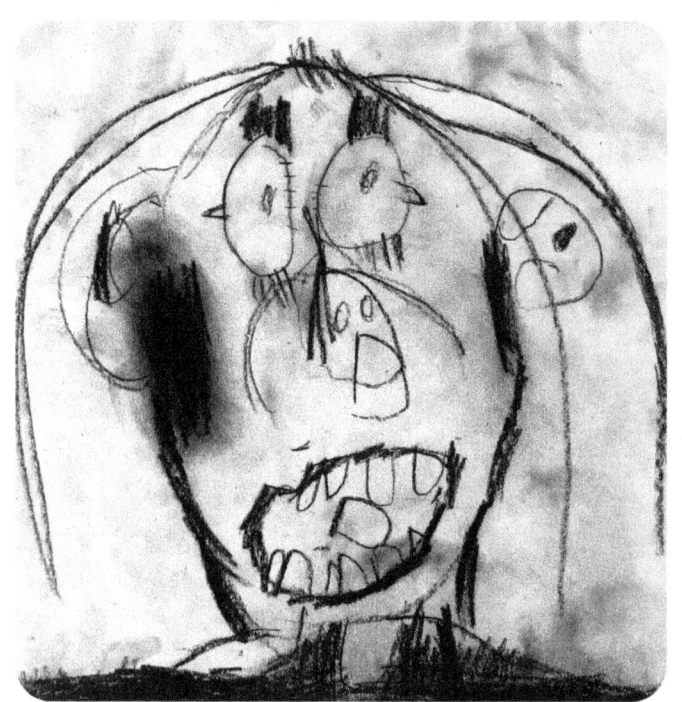 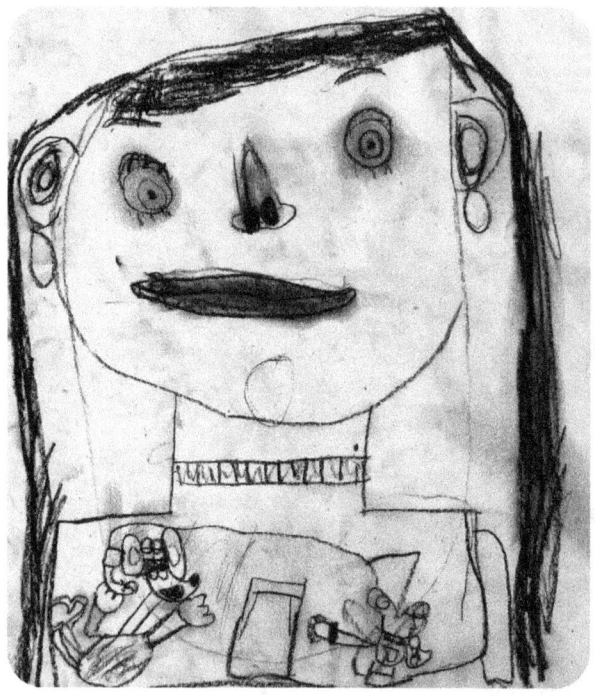

Sometimes the medium, or mark-making tool, behaves in a way the child does not intend but they do not yet have a solution to avoid the outcome. Sometimes the mark making tool will influence the drawing outcome as the child becomes more absorbed in discovering the properties of the media than the actual representation. Sometimes they get sidetracked by a problem (such as, "How do I create an area of tone without my marks being visible?") This set of portraits are very well observed and have a lot of important details. There is a combination of charcoal and graphite and there is a better understanding of the proportions of the face. There is the beginning of an interest in shading.

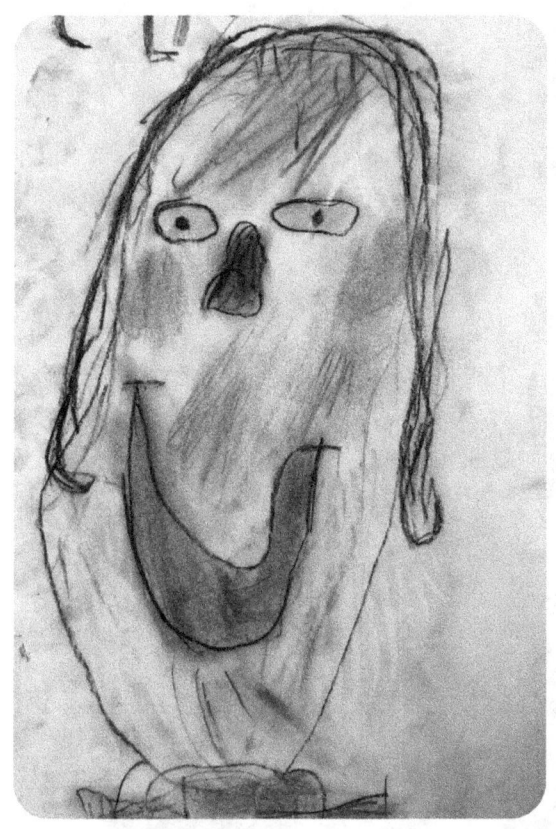
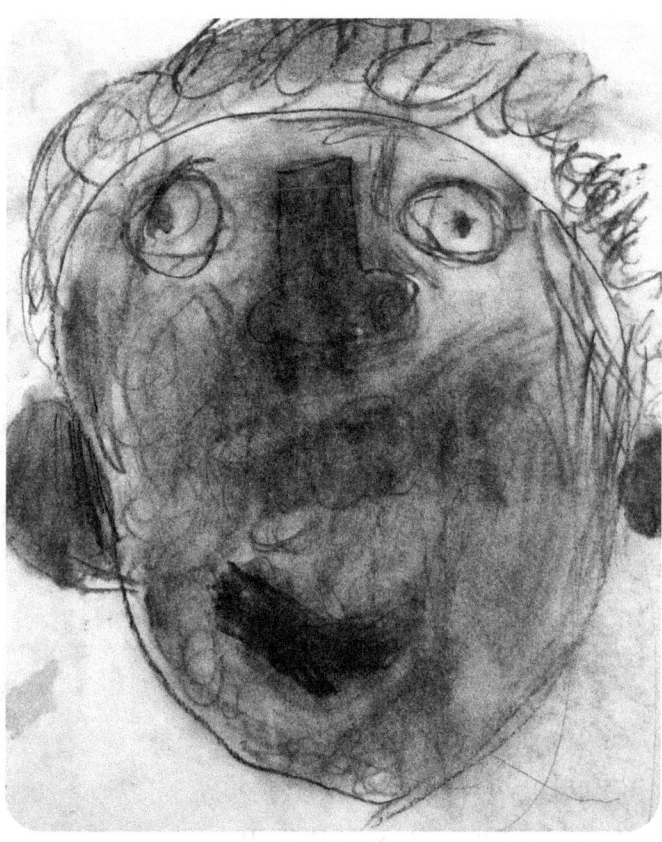

While drawing from observation is the best practice, it can also be challenging for young children as they have to sort their way through an overload of visual information to pick out the salient points. One way to cut down on the visual clutter and noise is to close one eye. Closing one eye reduces the depth of field so the observer sees the face as a collection of flat shapes. However, young children find it difficult to close one eye. Accordingly, I made photocopies of all the children's faces. This too flattens the image. It also gives children something they can draw on and touch if they want to get the feel of a line. I asked them to notice where the dark and light shapes were as well as the thick and thin lines.

It is also helpful to look at the work of professional or famous artists. Discussions with children about what they notice are encouraged. For example; 'It is darker under her hat', 'the light is shining on top of her hat', 'she is looking at us', 'he has just drawn her head', 'one eye is just a dark patch, and the other has more lines and details', 'the light lets us see one eye more clearly', 'there are shadows behind her maybe because she has a hat on', 'her nose and chin are lighter than the rest of her face and it makes them stick out more'

It seems to be a common myth that real artists lay down perfect lines and tones that need no adjustment. However, in reality, making a drawing involves a constant process of adjustment. We learn from artists that "mistakes" can become fortuitous accidents when we embrace them for their possibilities.

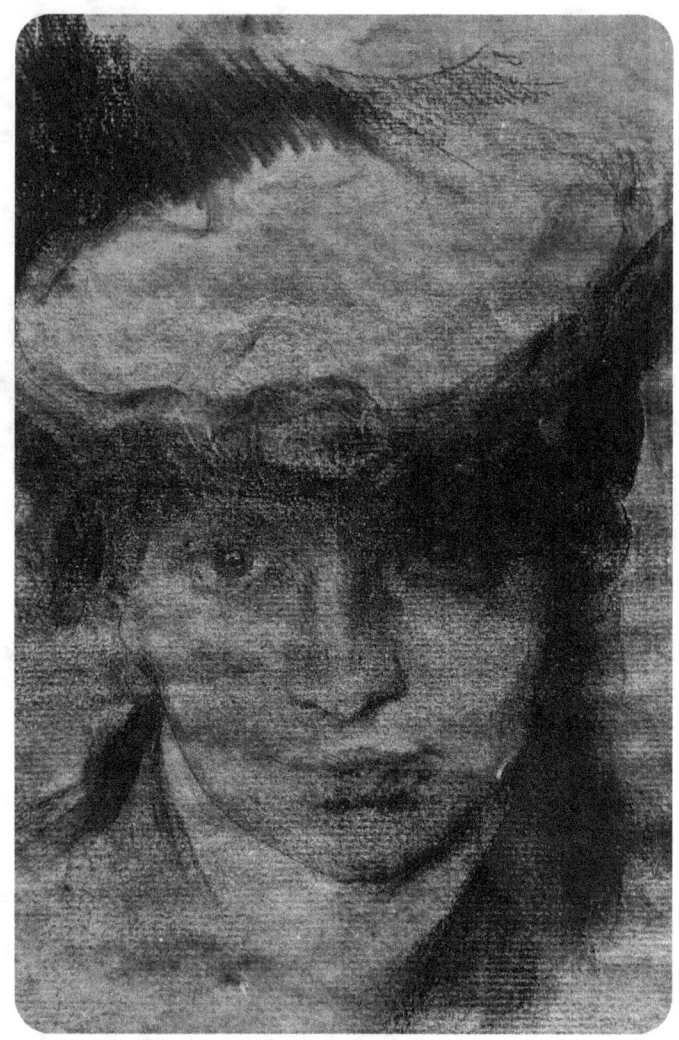

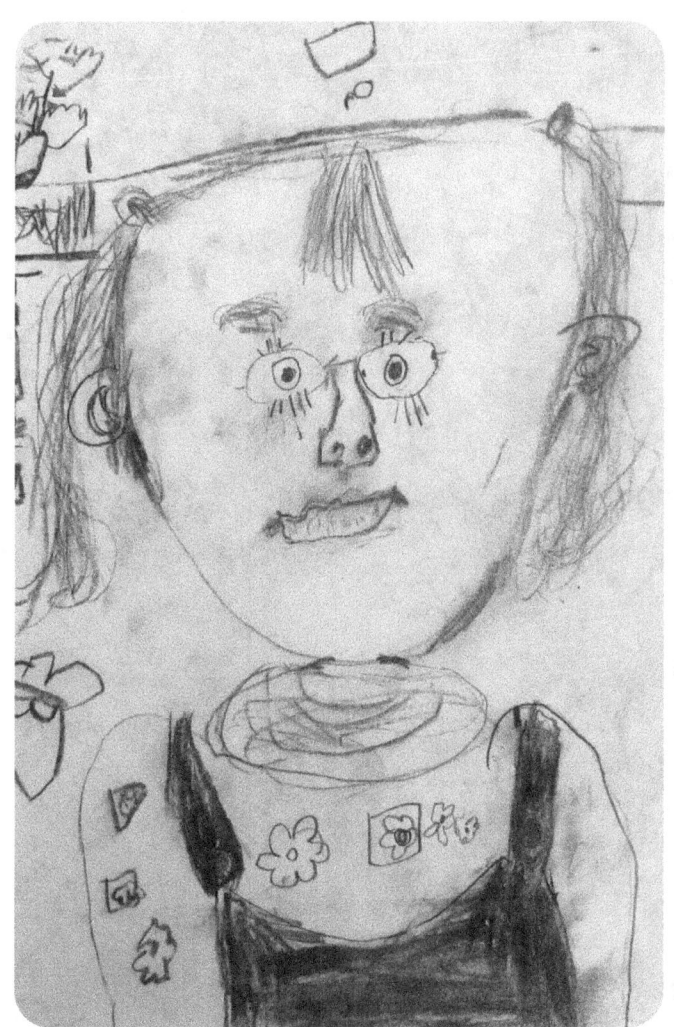

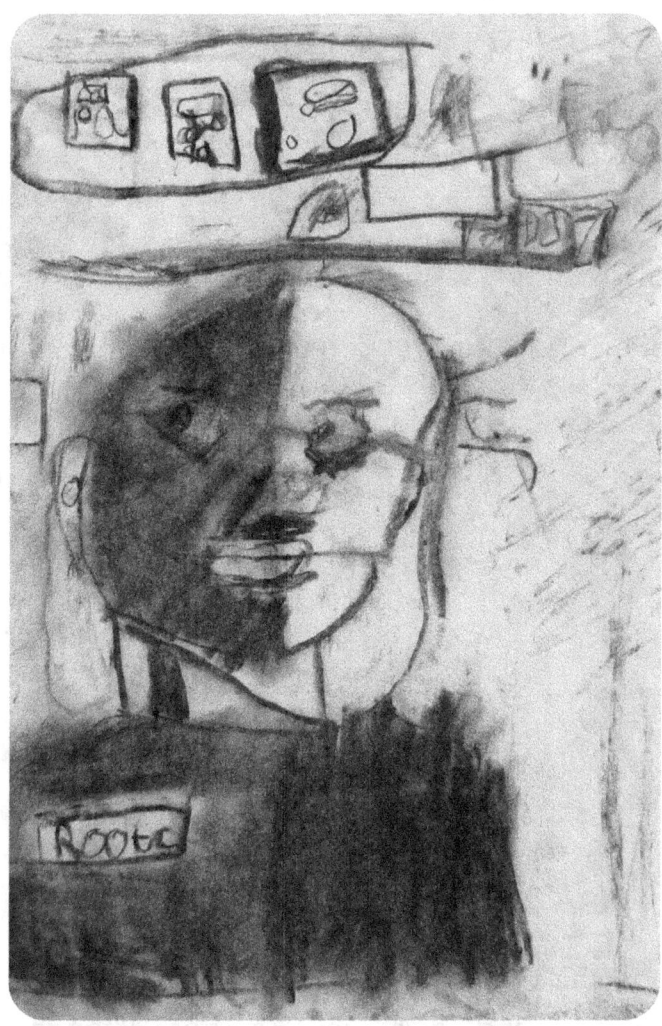

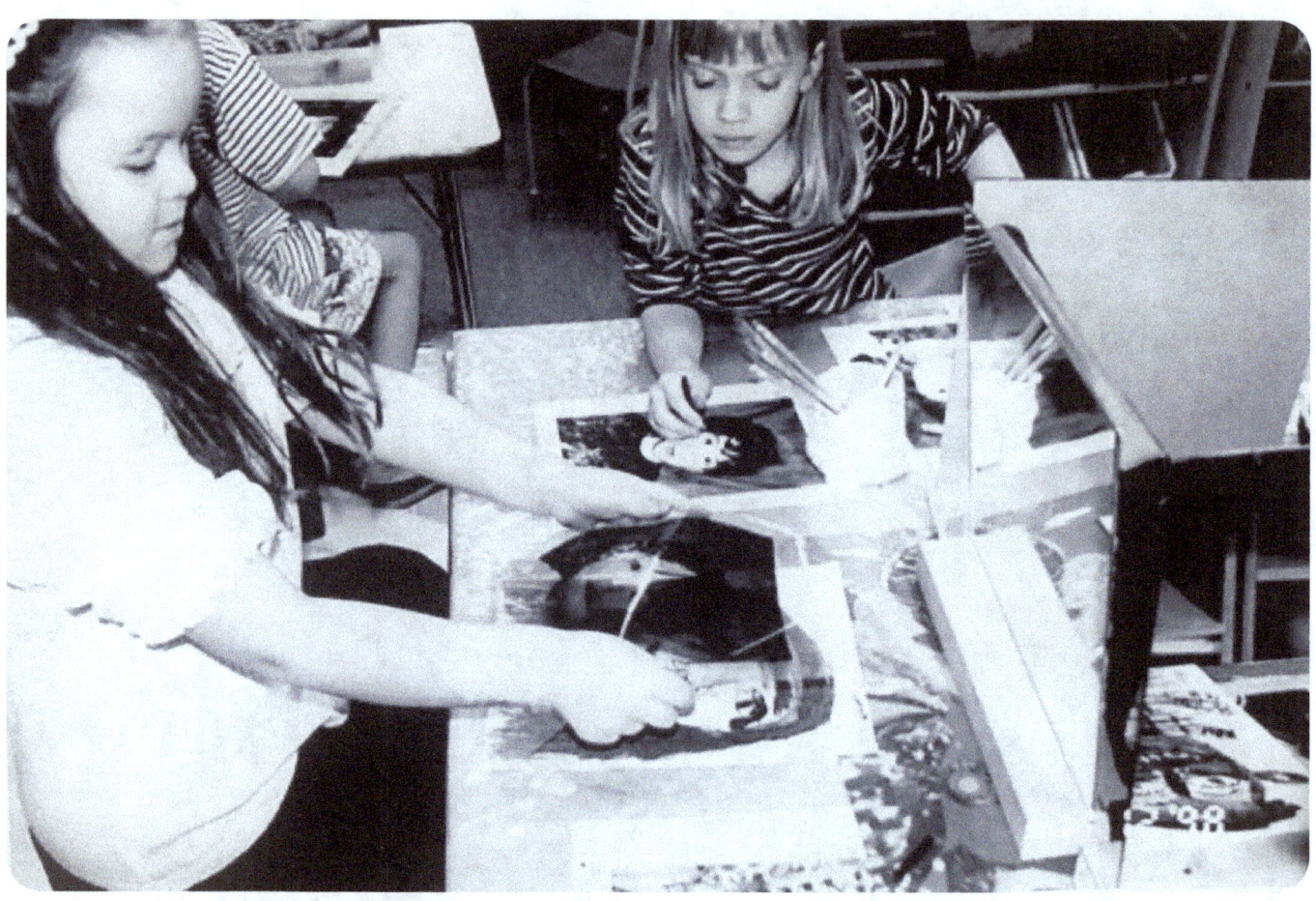

We challenged the children to hold acetate sheets of their portrait photos over their drawn portraits and adjust their drawings. When they looked through the acetate sheet of their photos they could see where a nose or an eye was misaligned, or an ear was out of place. The children were at first incredulous but soon found the process interesting and liberating. The children spent a long time adjusting and talking to each other about all the differences between their original drawing and the acetate.

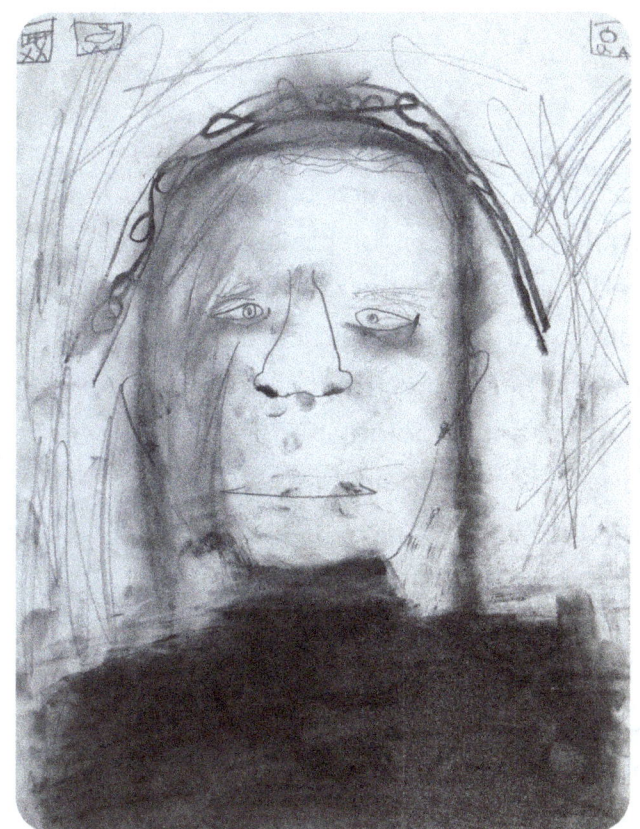

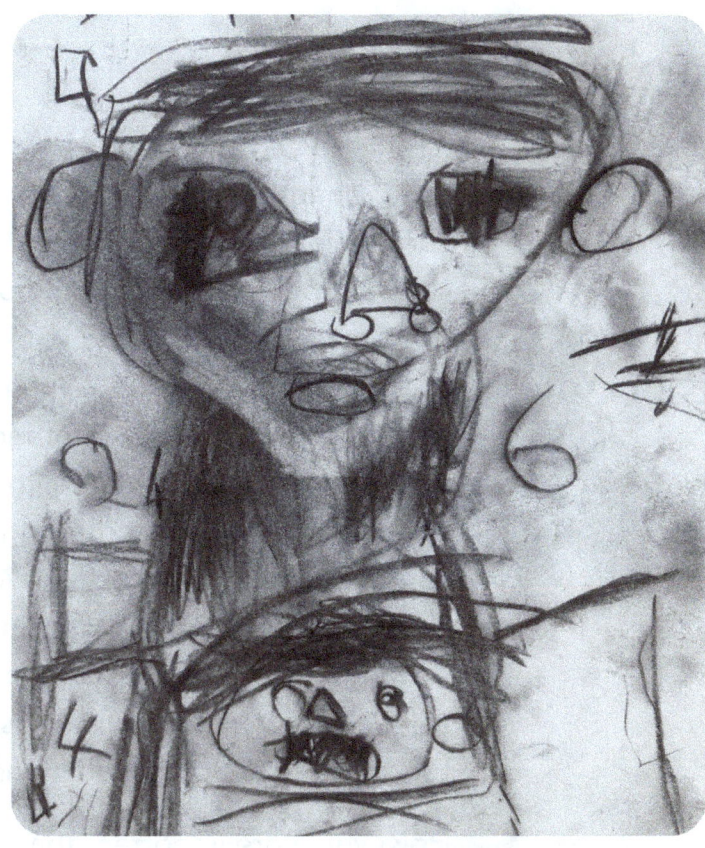

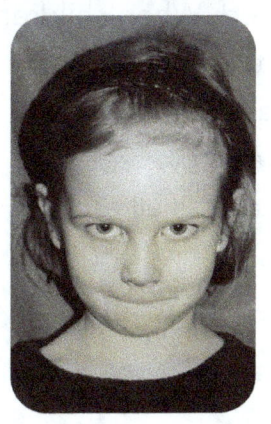

What interesting drawings this process initiated. The children spent a long time adjusting and talking to each other about all the differences between their original drawing and the acetate.

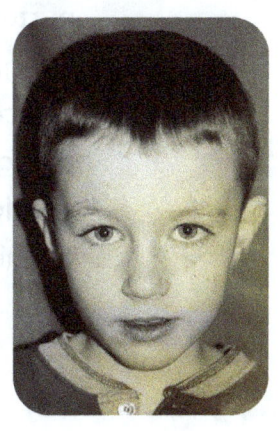

Conclusion

In this chapter I have tried to demonstrate how the arts can be core for learning for young children. In the Faces project we used several kinds of drawing and applied them across the curriculum. The drawing and labelling of anatomical drawings could be classified as a biology component. When drawing field notes the children were taking on the role of ethnographer/anthropologist and studying the social environment. Health and wellbeing was clearly addressed through the drawing and study of expressions for social competence. Measuring faces involved considerable mathematical skills in conjunction with drawing. We touched on art history through viewing other artists' work. Portraits extended children's repertoire of artistic skills in meaningful ways. Our project brought all of the above together and made connections across learning experiences.

However, more important than covering the curriculum is the nurturing of the disposition to learn and be engaged. When children are given the chance to make suggestions and determine the direction of their learning, their motivation to be actively involved at higher levels of thinking is clearly visible. Many arts processes provide similar excellent examples that are useful across all aspects of children's learning.

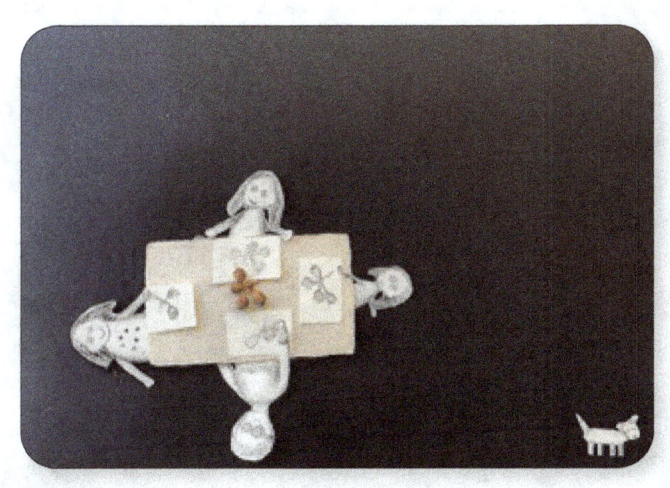

Chapter 3

~

Authentic media:
Clay with young children

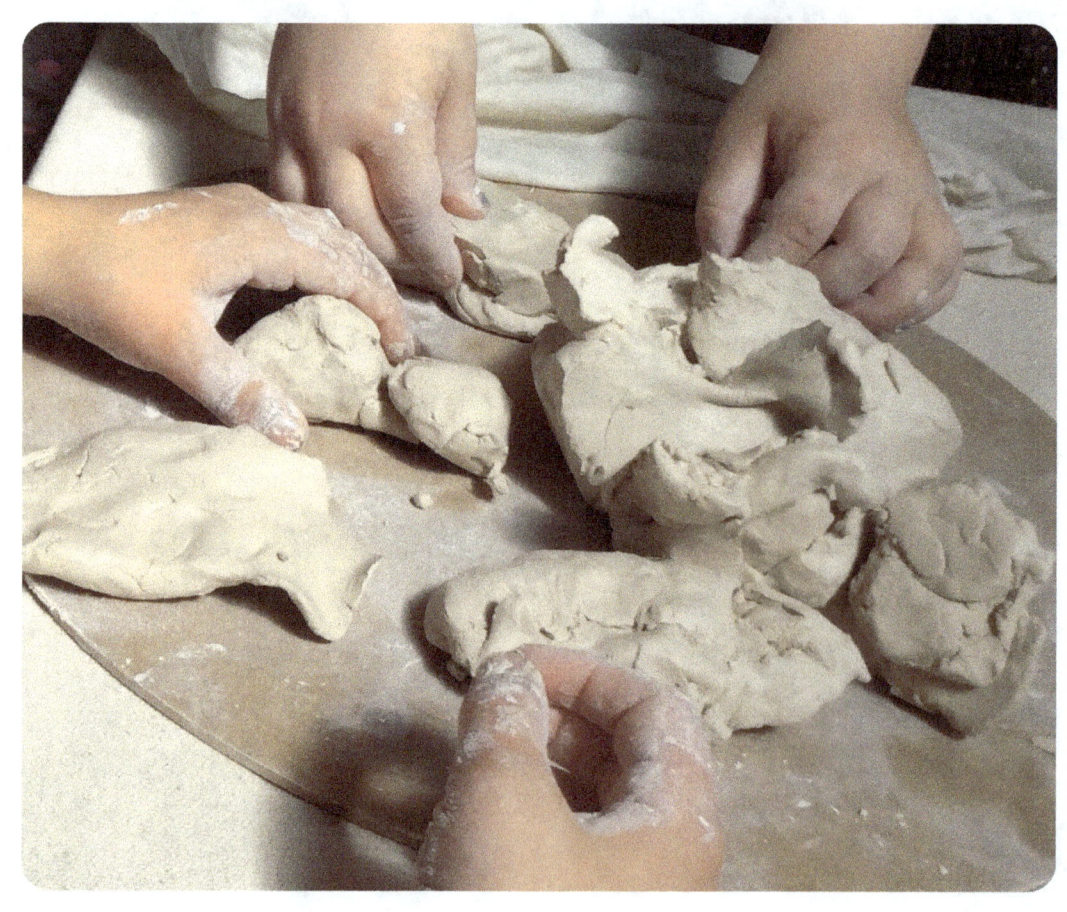

Clay is one of the essential media with which young children can represent the world. Like drawing, sand, water and blocks, it is one of the foundational media that young children should be given the opportunity to explore. It is a wonderfully responsive media that clearly shows the trace marks of everything that touches it. Clay immediately and honestly feeds back information about what the child has done. Children notice changes in the shape and texture of the clay with fascination. Clay is flexible and easily malleable. Children quickly learn that they can make almost anything they want with clay.

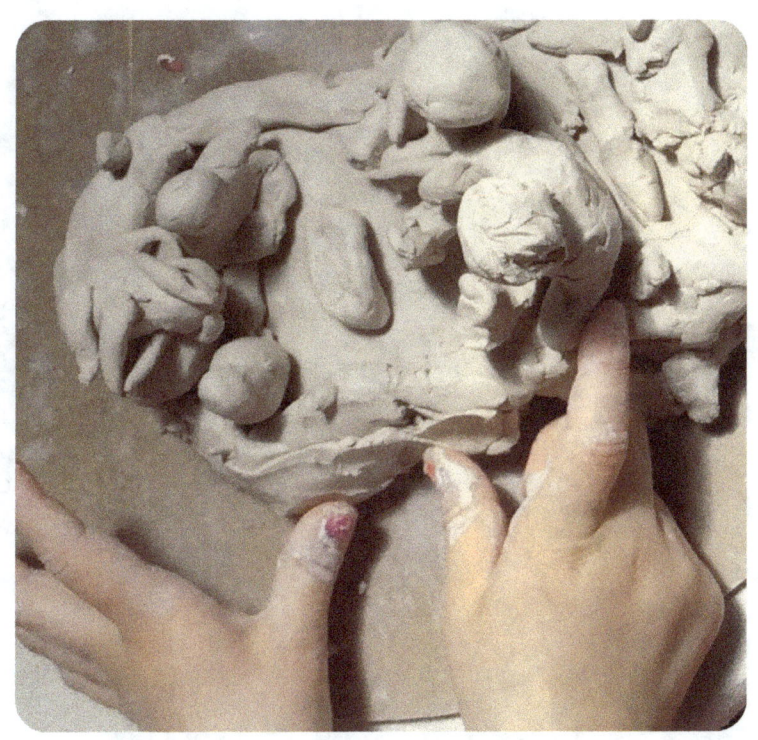

Children can use clay to represent their understanding of the world around them and to extend their thinking. Clay work presents many challenges that encourage risk-taking, trial and error and creative thinking.

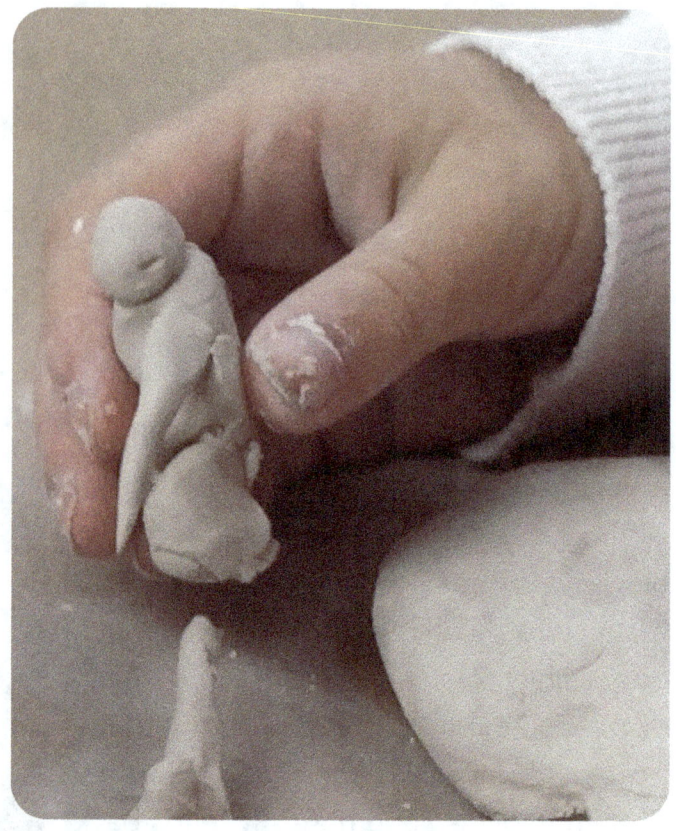

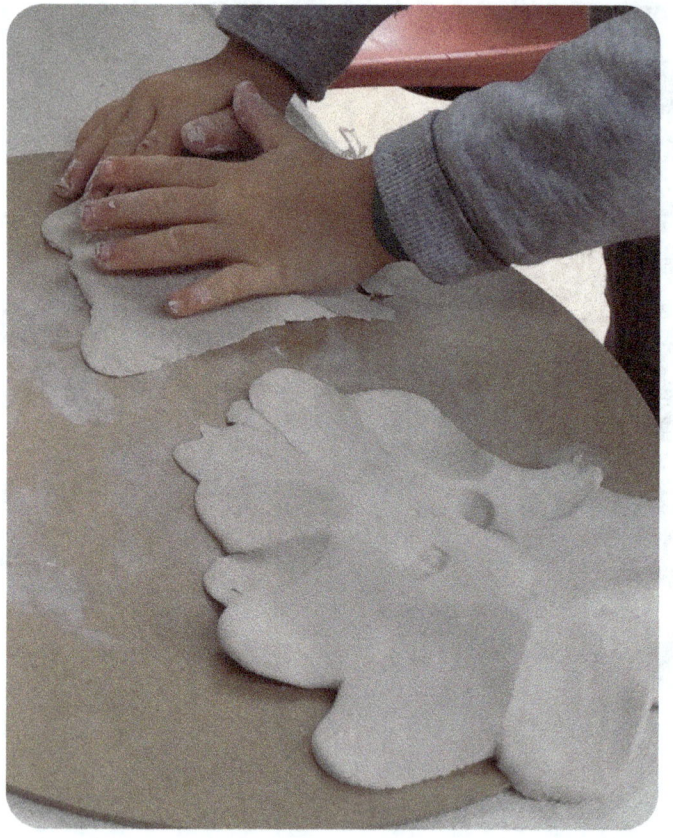

The sensory aspects of clay are attractive and beneficial for children. Clay has a calming effect and helps to settle emotions. It is a sustainable material that can be endlessly recycled and it should be offered to young children every day

The images in this guide contain a lot of information about the context for working with clay. The text is kept to a minimum so that you learn to become a good observer of details, e.g. noticing in one image that there are tiles on the shelves ready to display wet clay work. When this picture was taken it was a hot dry day so we had wet cloths over the work to stop it drying out.

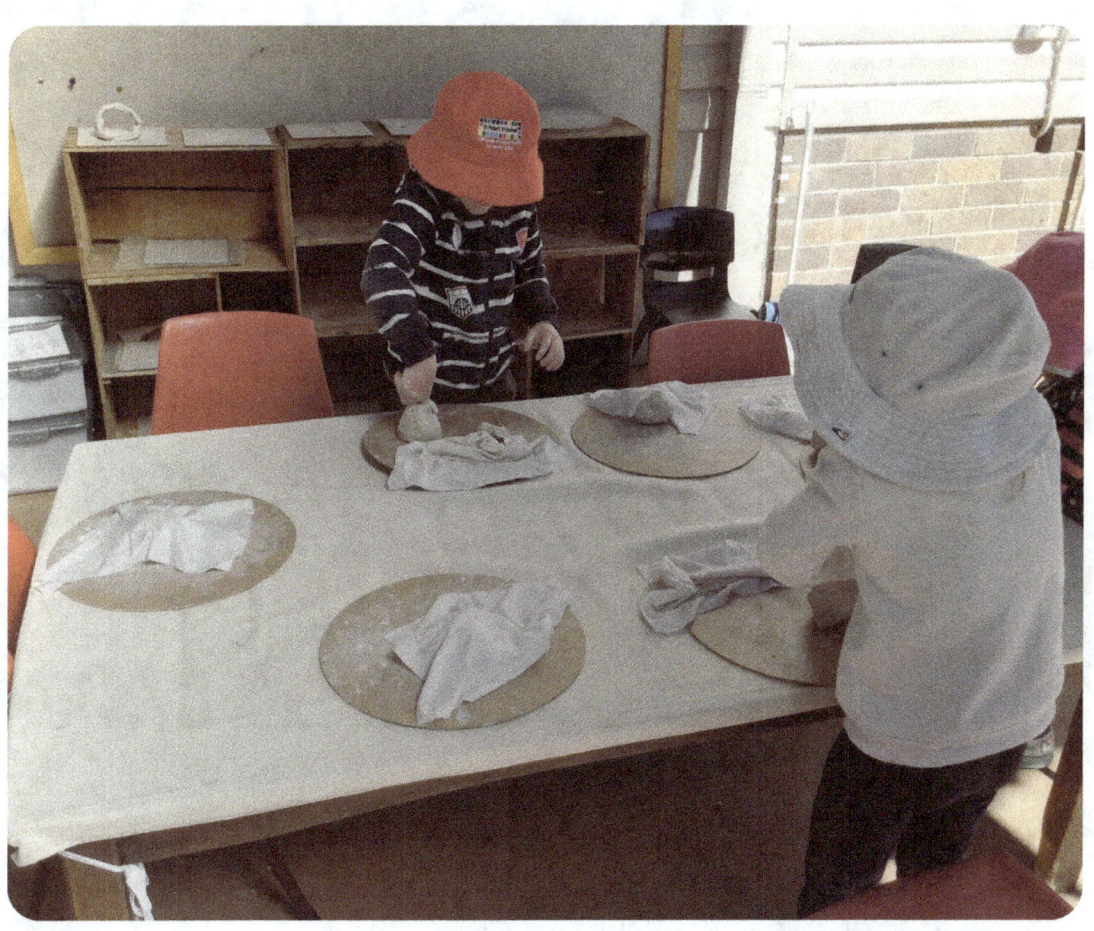

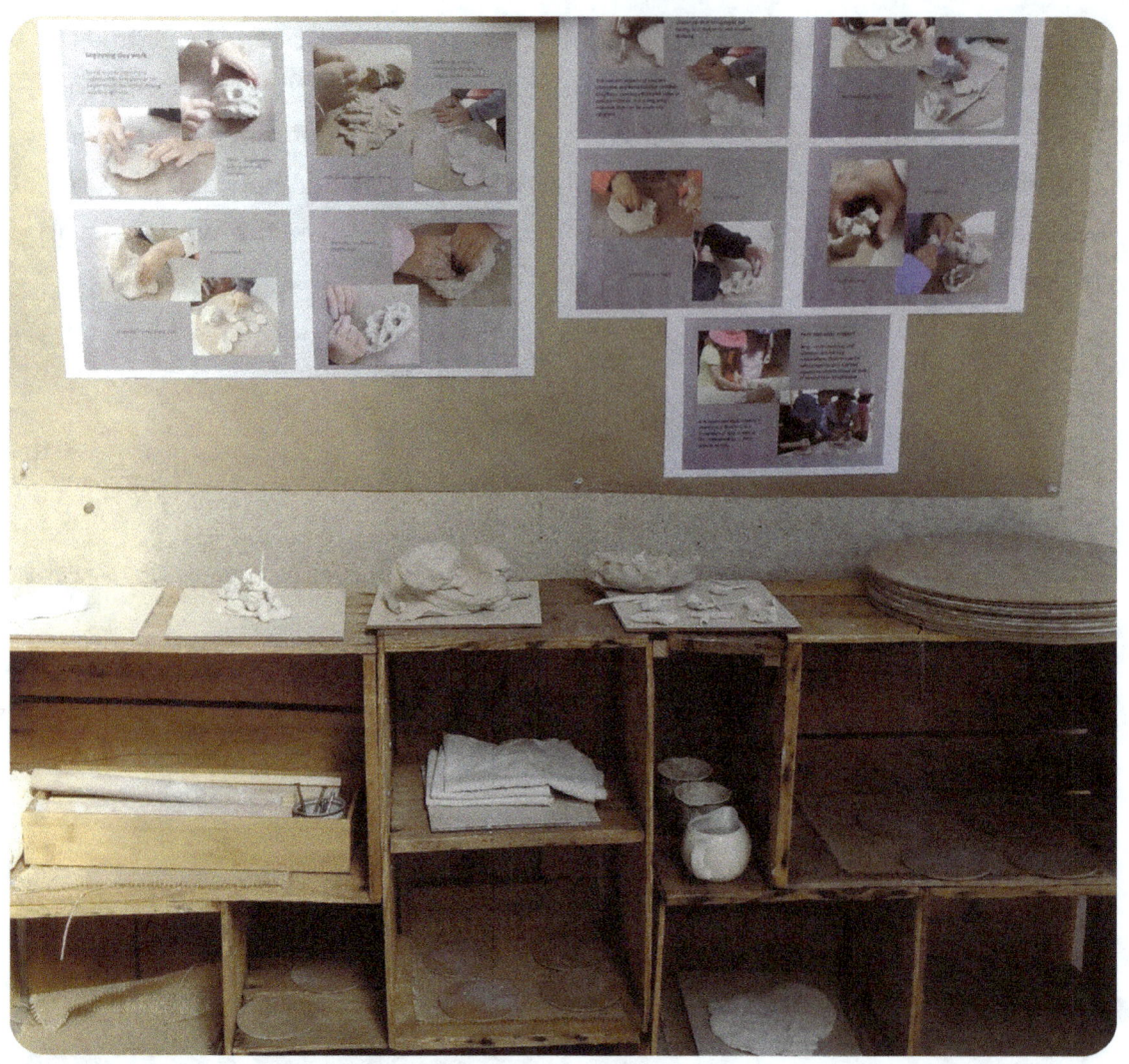

The next few pages contain practical information about clay for teachers. I will discuss spaces for clay work, some materials needed to work with clay, and the care and storage of clay. Then I will share some examples of young children working with clay.

❮ Space:

Ideally clay should be offered on an ongoing basis. This means careful consideration of a dedicated space for clay work with small groups. This space needs to have a washable floor, be out of the flow of traffic and have access to the sink. Here, shelves for displaying finished work are made out of recycled apple boxes.

Clay: **❯**

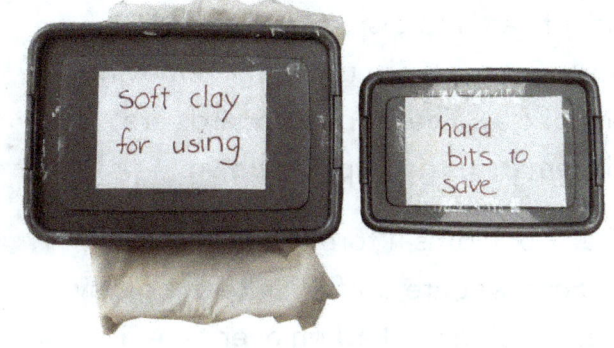

I prefer a soft, moist grey earthenware clay. You will need about 1 kg of clay per child. You can buy this from a pottery supply store or ask your local pottery club or potter. You need airtight containers to store the clay and keep it moist, and a smaller container for recycling

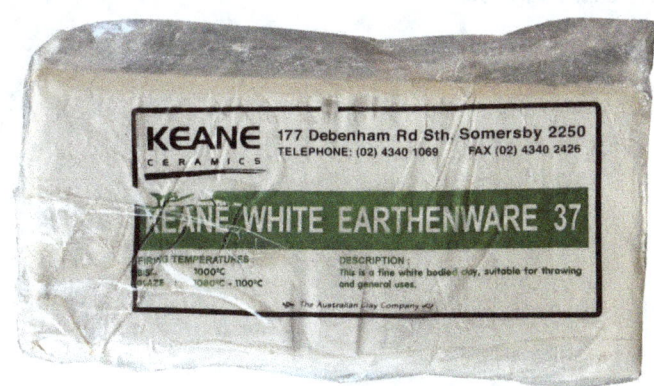

Other related materials:

Several wooden boards and/or ceramic tiles for working on and other bits of cards to display and store work. Scrapers are useful for removing bits of clay. These round boards are placemats turned upside down.

A box of cloths (I tore up an old sheet) you can wet are useful for keeping clay that is being worked on over time nice and damp. Wrapping the cloth with clingwrap will retain moisture on the hot dry days.

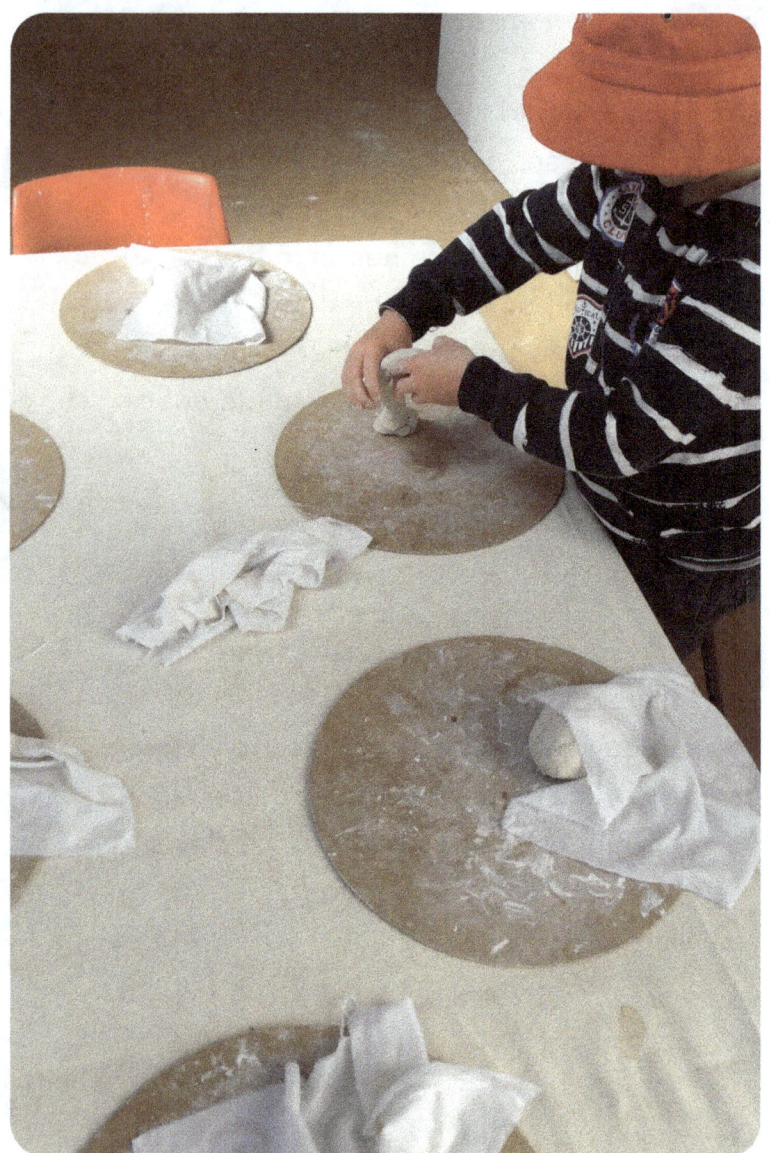

Slurry pots and brushes are needed for joining clay.

A cutting board and wire clay cutter is useful for getting even thicknesses of slabs of clay. The wire, or fishing line, can also be used to get stuck models off the base.

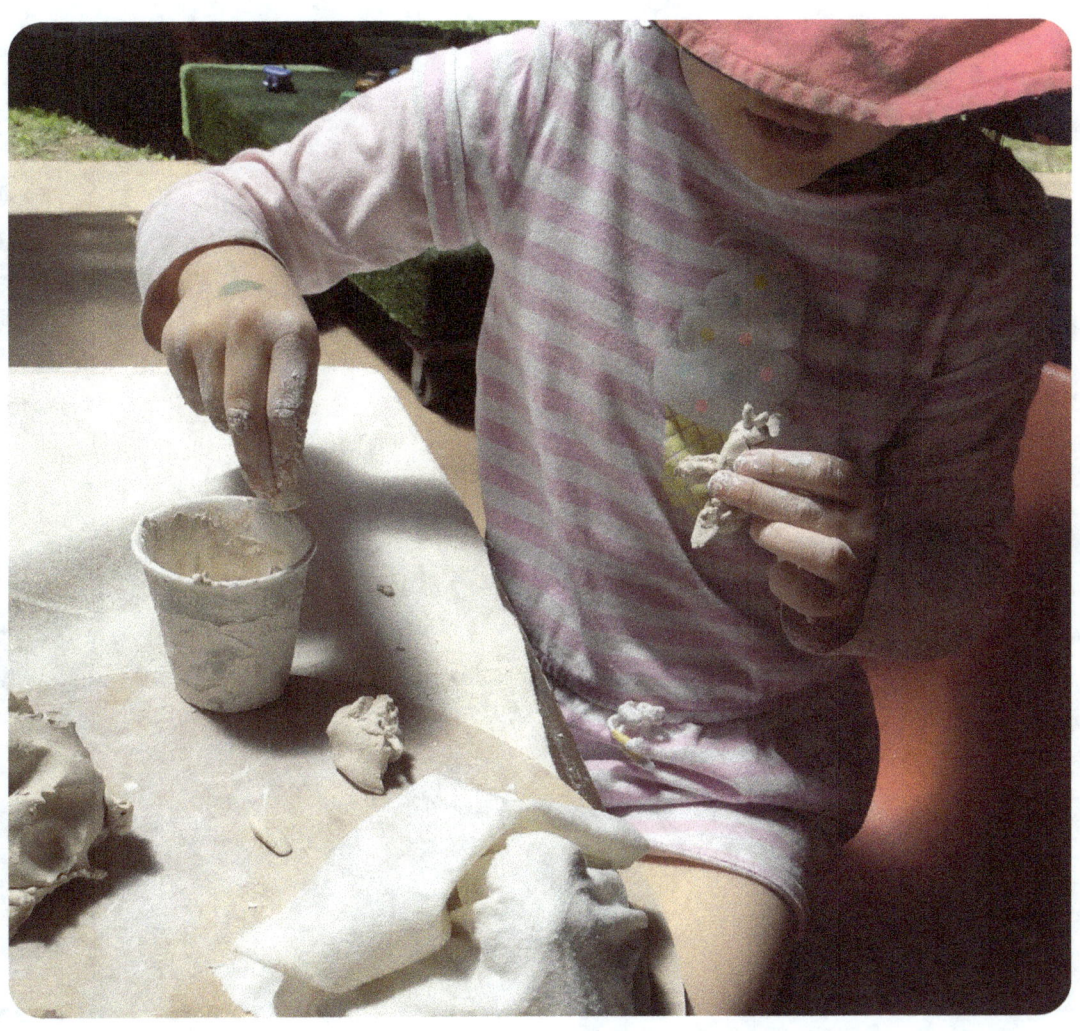

Children's hands make the best tools for manipulating clay. The more direct contact with the clay the children can have the better they can learn to feel how the clay reacts under all kinds of conditions.

There are many tools and materials you can use and combine with clay, but I will leave that for later as it is important that children only use their hands to start with.

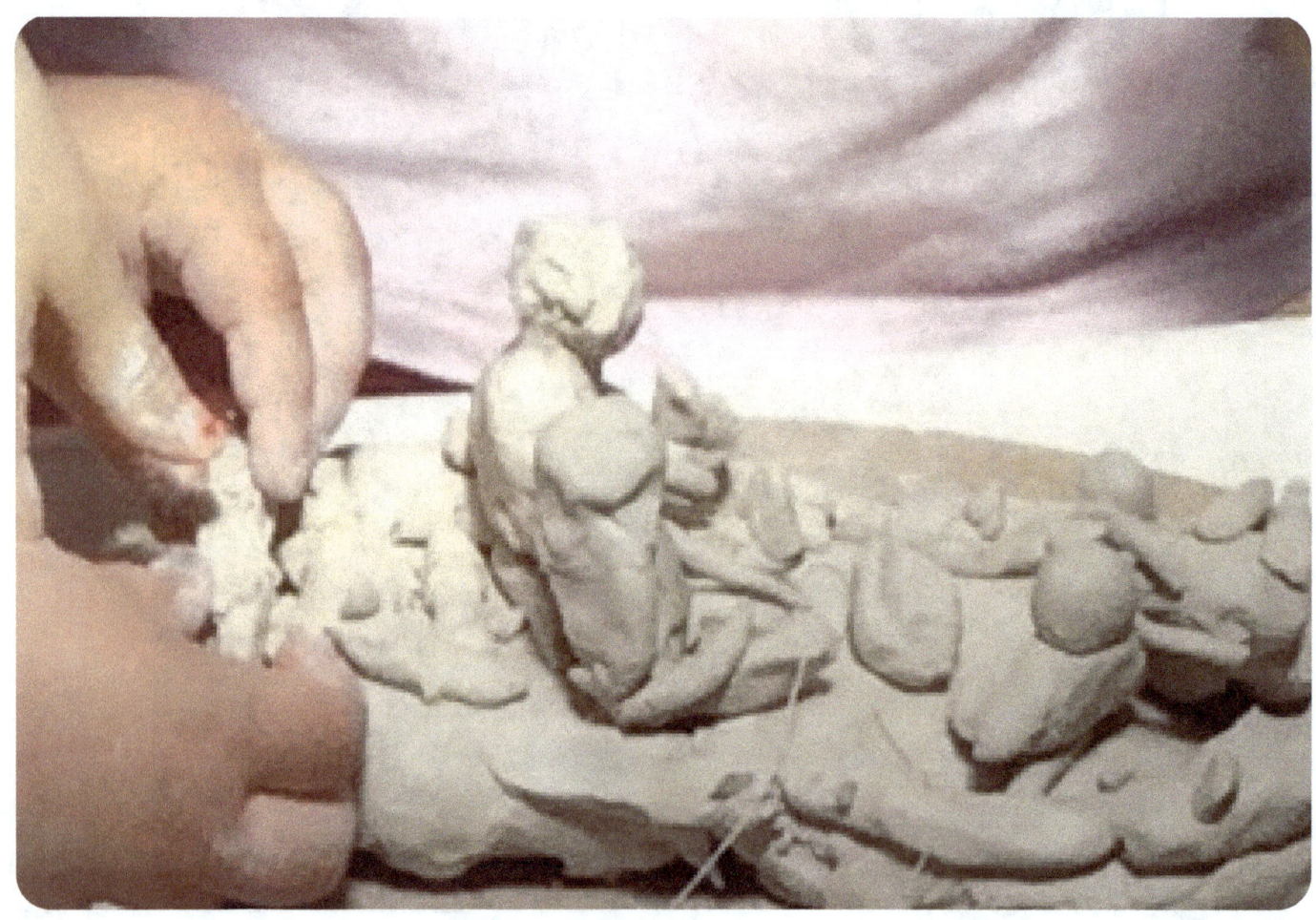

Care of clay

Clay is very economical, especially if you don't fire it. But it does need to be cared for to keep it soft and moist to use. Clay that is old and hard is discouraging to work with. You can test for the right consistency of clay by rolling a piece into a small cylinder about one centimeter thick and five centimeters long. Then gently bend the cylinder into a right angle. If there are cracks on the bend then the clay is too dry and needs some water added to it.

Clay can be kept ready for use by rolling it into apple sized balls that are placed in an airtight container with a damp cloth covering them, and the lid on tight.

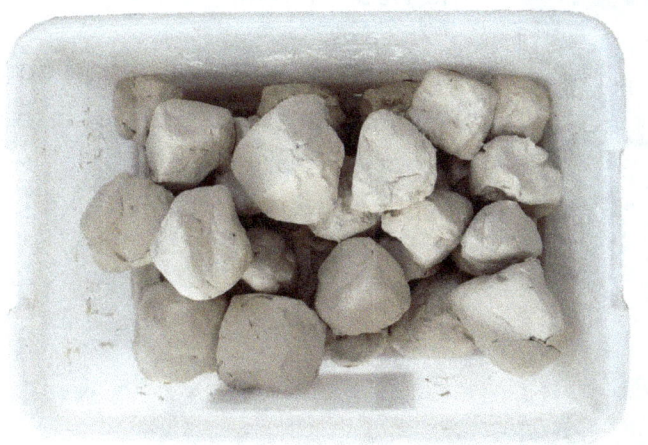
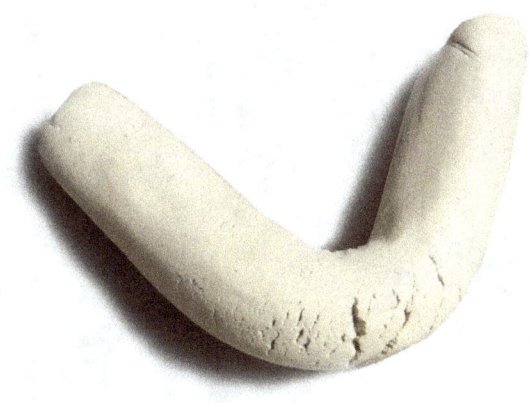

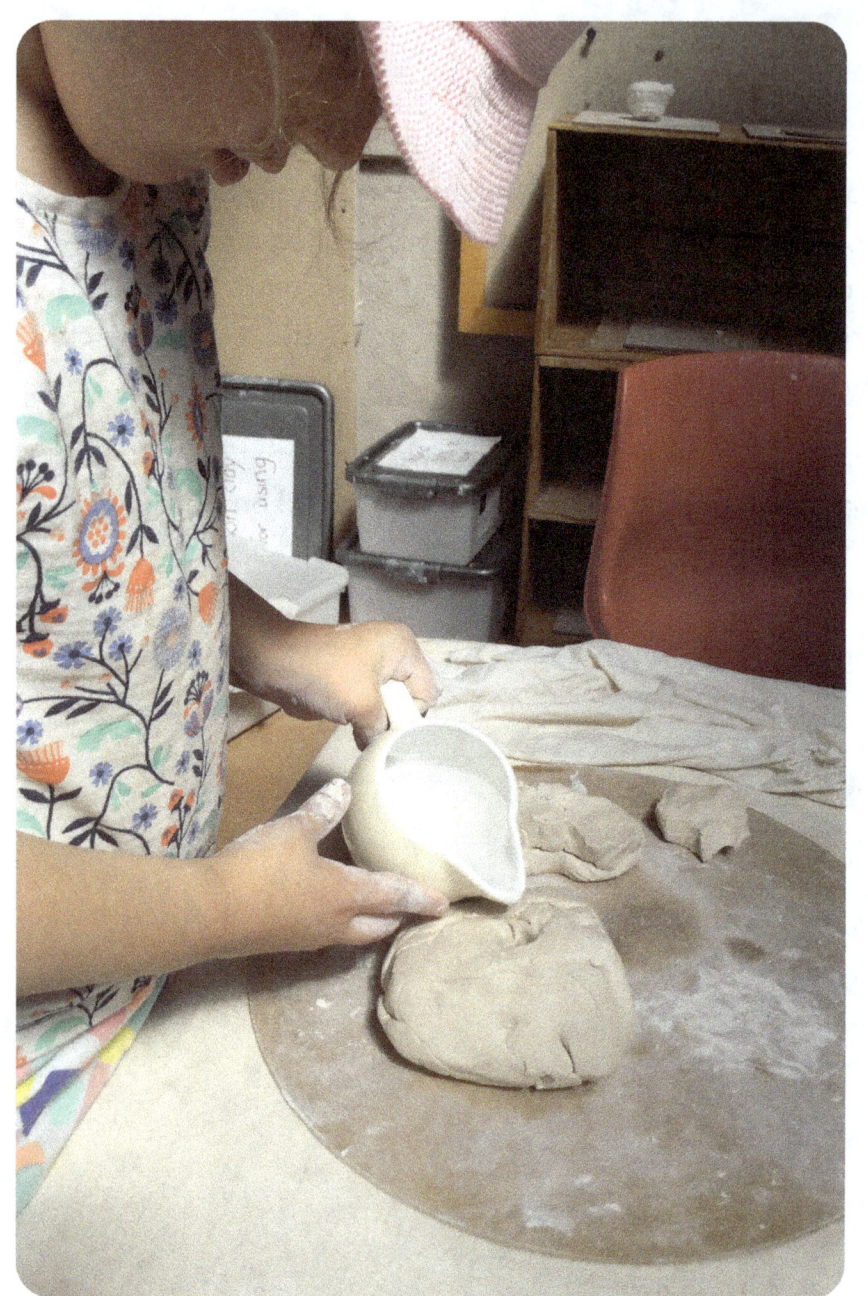

The children should also be taught how to look after clay so that it is at its best for modeling.

When they have finished working with their clay, they roll it into a ball, put a big thumb hole deep into the middle and fill it with water and cover it over trapping the water inside.

They can experiment to find out how wet clay should be for it to be good to work with.

Old clay and clay scraps can be saved in a similar container and covered with water to break down into sludge. When all the bits are soft the water should be skimmed off and the clay left to dry a little. When the clay is firm enough it can be wedged into a nice pliable and moist chunk. There are some good You Tube videos that teach you how to wedge clay.

Care of clay can be built into routines and the tasks shared. Children can learn to clean their boards, put their small clay scraps in the recycle tub and to roll their unused good clay into a ball, moisten it and store it. They need to decide which clay models they want to display and which will be recycled.

It is rare that preschools have facilities for firing clay, so I have not discussed this aspect of working with clay. In preschools, typically clay is left to go hard, but it is fragile and not durable like that. However, it does break down in water and can be used over and again.

If you are lucky enough to have a kiln then it opens up longer term possibilities for clay. The internet has many tutorials on firing clay.

Fingers first

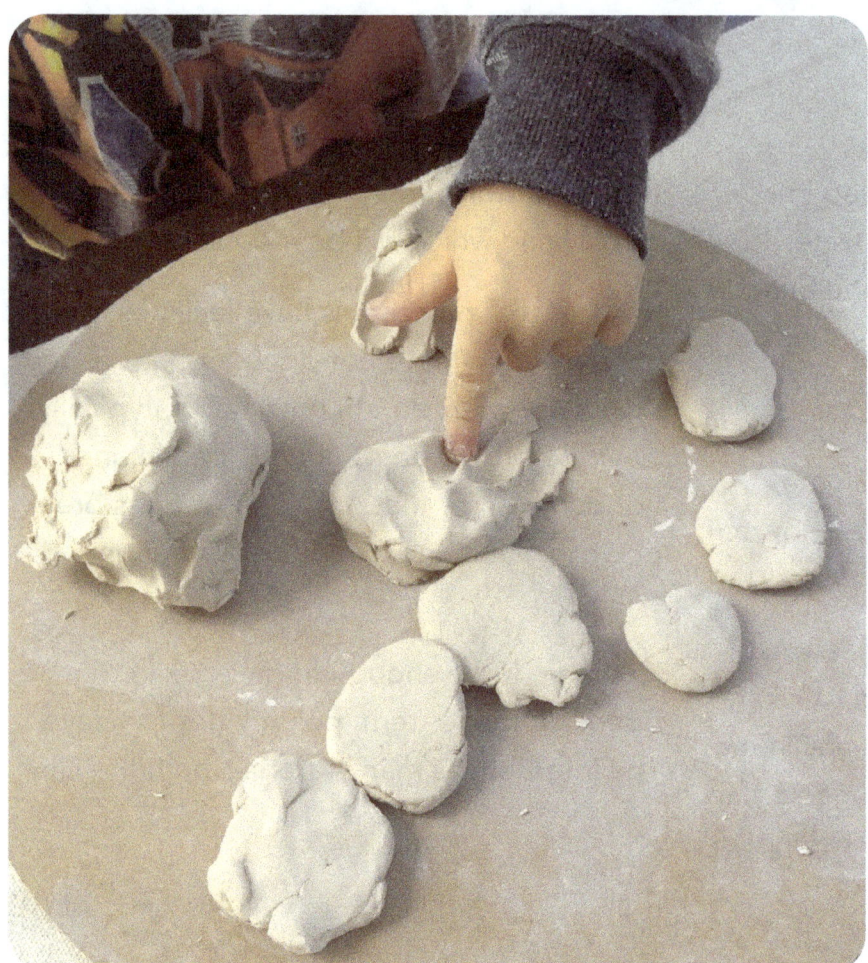

Children need lots of direct contact with clay so that they get to know it. They need time to learn how tall they can pile it, how small they can pinch it and how they can roll it, ball it and flatten it. This embodied understanding of clay is essential for gaining the skills needed to represent their ideas.

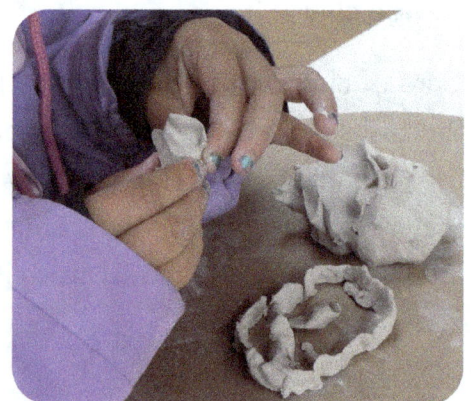

Clay tools introduced too soon can distract from the qualities and potential of clay so it is best not to introduce tools until the children have had many weeks of using their hands.

Clay has so many possibilities. With careful noticing and dialogue around clay explorations children can be encouraged to gain a broad repertoire of techniques as well as extending their imagination.

They will discover how to roll clay, how to get fine details, how to smooth out the rough bits and how to join two pieces together. They will create representations of things around them. They will become good problem solvers and good observers.

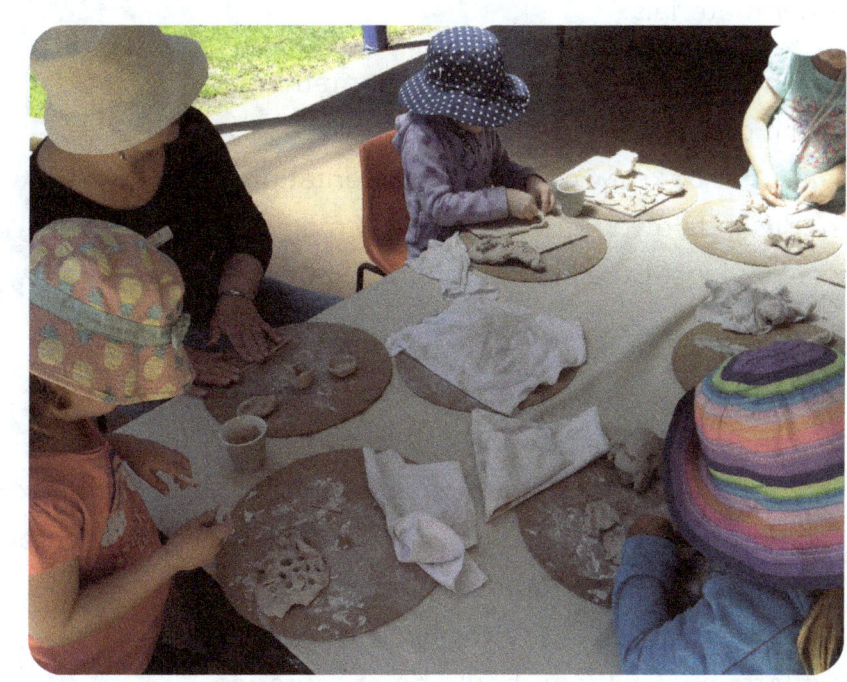

The adult's role is one of 'guide on the side', interested observer and provocateur. We can bring children's attention to details and offer challenges as well as appreciation.

The adult works with children to support and to extend their thinking and encourage them to elaborate on their ideas.

STOP

Many educators are too keen to introduce sticks and other natural materials to clay. However, the problem with doing this is that it reduces the clay to just a base or prop for other materials.

When clay is used as a prop for something else it deprives children of opportunities to really get to know clay as a representational media in its own right. Try to allow many weeks of just pure clay with no additions.

Within the context of early childhood education, clay is first and foremost an art media. It should be used to support children's learning about their world and promote creative thinking. Creative thinking is divergent and generative. It involves trial and error, extensive research, and exploration. Children should be encouraged to explore both the media and their own ideas and questions.

The following few pages demonstrate some

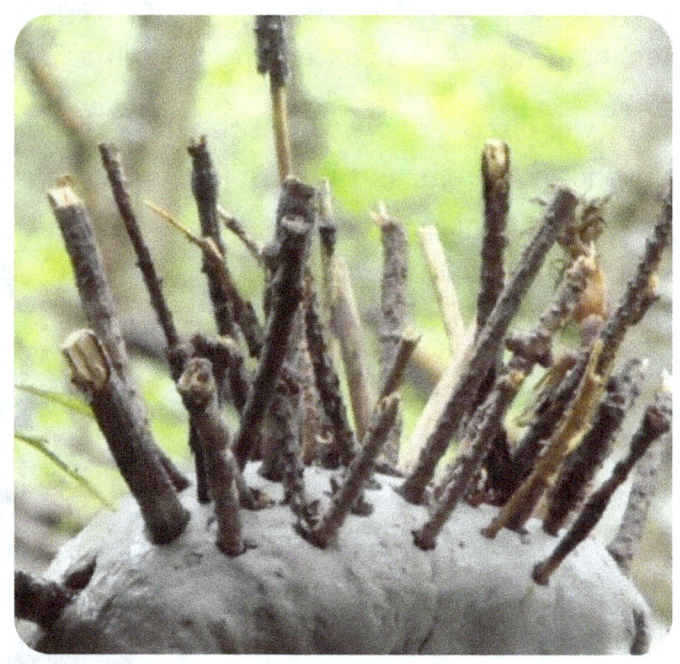

of the explorations children made when presented with clay for the first time.

It is important that you also try similar explorations.

In particular, flattening, building up, linking, joining, making holes and spaces, marking, coiling, rolling, small parts and assembling large structures.

Exploring the properties of clay

Multiple opportunities to explore the properties of clay are needed. Many children will not yet have experienced clay so plenty of time and support is required for them to fully get to know and understand all of its properties.

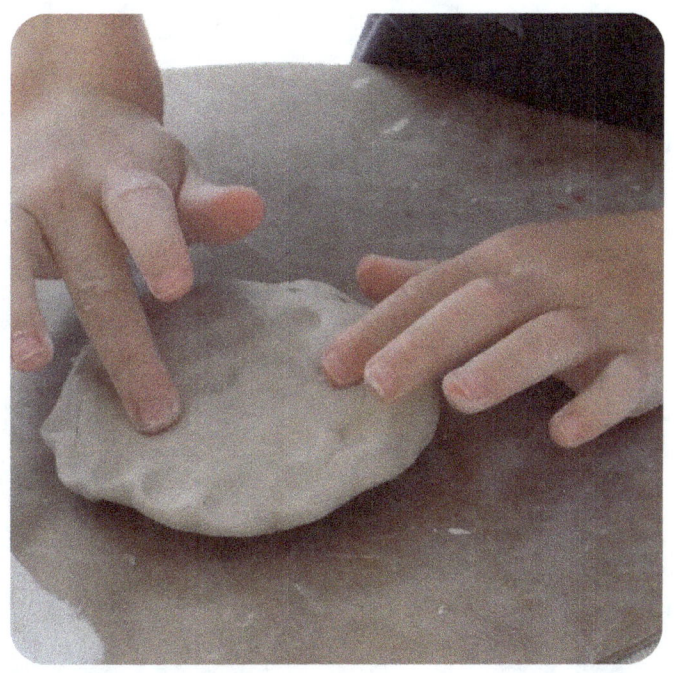

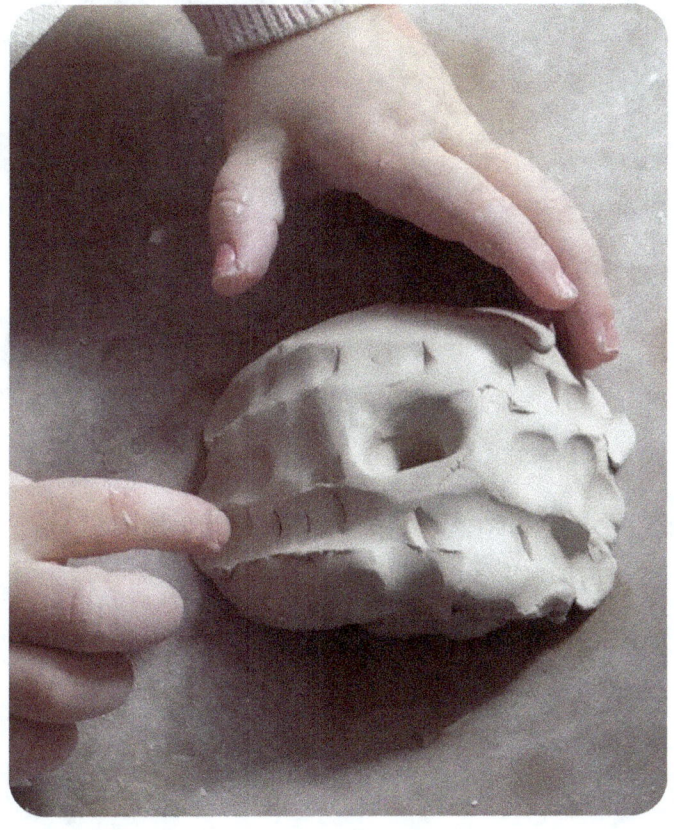

They can do this through the thoughtful handling of clay and noticing what happens when it is poked, pulled, squeezed, stroked, flattened, rolled and scratched.

Don't rush into teaching how to making things, rather affirm what they are trying to make.

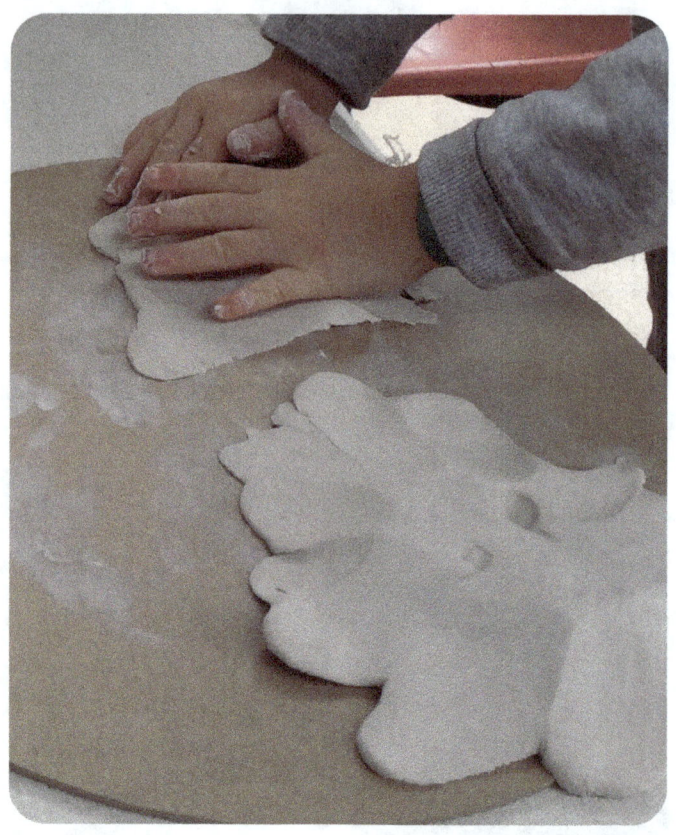

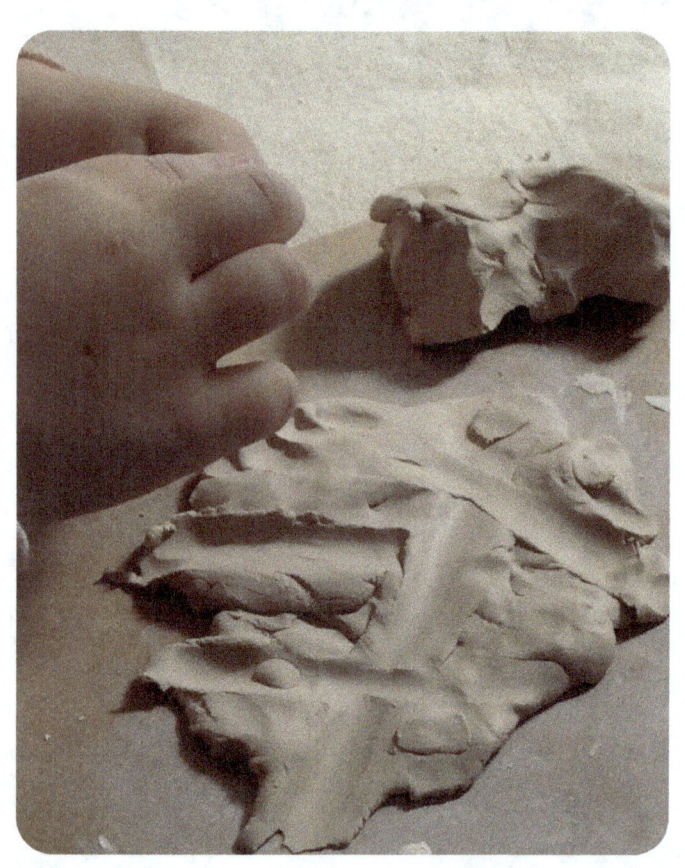

Here are some actions that will demonstrate the properties of clay.

Actions: flattening, pressing, smoothing, hand prints, slopes, pathways, slides.

Properties: soft, pliable, responsive, strong.

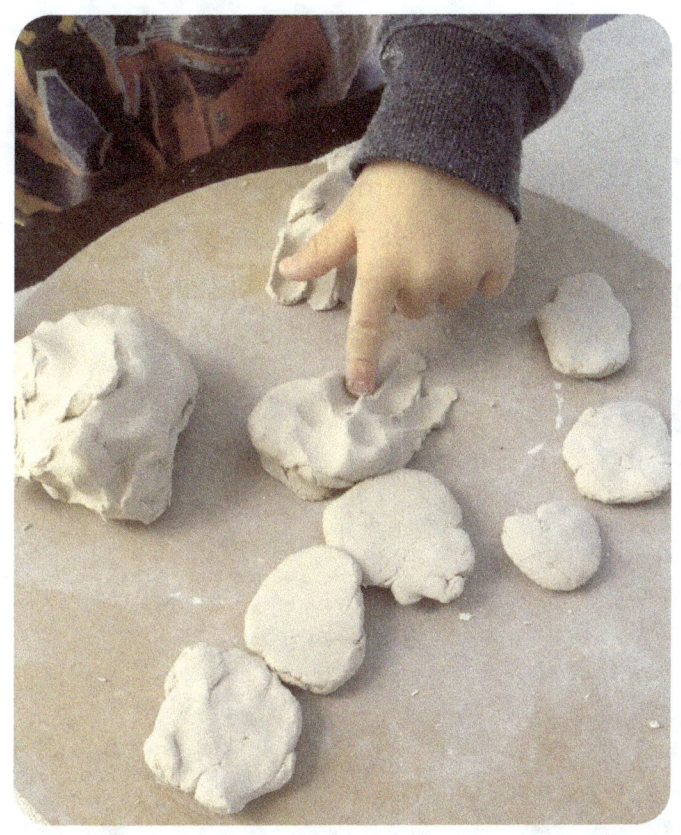

The tactile properties of clay are very inviting for young children. The stepping stones and slide are slippery.

This five year old is exploring how smooth she can make the clay. She wants to make a smooth bed.

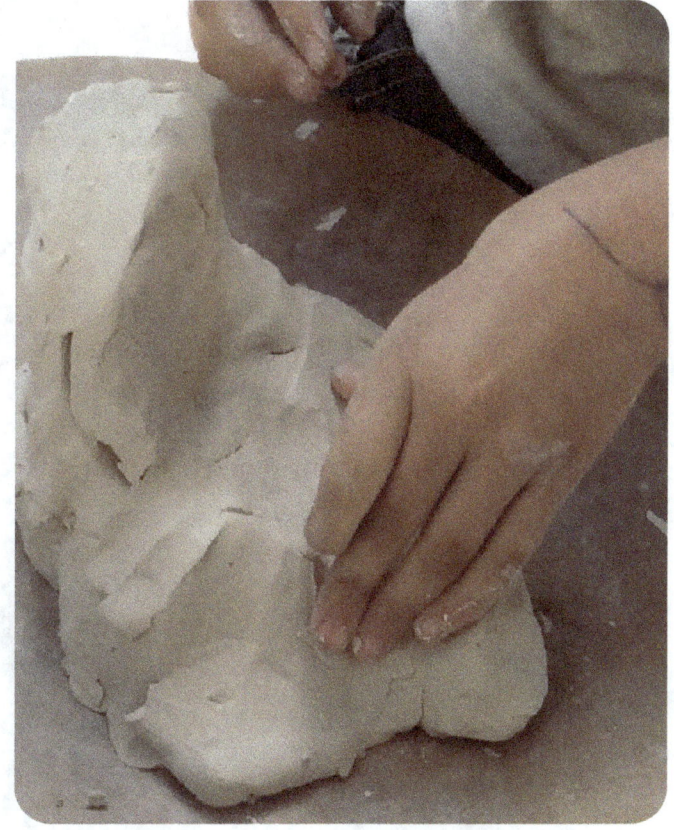

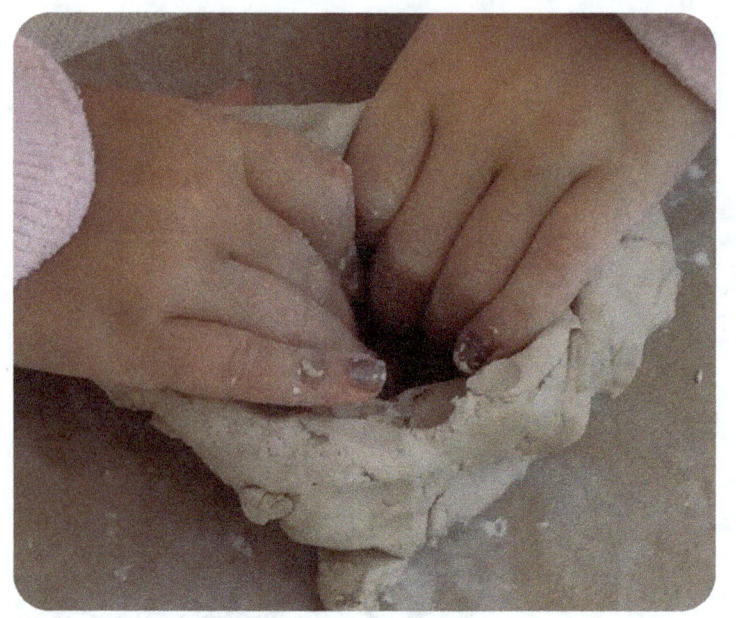

As the clay becomes more familiar and some techniques are learned it is much easier to construct some of the things they want to represent.

Along with representation comes narrative actions.

The worm has a big story around him.

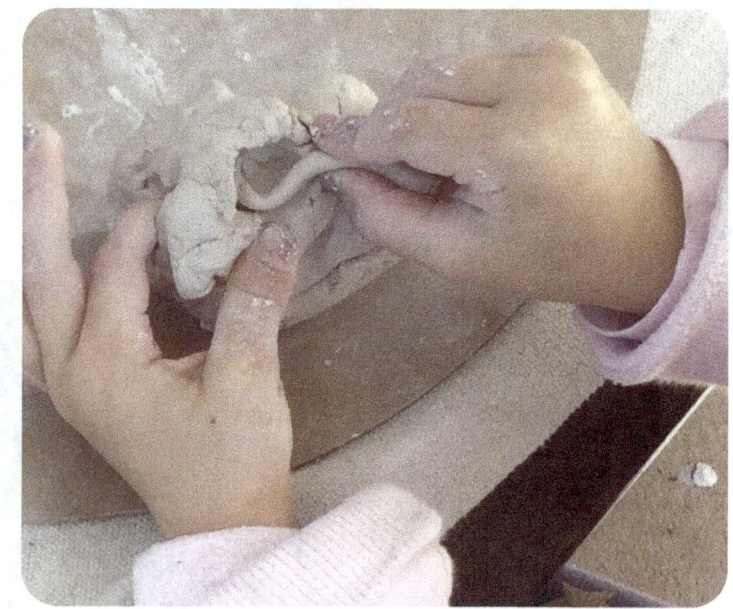

'A place for fish eggs'.

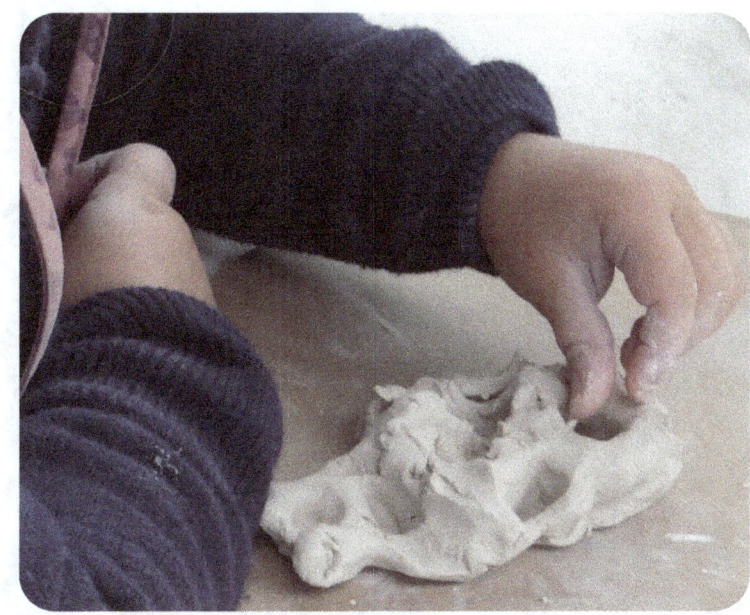

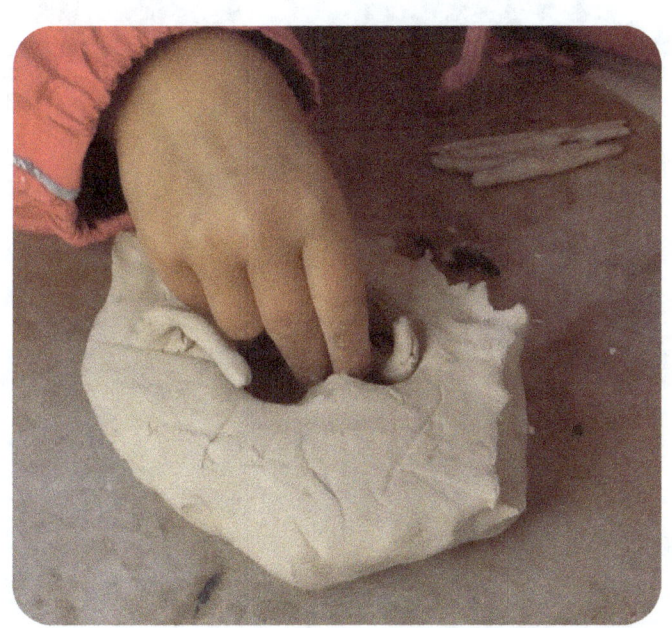

The worm house.

Birds in a nest.

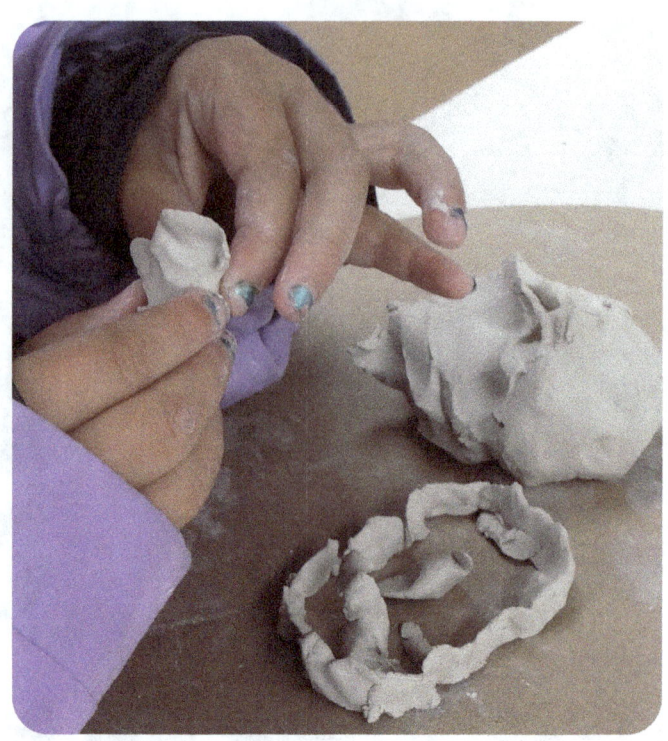

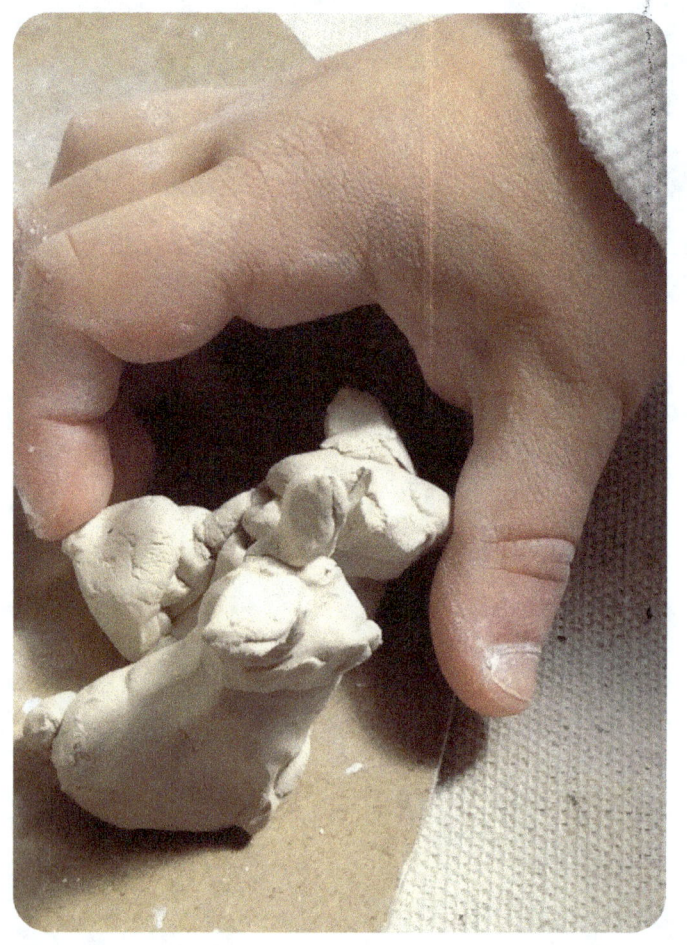

Two rabbits.

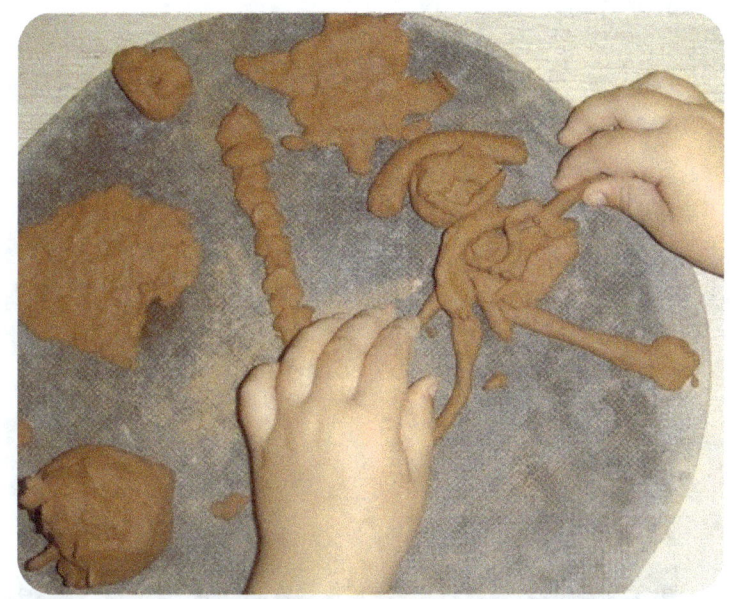

Coils are very versatile. They can be used to construct almost anything.

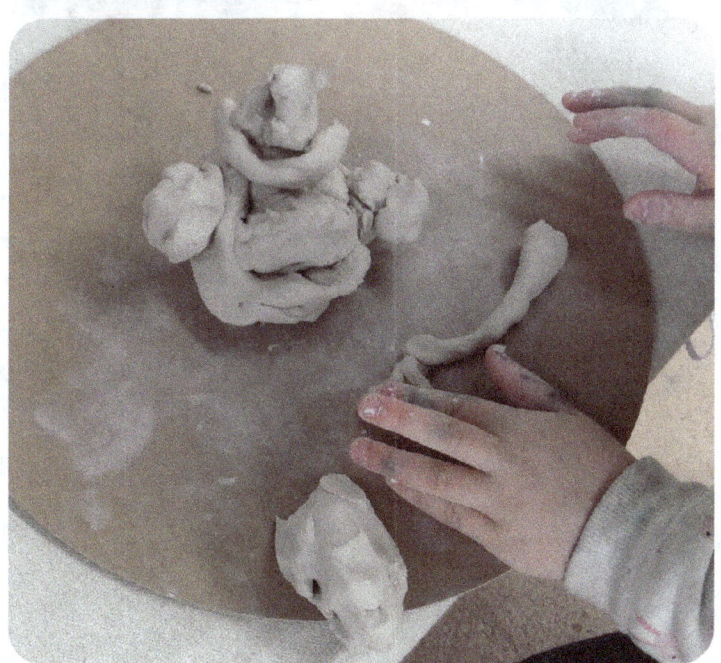

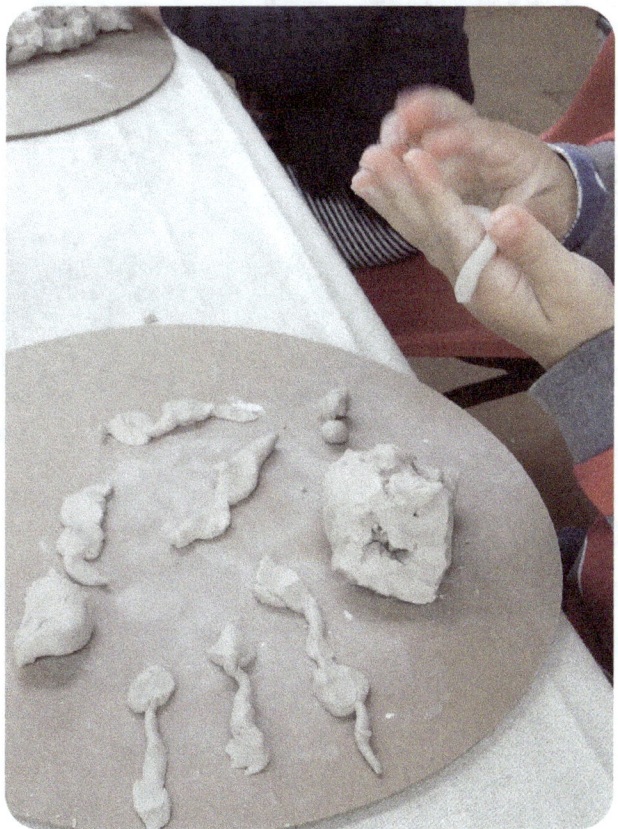

~ 109 ~

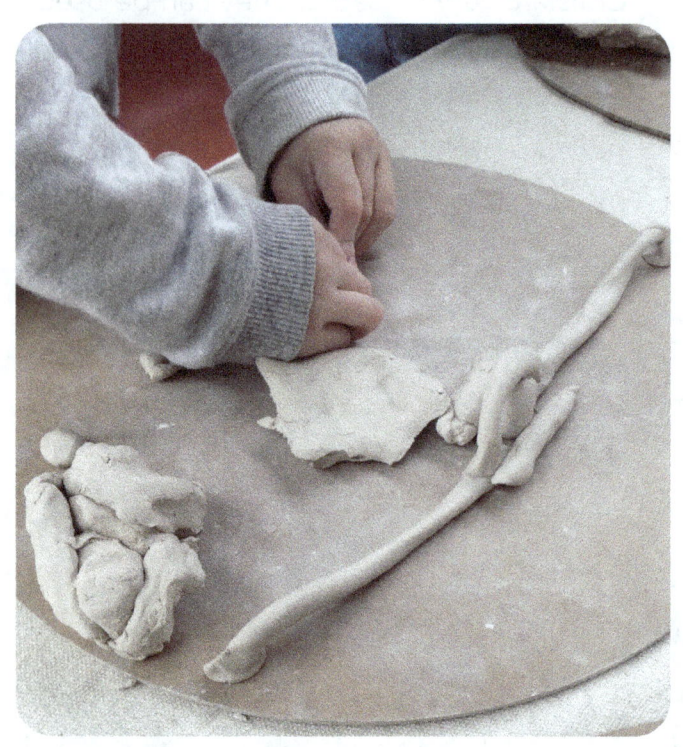

Coils are wonderful to draw with. Children make quite complex relief pictures from coils.

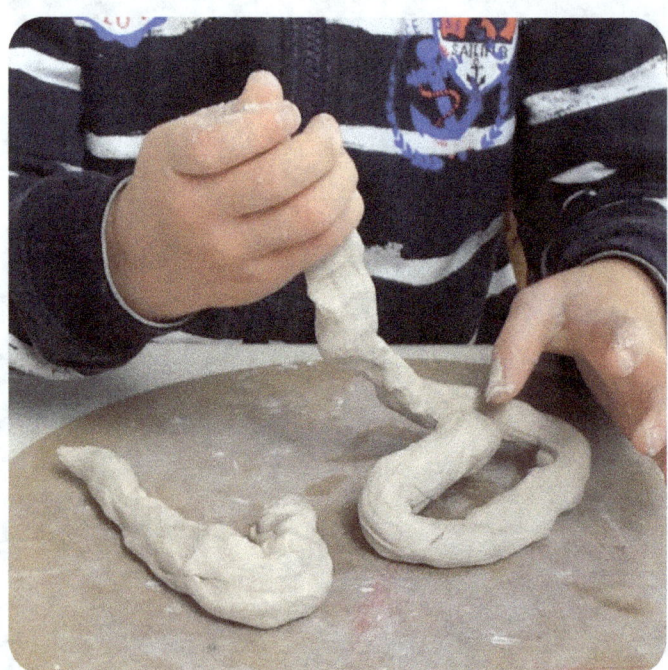

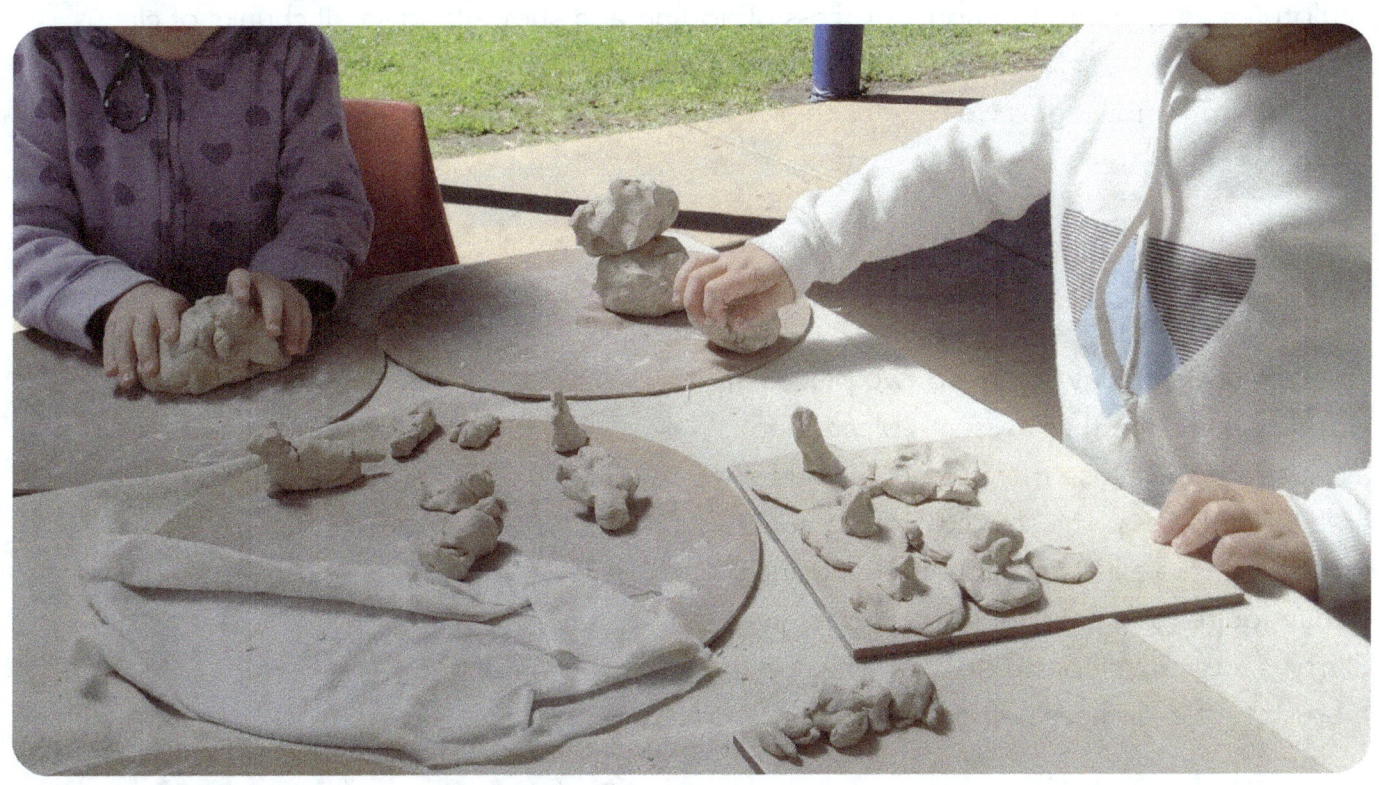

Small groups of children will work together to create elaborate play events and narratives. They share ideas and techniques as well as develop stories that flow from day to day. A wet cloth stops the figures from drying out overnight.

Adding and subtracting clay

Sculptures are created through a process of adding and subtracting small chunks of clay. When creating with clay we are thinking about a three dimensional object. This is very different from drawing as we have to think about the front, sides and back of an object as we make it.

Slab work

To make slabs of clay you need two pieces of wood of the same thickness and place them as illustrated. You use them to guide you to an even thickness. The slab can be cut and joined to make all sorts of structures. Using slabs requires a mastery of slurry and joining. Slurry is a thick clay paste that is applied with a brush to the surfaces being joined.

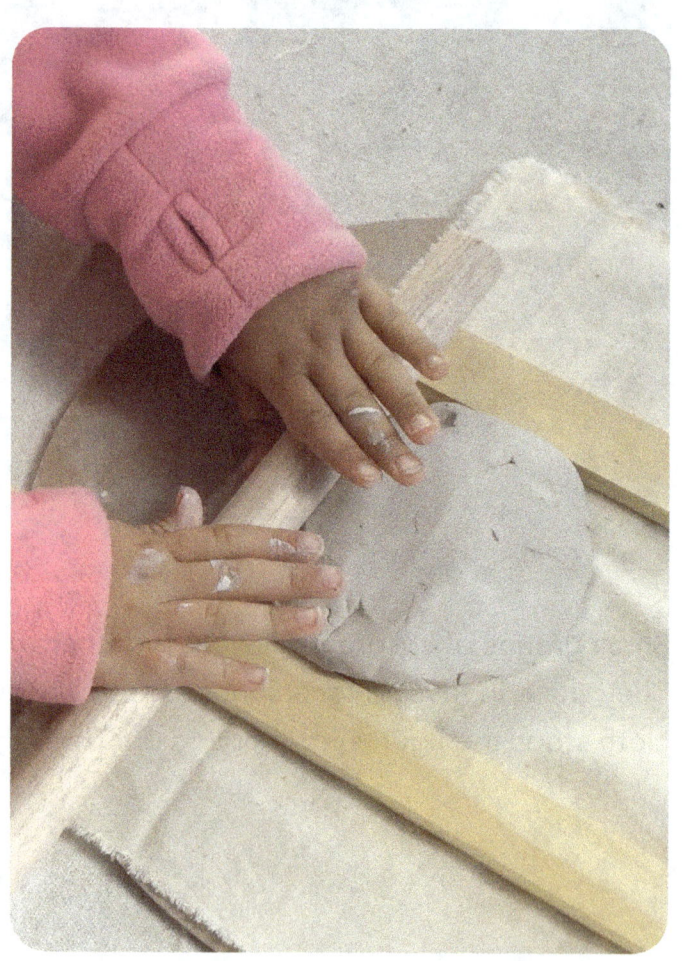

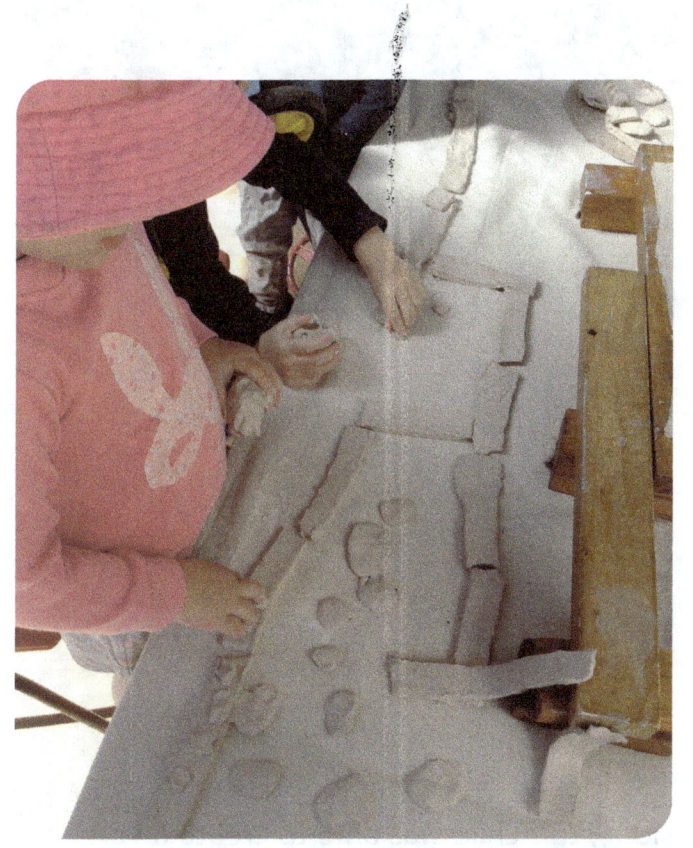

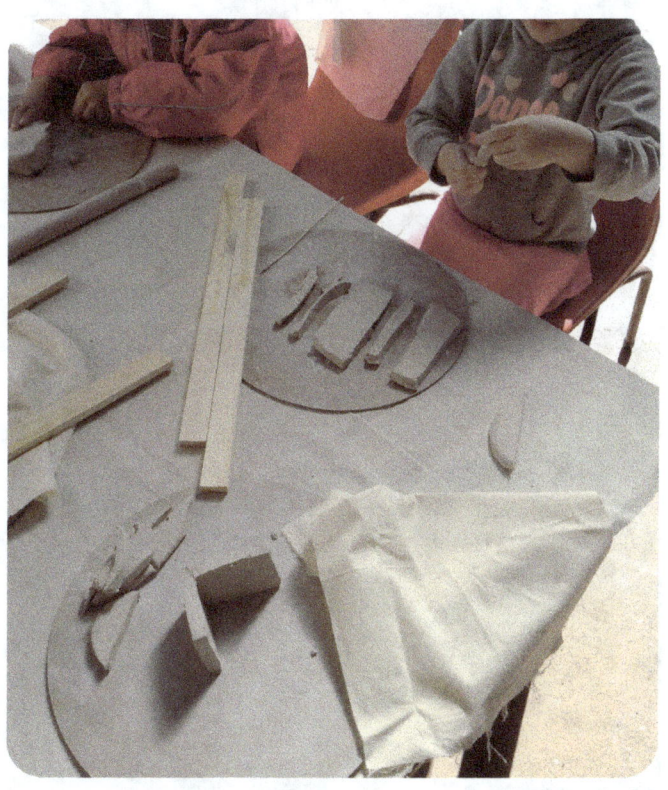

These children are making roadways from slabs. Next to the roads they made the houses in their neighborhood.

These children made a room out of slabs. They made small figures to go in the room.

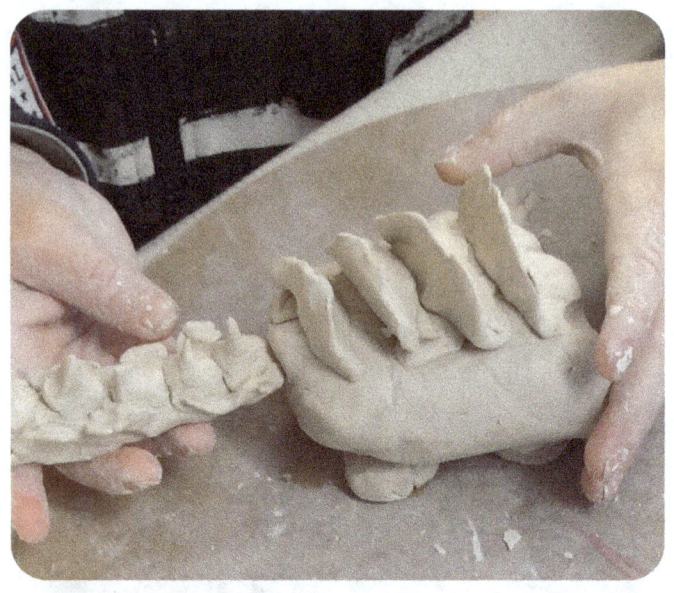

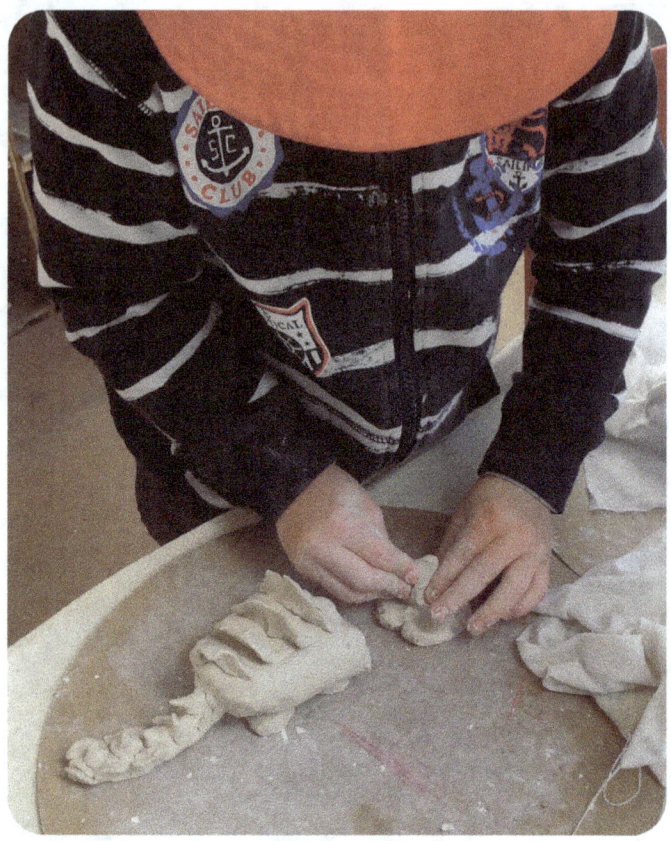

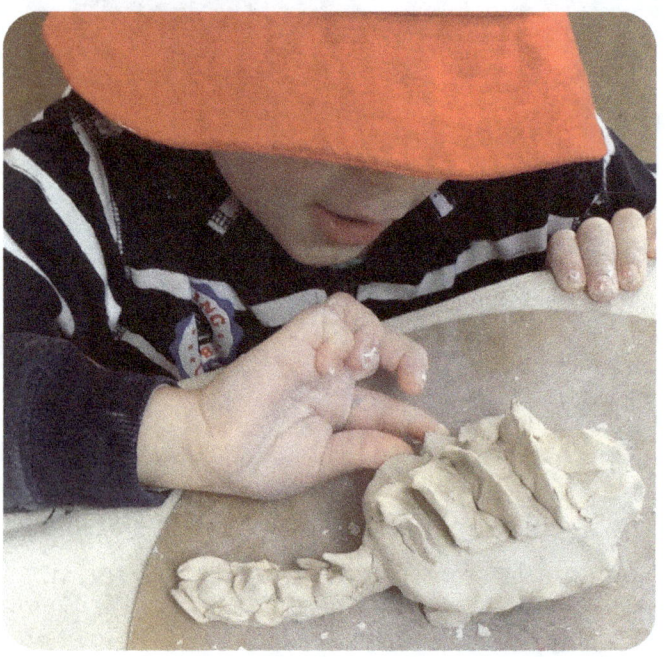

The making of stegosaurus.

Through a process of adding and subtracting, and some good use of slurry, this child was able to create a very satisfactory rendering of his favorite dinosaur. Notice how carefully he is pinching the scales on the side of stegosaurus.

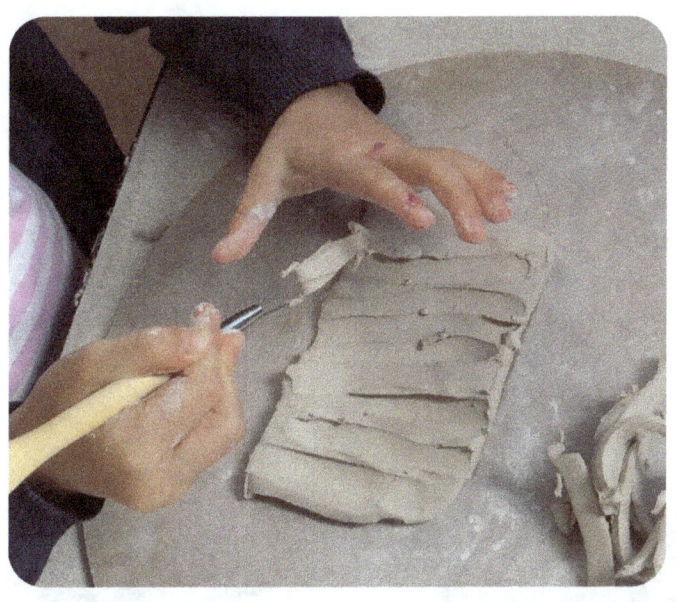

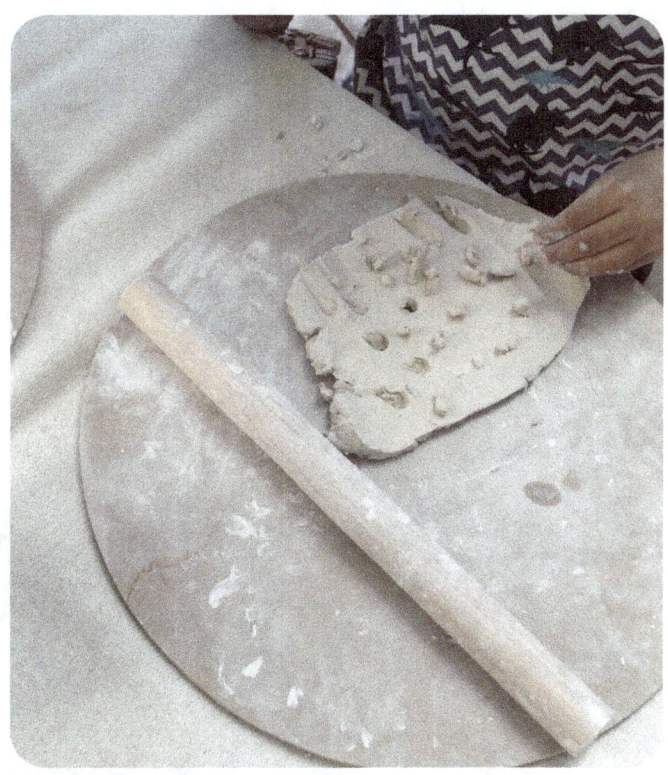

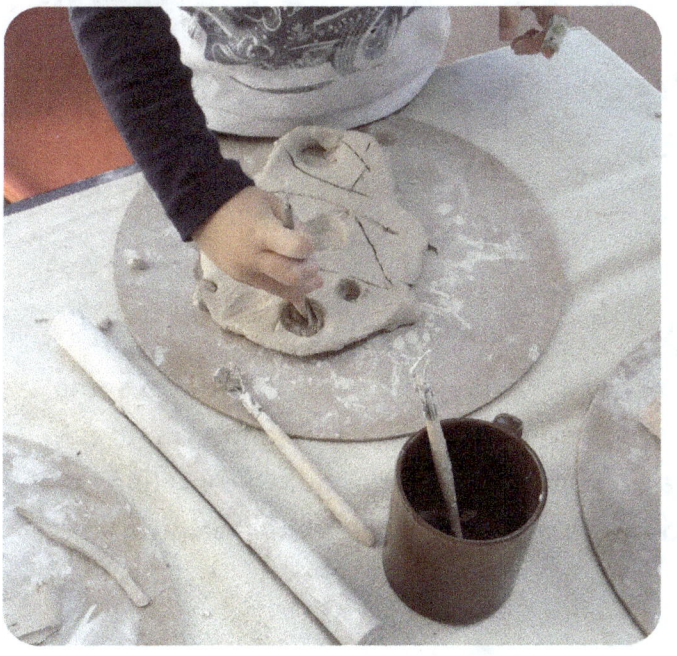

Tools for clay

There is a range of tools you can buy for working with clay. Some are all wooden and some a mixture of wood and metal. They are useful for making marks and texture on clay. They are also useful for smoothing hard to get to joints. You can also create texture with found objects like shells and cones.

~ 115 ~

Clay tends to be functional for young children. They are usually not so interested in creating objects for admiration but rather prefer to make things they can use and play with.

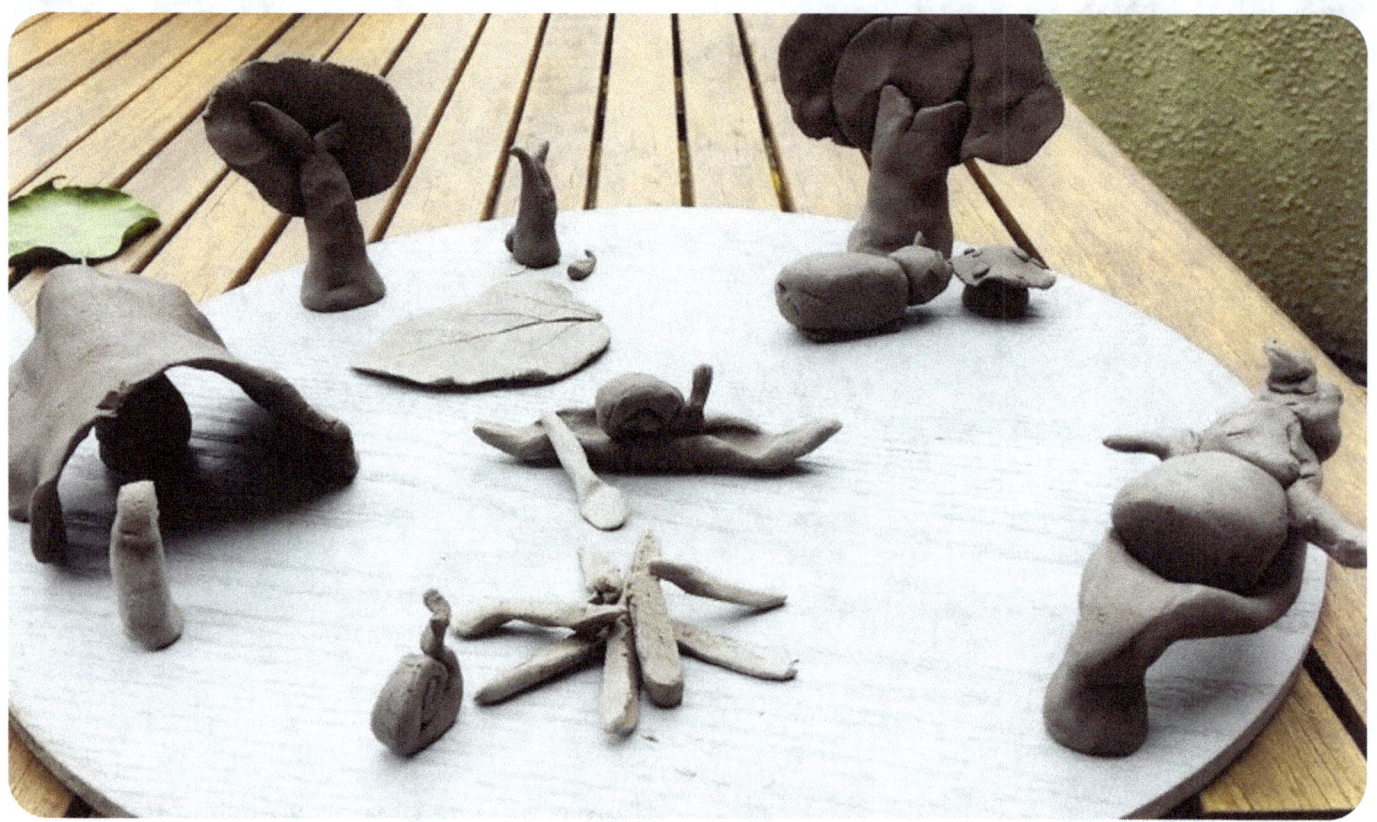

This child spent several days recreating a camping holiday she had been on, but with some of her favorite characters like Olaf and penguin. Olaf and penguin were visiting from the South Pole via magic carpet. Olaf has a comfortable hammock and penguin a tent. Snail and penguin roast marshmallows at the campfire and sing songs. The figures were painted to give them more character.

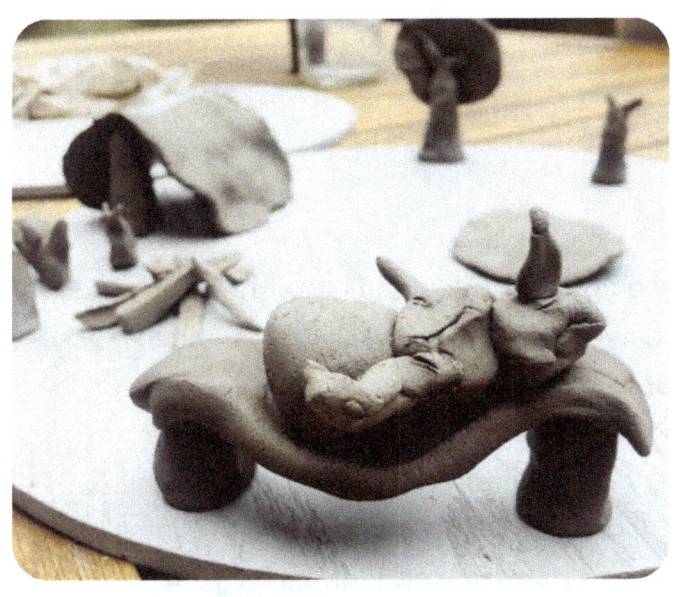
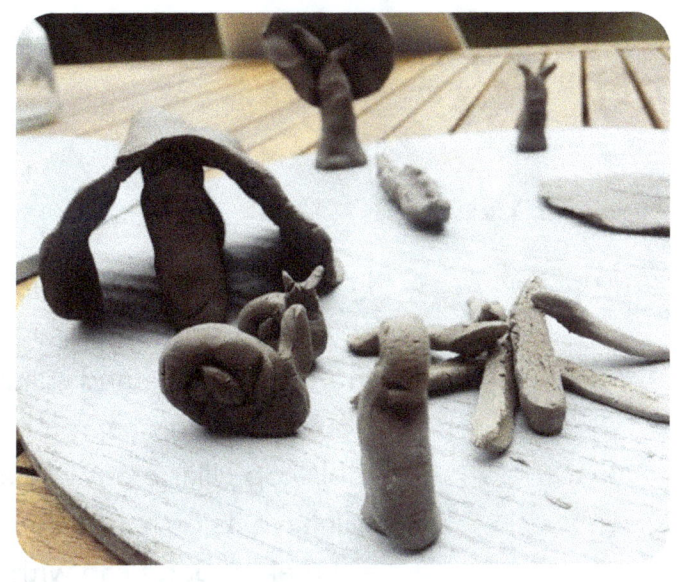

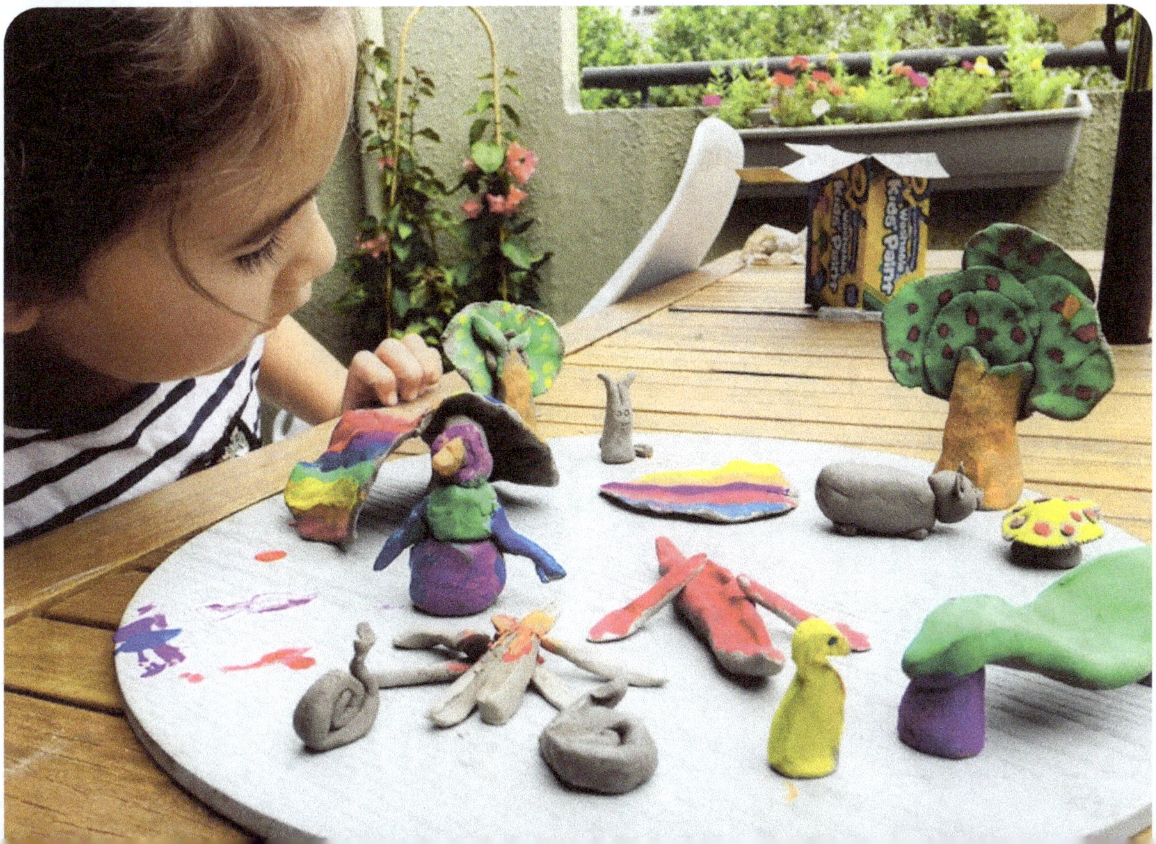

Conclusion

I hope this chapter has inspired you to work with clay with young children. Consider replacing playdough with clay. Clay is so much more expressive and sustainable. The possibilities are endless, from one child's camping scene to a large group making a whole table top village out of clay. Try using different kinds of clay. Each will have its own affordances. Consider doing a sawdust firing in a metal garbage can with a few air holes poked in it. Layer your sculptures in the sawdust and set light to it. It will burn down and leave your clay with beautiful markings.

Enjoy working beside children and learning with them. If you are pedagogically engaged you will notice and support their many amazing ideas.

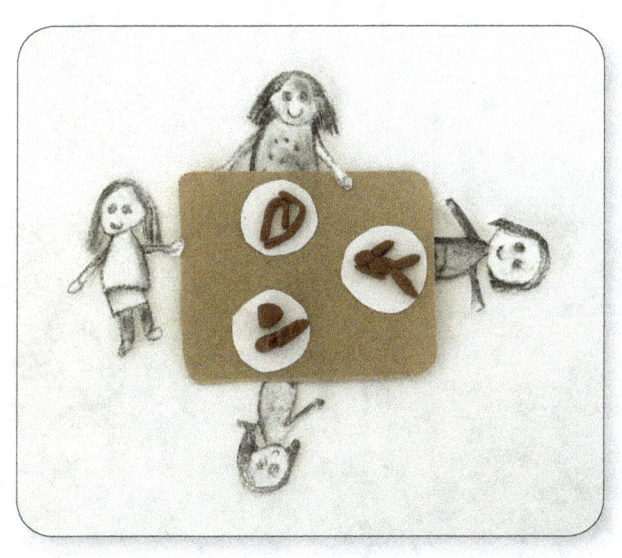

Chapter 4

~

Mark making

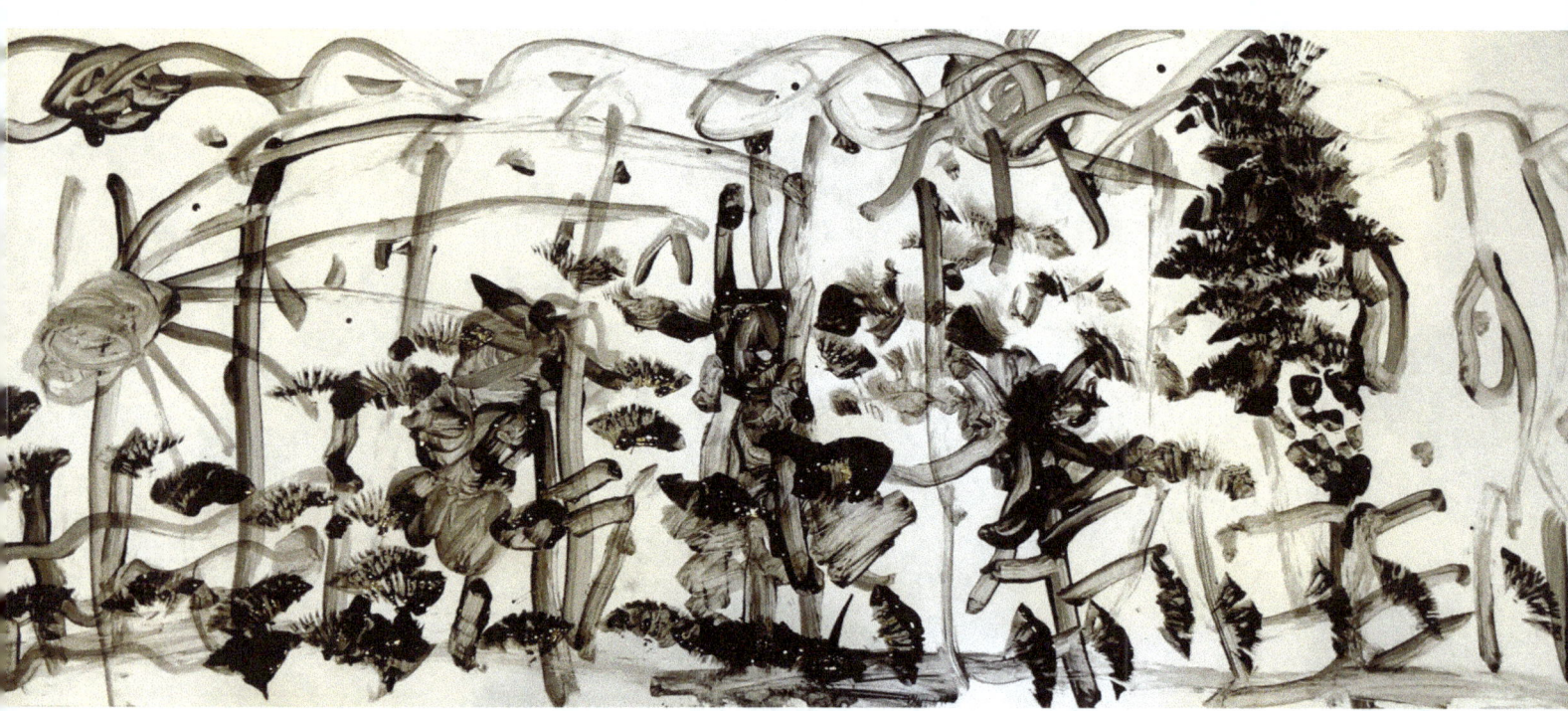

Nature brushes

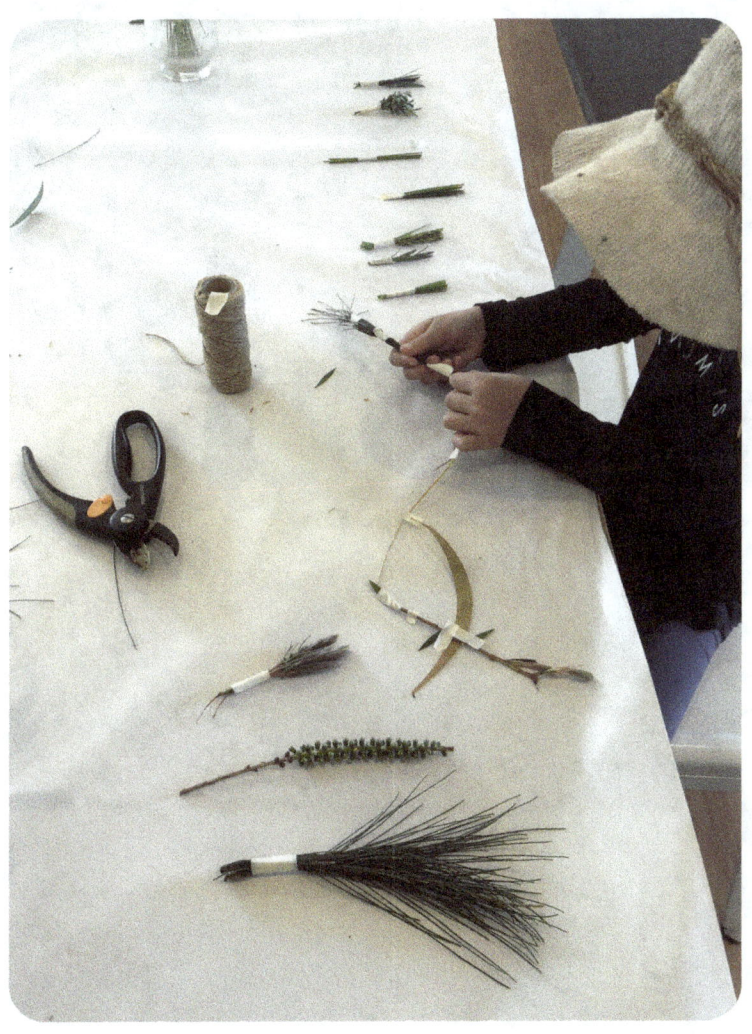

Drawings and paintings are made up of marks. Different tools make different marks and have different affordances.

The children in this project are making their own drawing or painting tools. By closely examining the tool, children's attention can be drawn to the relationship between the shape and texture of the tool and the marks it might make.

We also wanted the children to make informed decisions about the kind of tools they use to represent their ideas. The process of selecting materials and making nature brushes focuses attention on the mark making characteristics of their tools.

Making tools out of plant material was a precursor to a closer look at the different kinds of paint brushes.

Attention can be drawn to the shapes and textures of assorted twigs, leaves and grasses by inviting the children to make simple graphite drawings of them.

Observational drawing of the materials the children have collected to make tools and nature brushes assists in focusing the children's attention to detail. It helps them notice the thick and thin, rough and smooth.

When children draw together they learn a lot from each other, especially if the teacher encourages discussion about what they are drawing and what they notice.

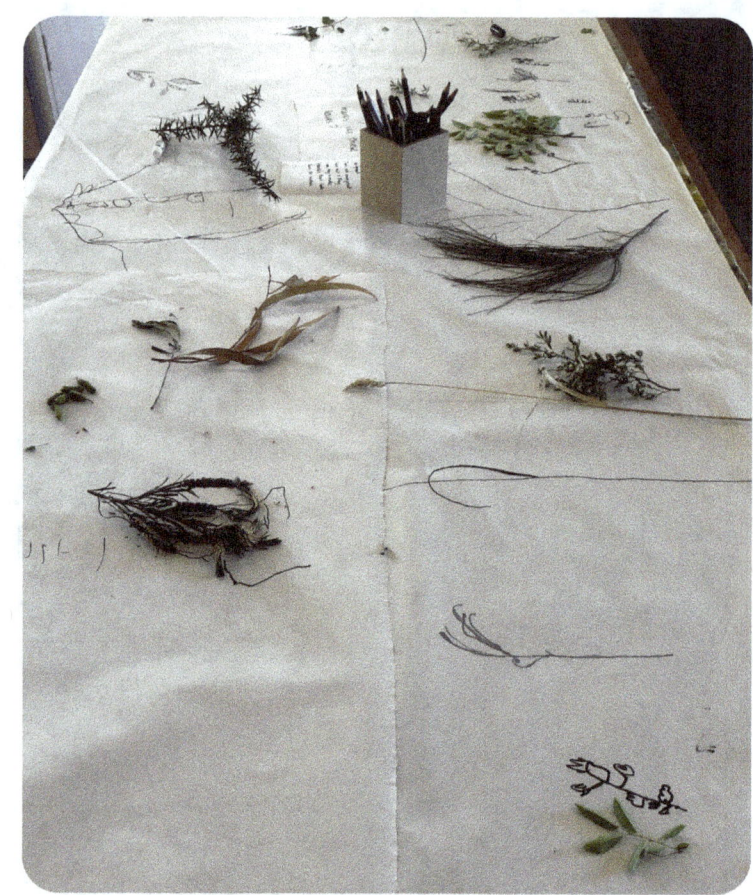

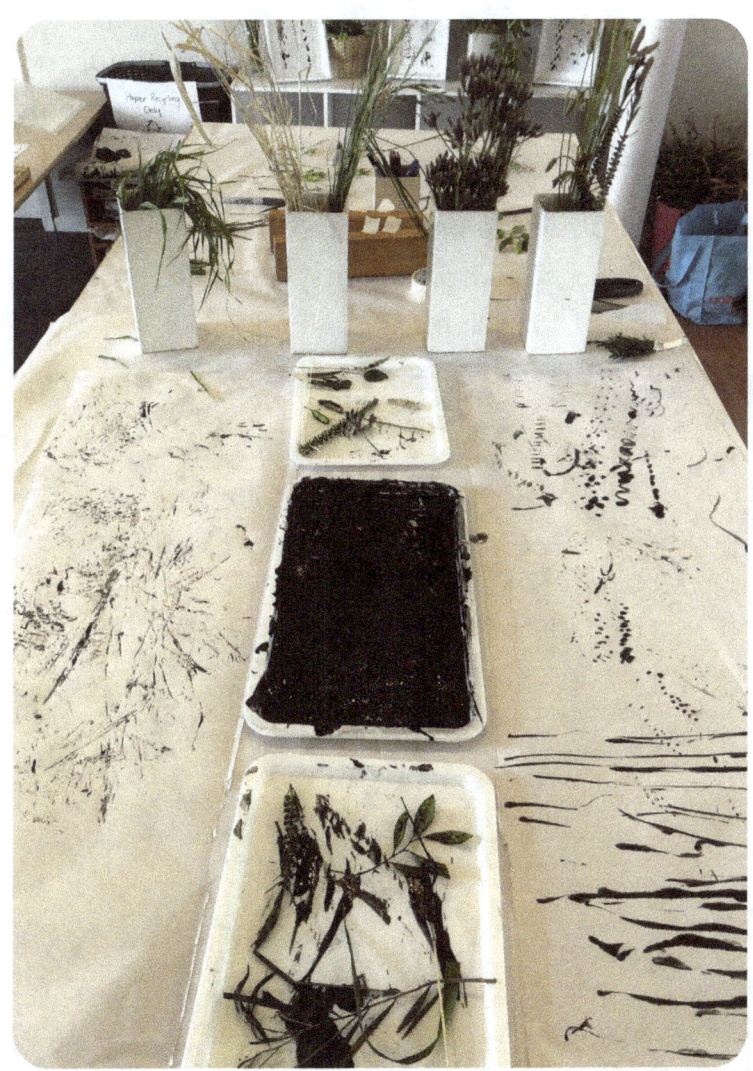

Creating a safe and interesting environment for making and experimenting is important. We covered a long table with plain newsprint paper to encourage shared drawings and opportunities for children to work together and learn from each other.

One end of the table was for making mark makers. The other end was for using those mark makers.

Black tempera paint was put on thin sponge laid in a tray. Two more trays were for putting the wet mark making tools when not in use.

At the other end of the table jars of plant material, tape and string were provided for tying together different plant materials into mark making tools.

Teachers worked beside the children and supported their experimentation.

Plain black tempera paint provides a sharp contrast between the mark the tool makes and the paper. The paint is thick enough to stay on the tool but not so thick it clumps. There is no distraction of colour.

We wanted the children to be thoughtful and intentional when choosing mark making tools to express ideas.

Too often the only choice offered are large, fat and blunt brushes that produce just one kind of thick line.

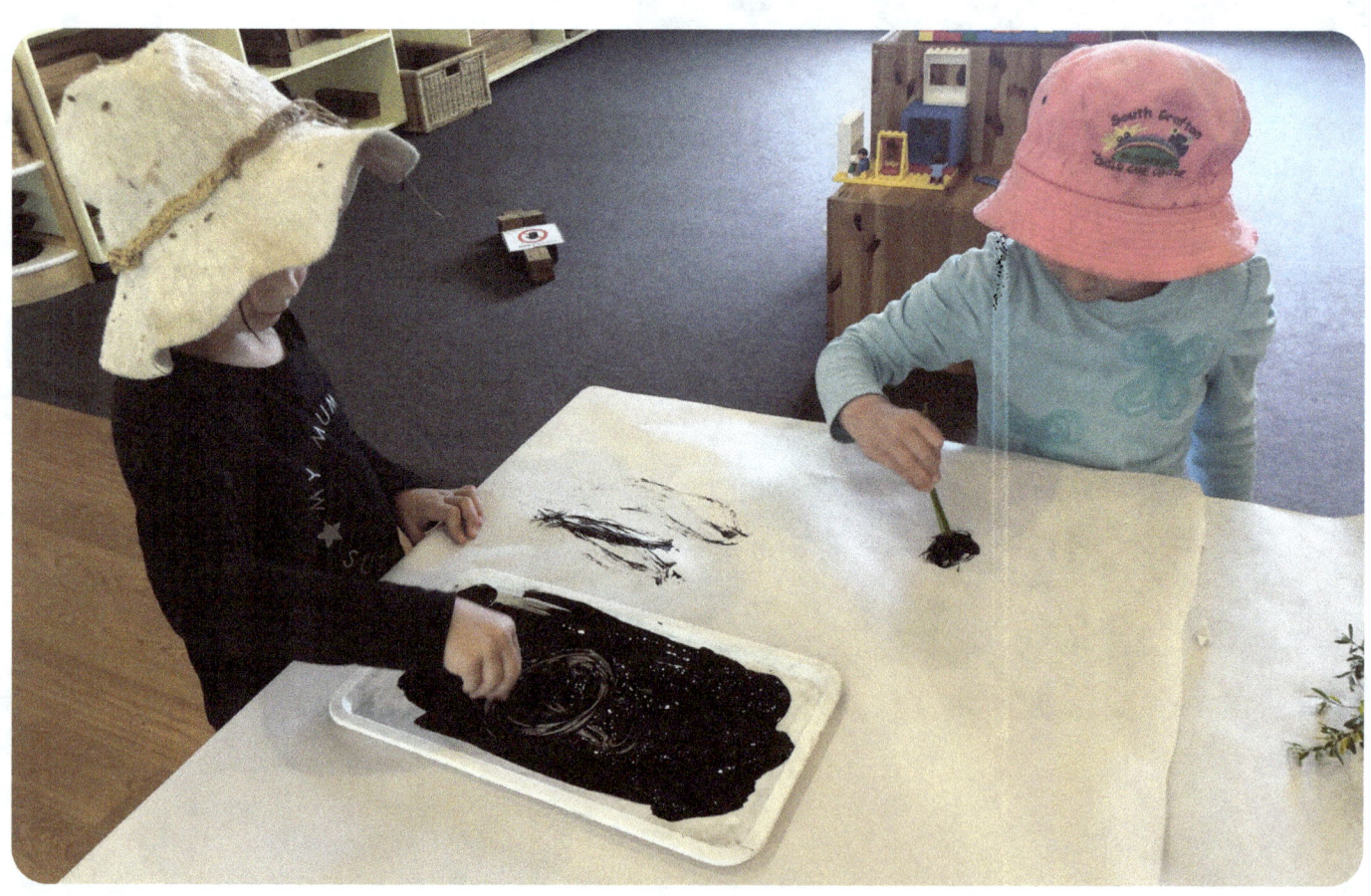

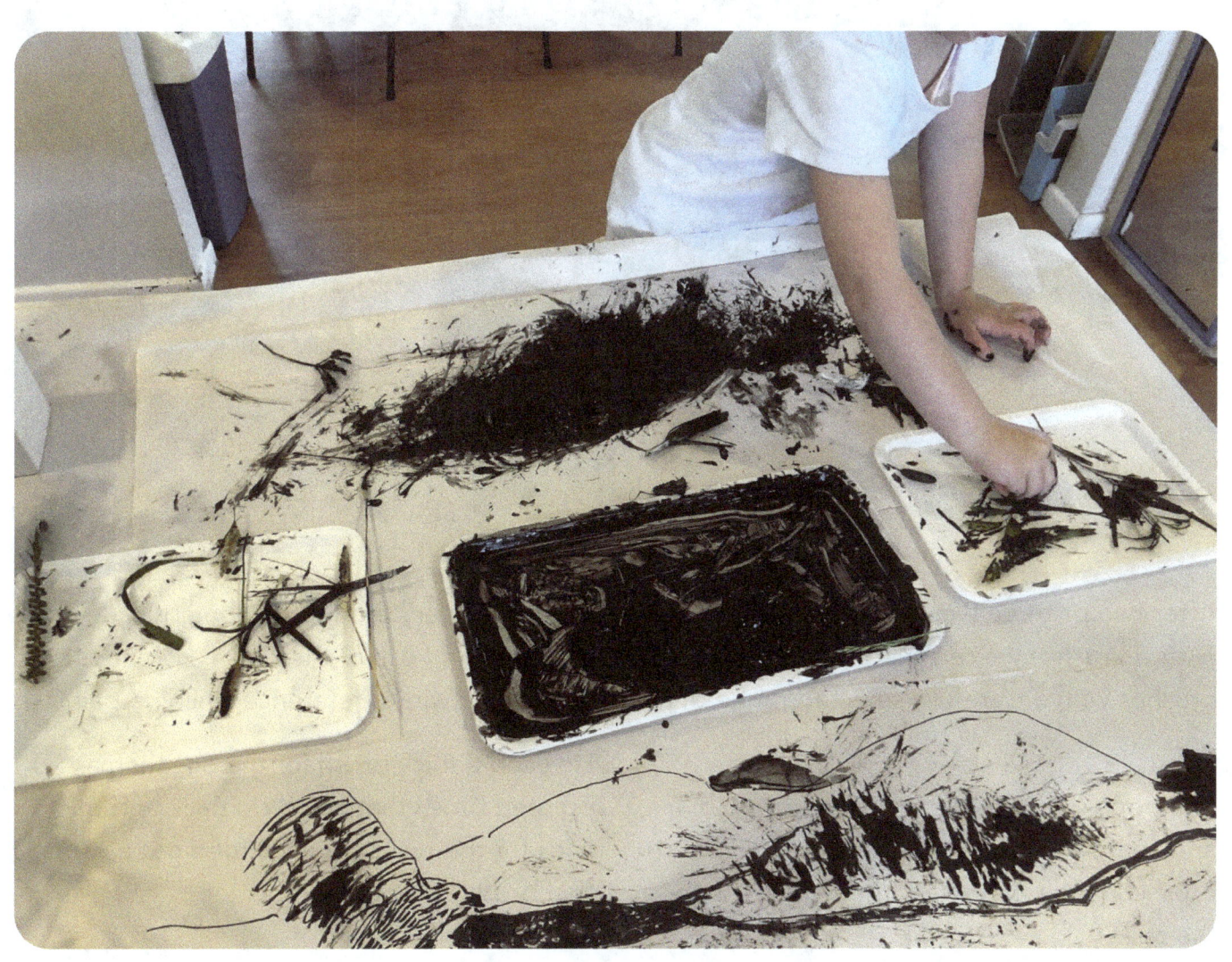

Looking at brushes and the marks they make

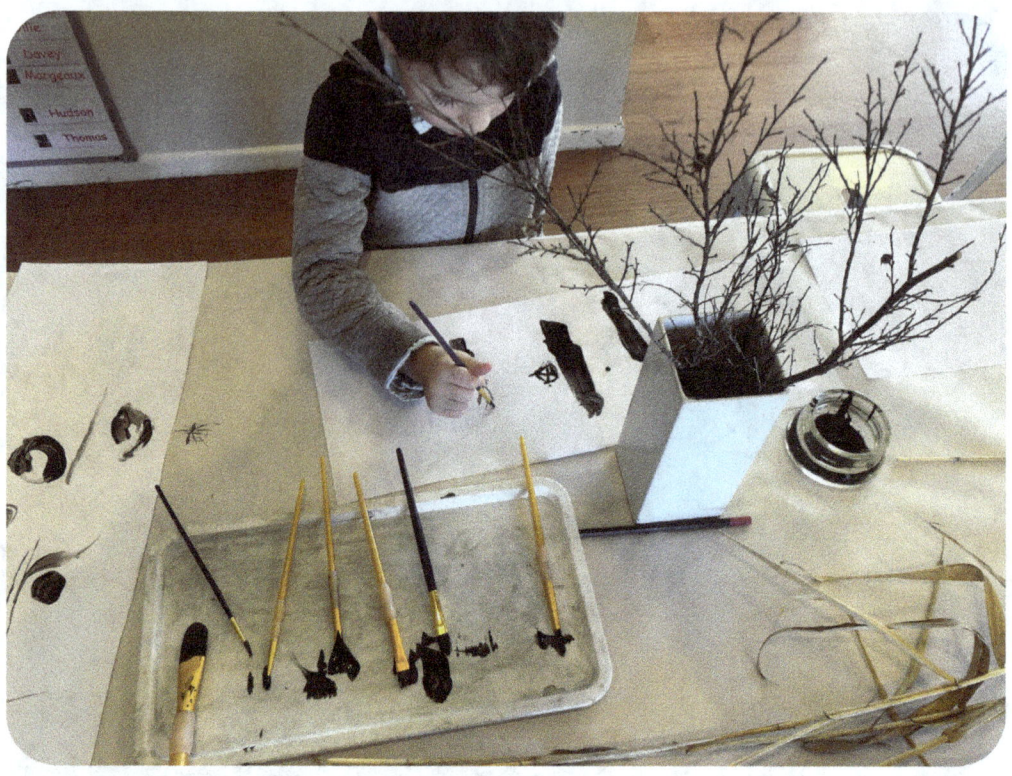

After two or three weeks of exploration with nature brushes we replaced the plant made brushes with a carefully selected range of art brushes.

Our hope was that the children to would anticipate the different kinds of marks the brushes made and select the best brush for the task.

Grayson is very thoughtful about his selection and use of the brush. He choose a very spiky twig to reference while he painted.

He used a thick brush for the pot then a pointed brush that could do thick and thin lines for the twigs. He also tried out a very thin brush.

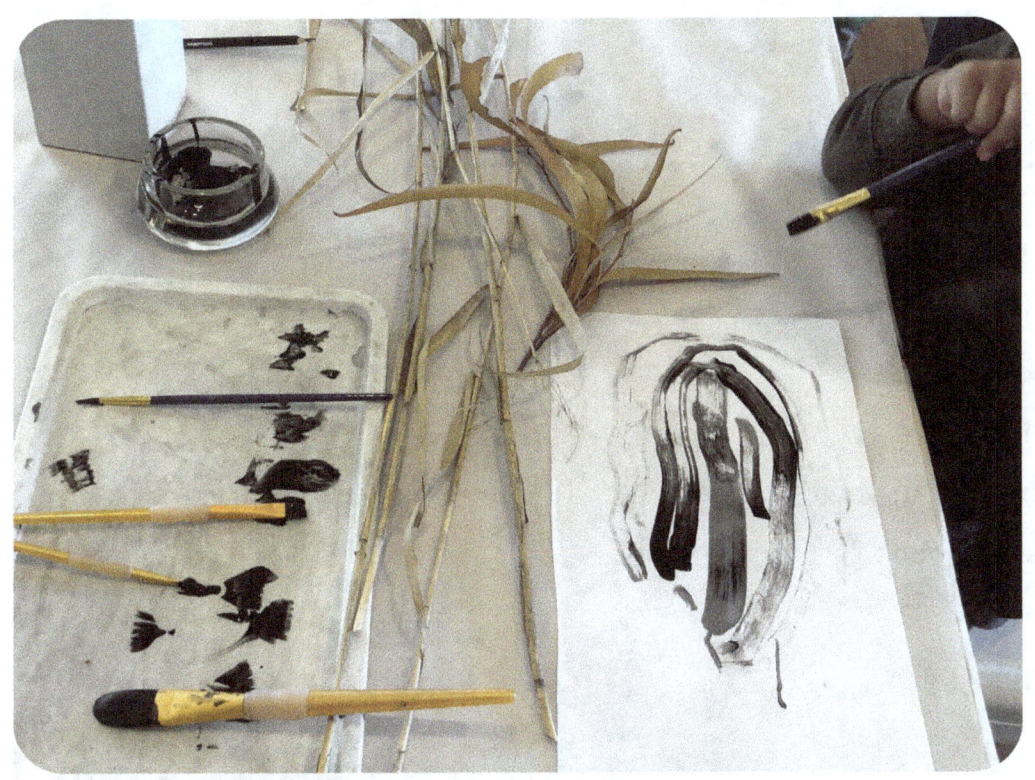

Before this child began painting we talked briefly about the shape of the brushes and wondered what kinds of marks and lines they made.

We contemplated what brush might make lines like the grasses.

Using a wide flat head brush the child discovered she could get many different widths of lines depending on how she angled the brush.

We provided visual prompts to reference while painting.

For this child it was a challenge to find a brush that could represent the feathery seed head.

She tried several brushes but none of them satisfied her.

She did however manage to paint the stalks and leaves.

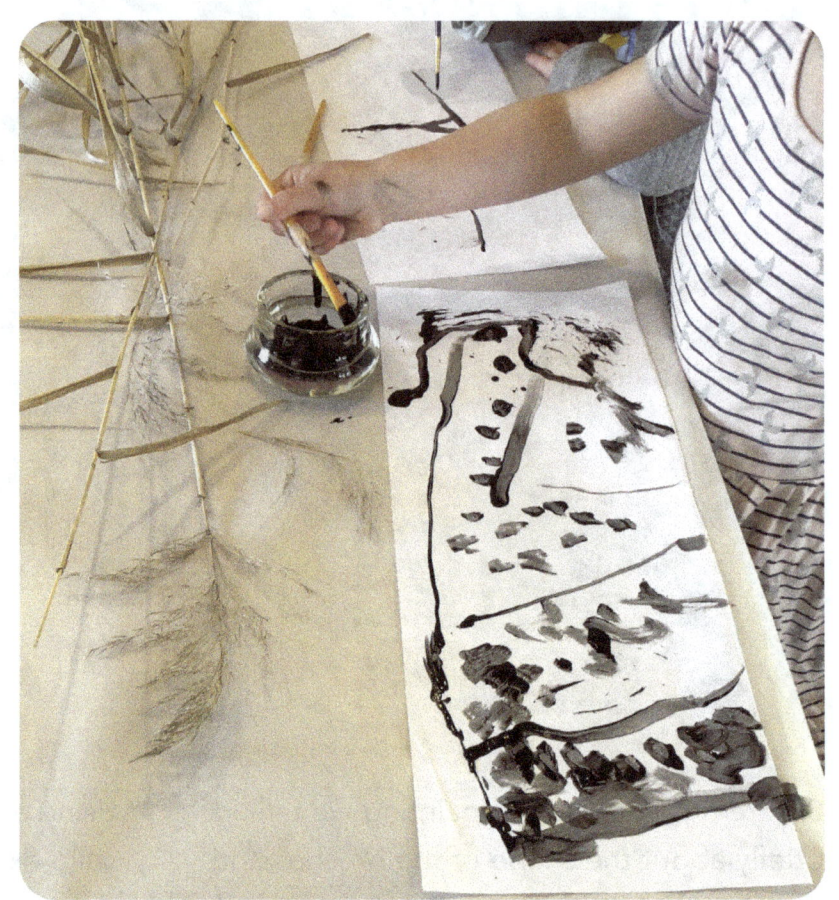

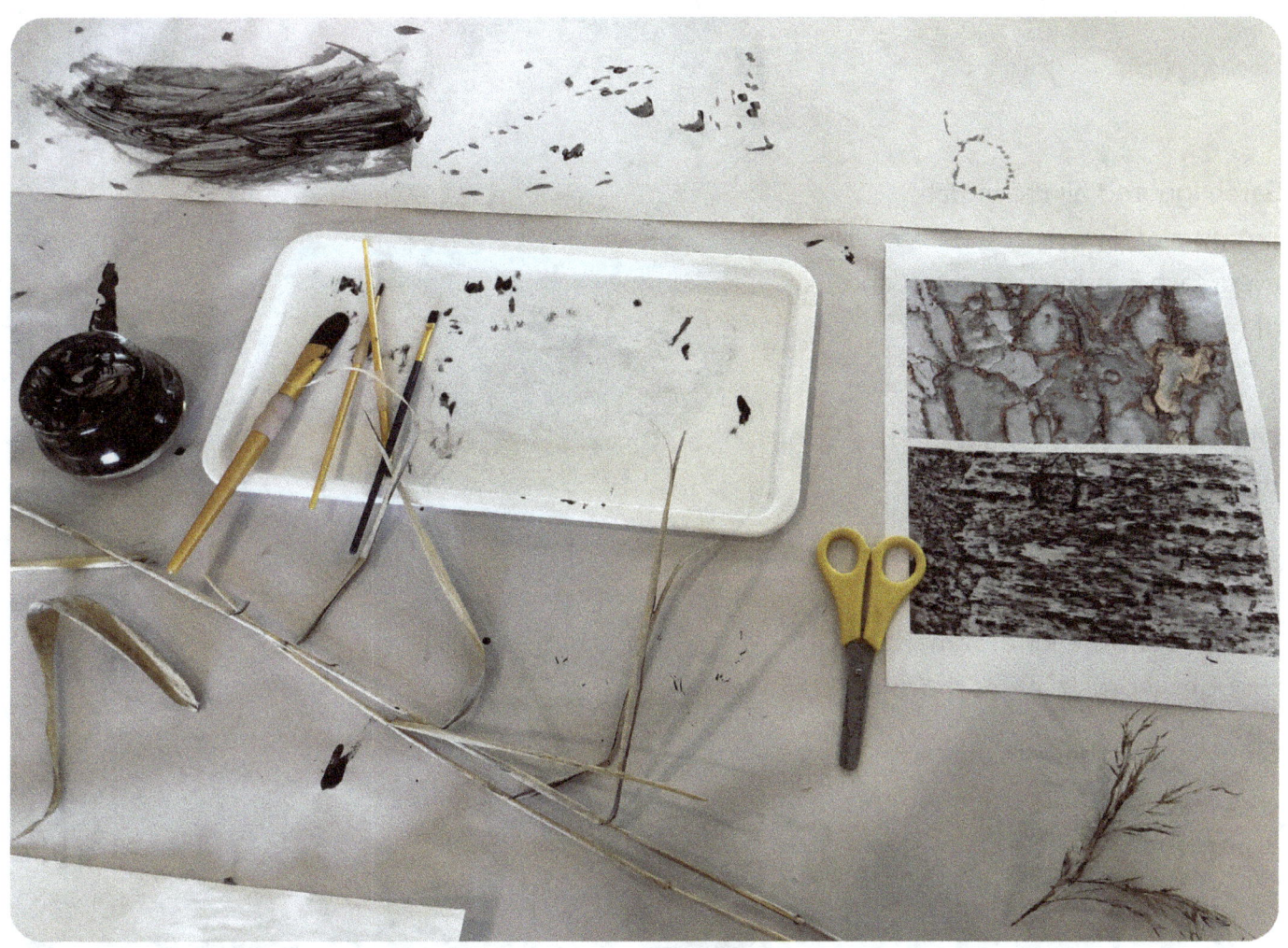

Selecting the right brush for the job is not easy.

Sam has tried to reference the two types of bark as depicted in the photo.

He has discovered that the amount of paint you have on your brush also influences the mark it produces.

Sarah ignored all the visual prompts and instead systematically tried each brush to see what kind of mark it would make.

She noticed that the mark changed when the paint on the brush began to run out.

She came back several times during the morning with new ideas about the kind of mark she thought a brush might produce.

She noticed that brushes with less bristles made a thinner and lighter mark.

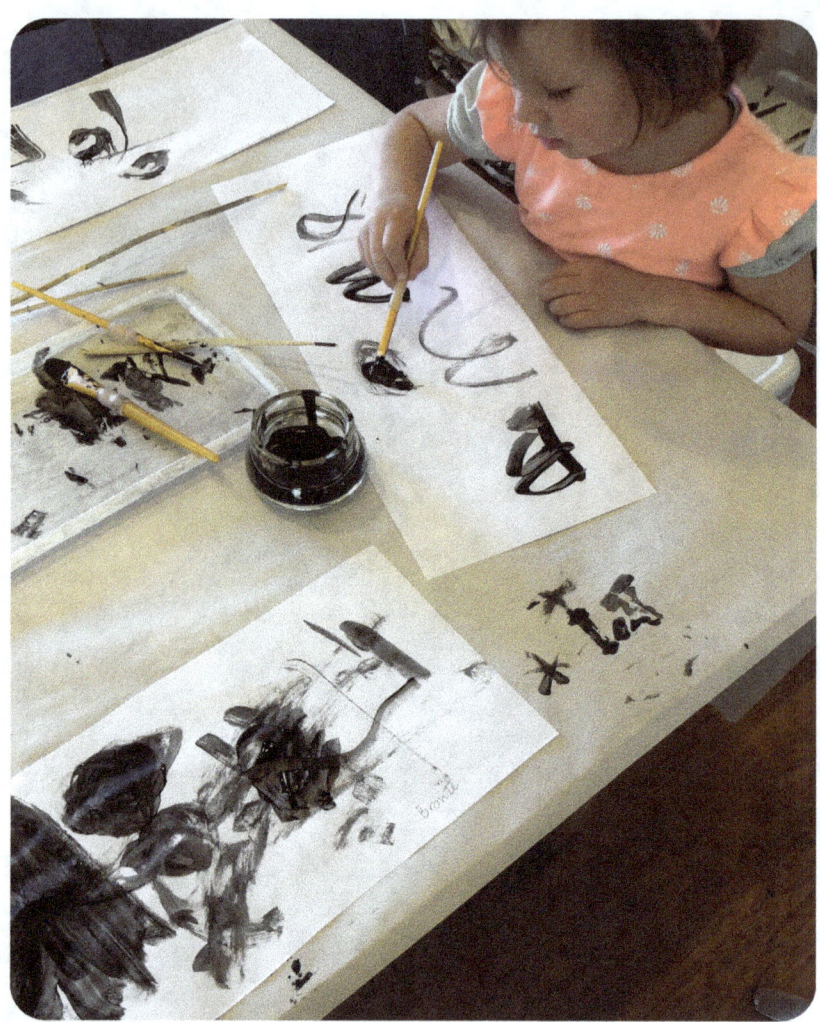

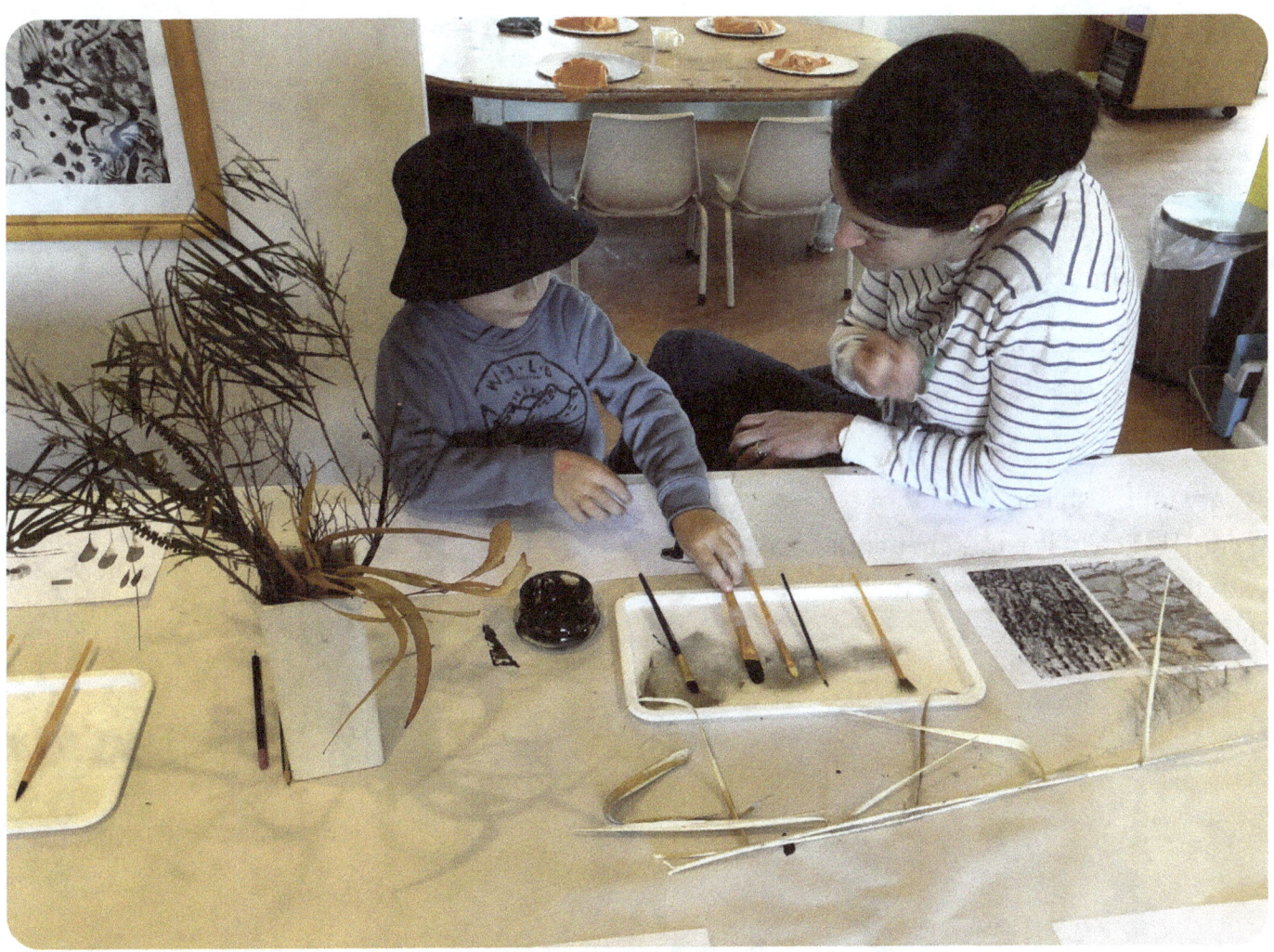

Louise, the teacher, spent time examining and talking with this child about the shapes of the brushes before they were used.

Their conversation helped him become more aware of the differences and so be more intentional about the choices made and the results he was aiming for.

One of the challenges for the children was to load their brush with the right amount of paint.

They tend to use way too much and it is too thick to do anything much with it.

A very fat brush carries a lot of paint. This child is experimenting with the brushes to see what different loads they carry.

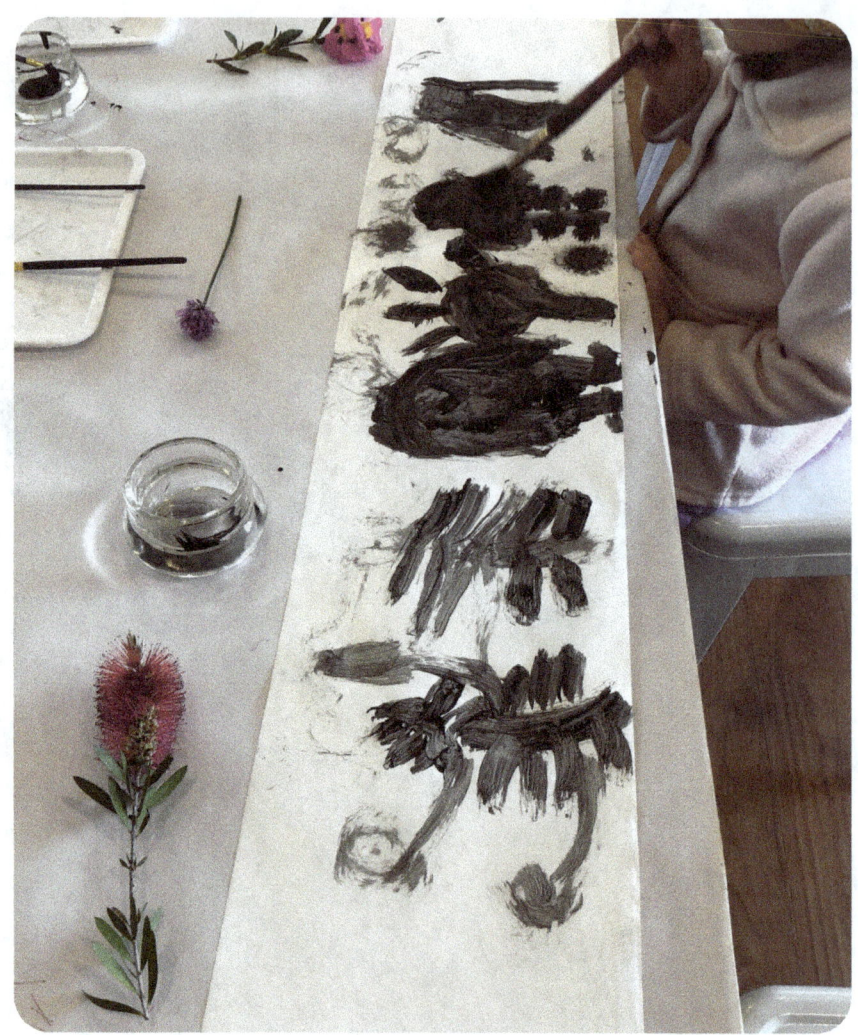

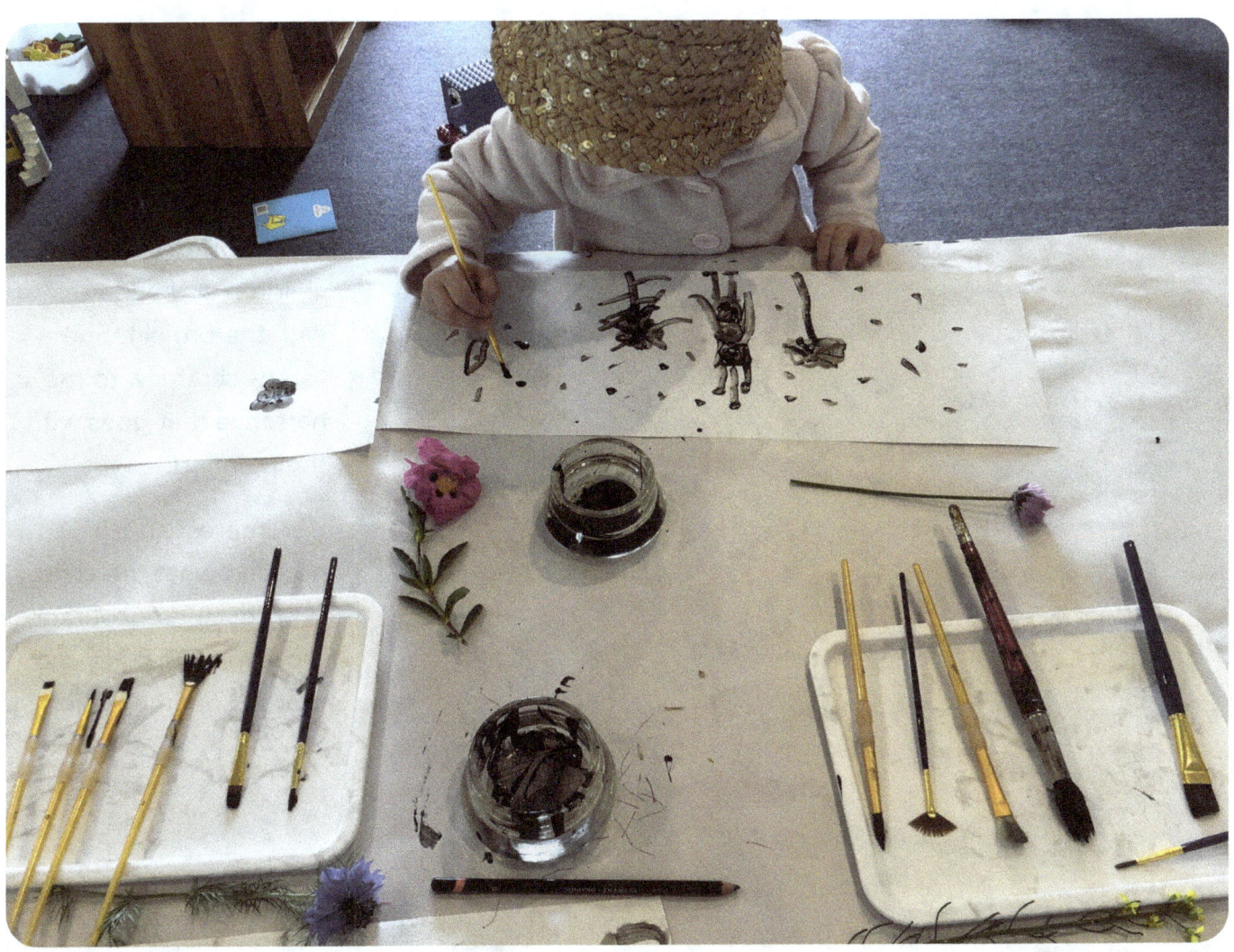

She takes fresh paper and carefully loads the brush with just the right amount of paint.

She paints a flower, a person and lots of stars.

It is a combination of what she sees in front of her and her imagination.

She is more confident in her ability to manage the paint and select the right brush.

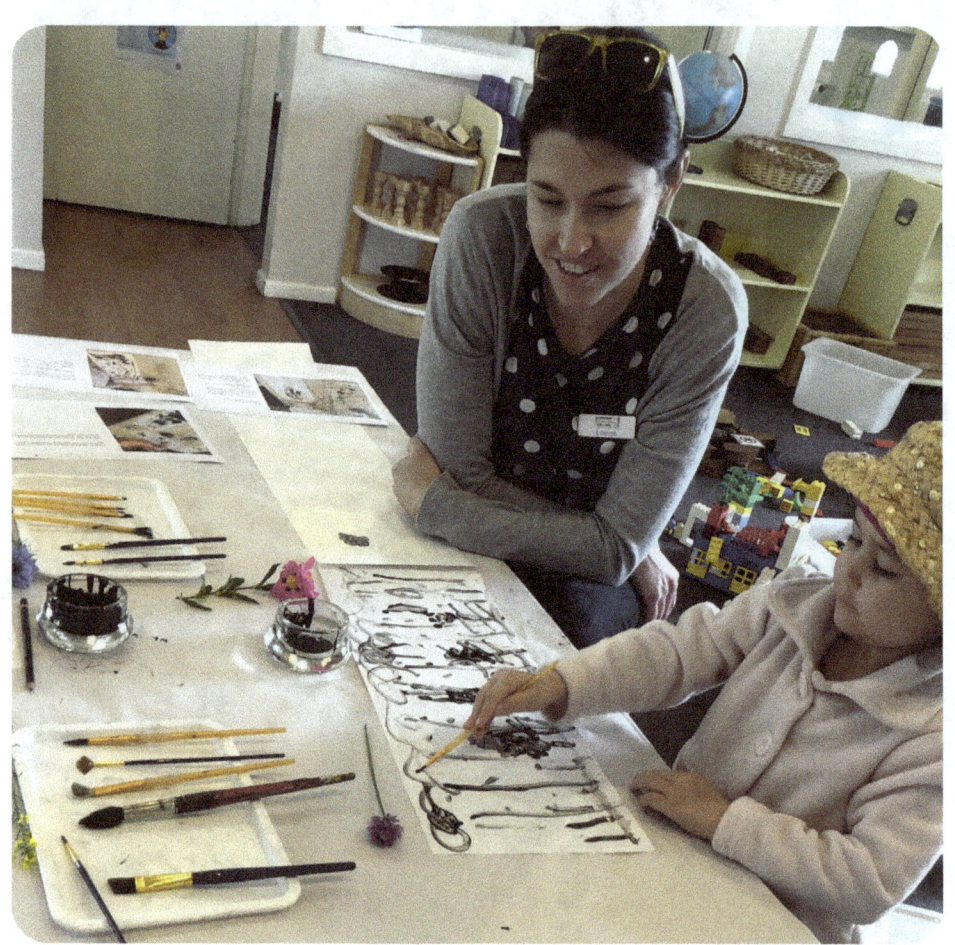

Louise often sits with the children and engages with the project. She listens carefully to the narrative that goes with the painting.

Her interest and noticing what the child is producing encourages more mark making and more experimentation.

Using water with paint to create a wider total range; Trees, flowers and stars.

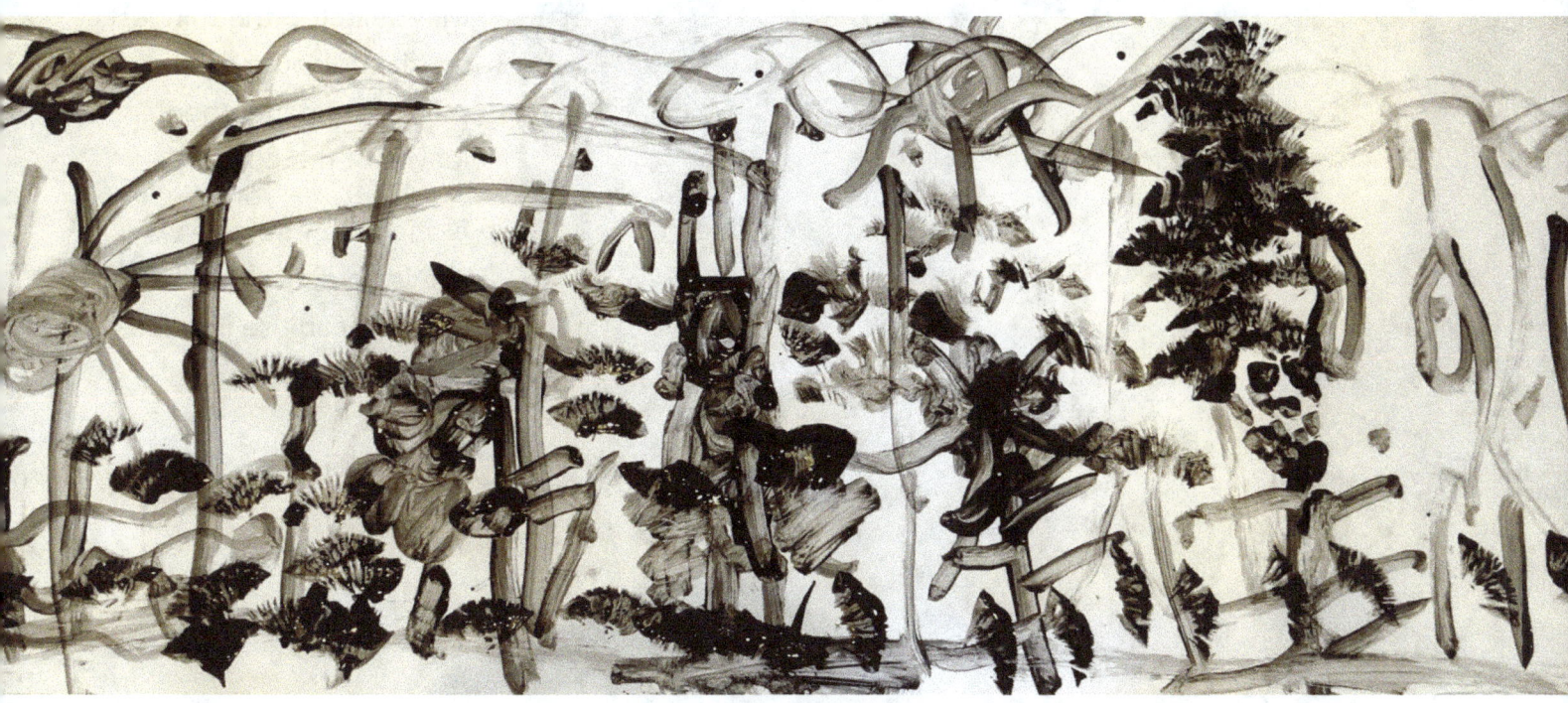

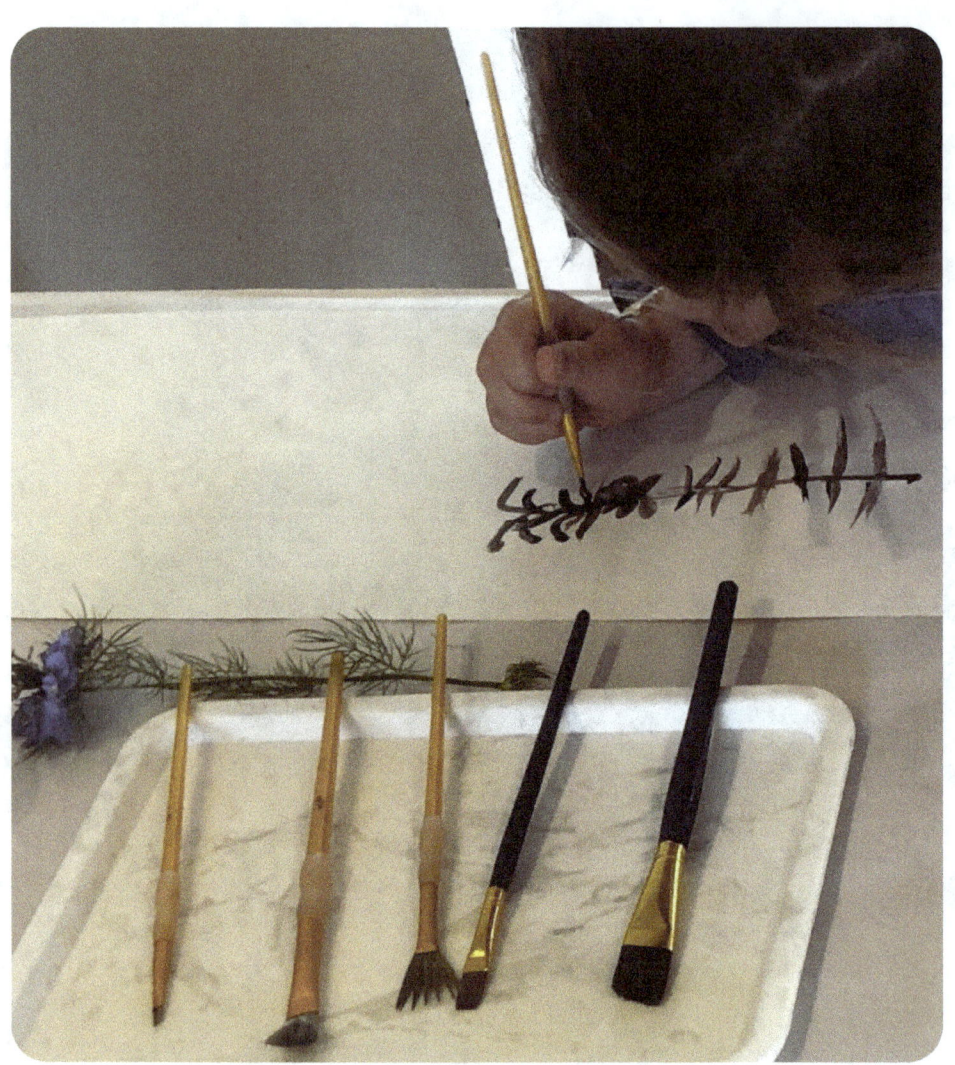

May selected the thinnest brush she could find to paint the fine feathery leaves of the flower.

Notice the effective way she is holding the brush so that she can use just the tip of the bristles.

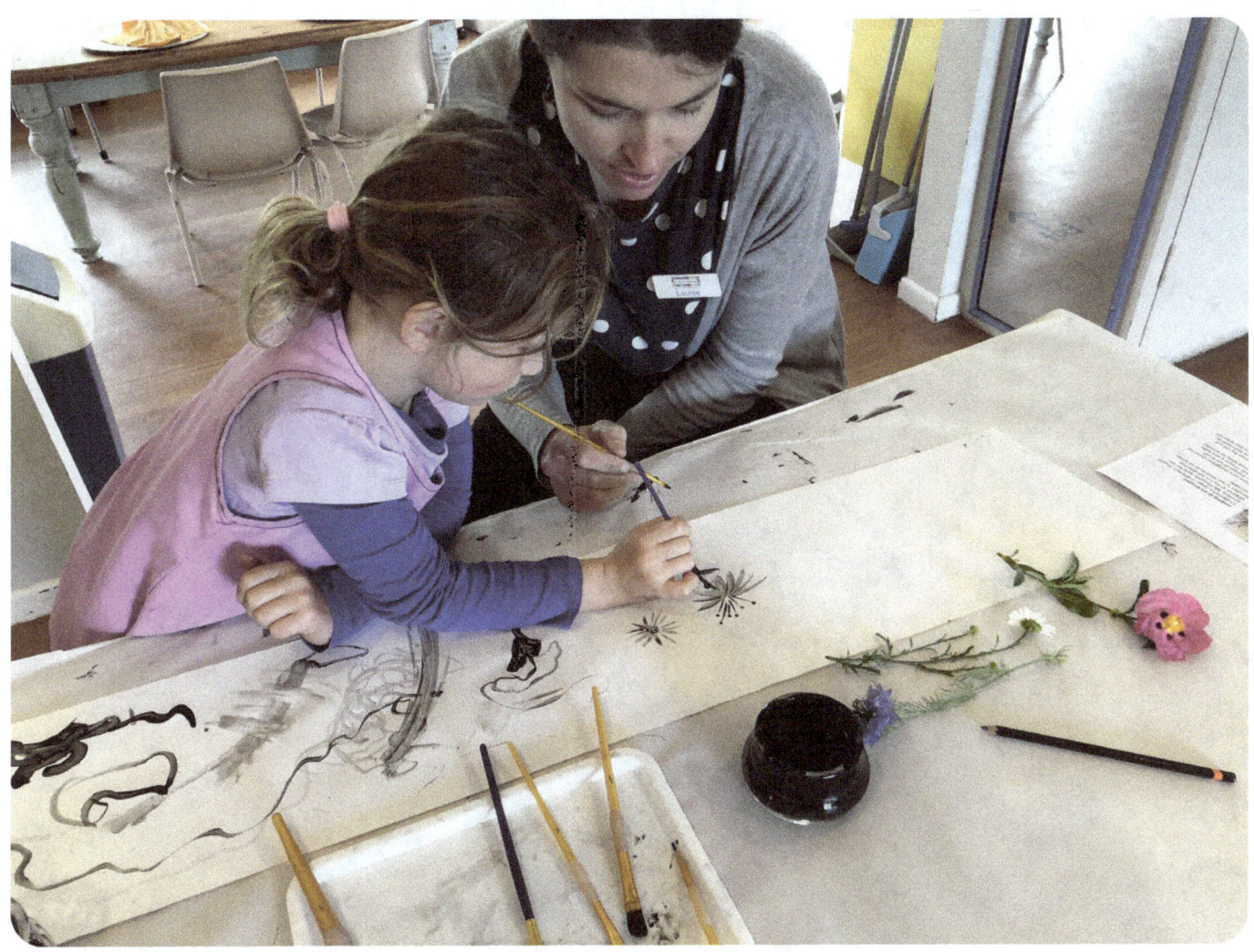

Working on a flower portrait together.

Looking at the marks the brushes leave.

Trying to match the brush marks with the plant being painted.

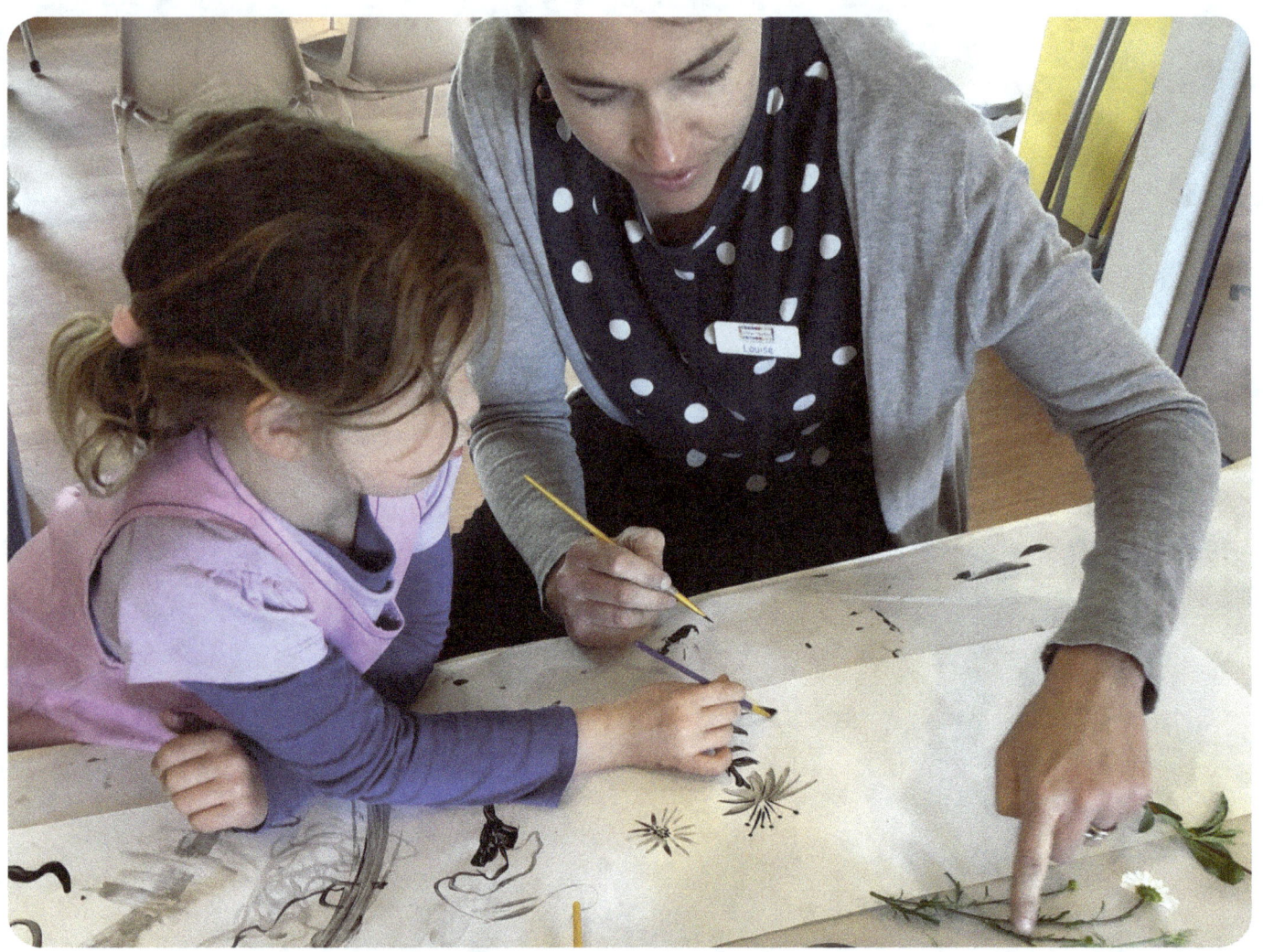

Teachers play an important role in modeling painting and drawing strategies, raising awareness of what is on display and the techniques needed to depict them.

Here there is a serious discussion about the shape and texture of the plant, which brush is being used and the kinds of marks that are being made.

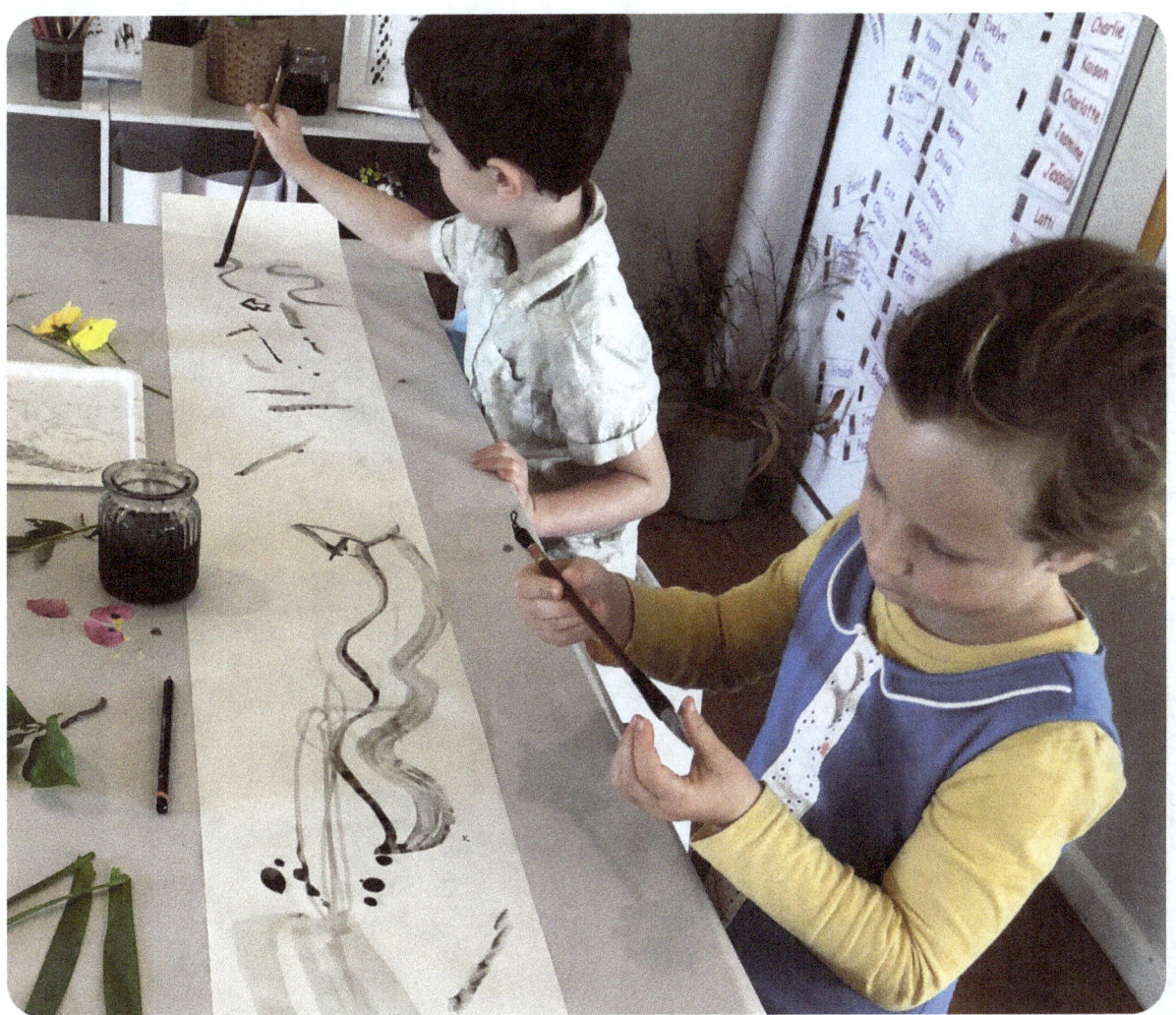

Chinese ink brushes and ink bring another level of exploration into the classroom.

These brushes and ink do not behave the same as paint and art brushes.

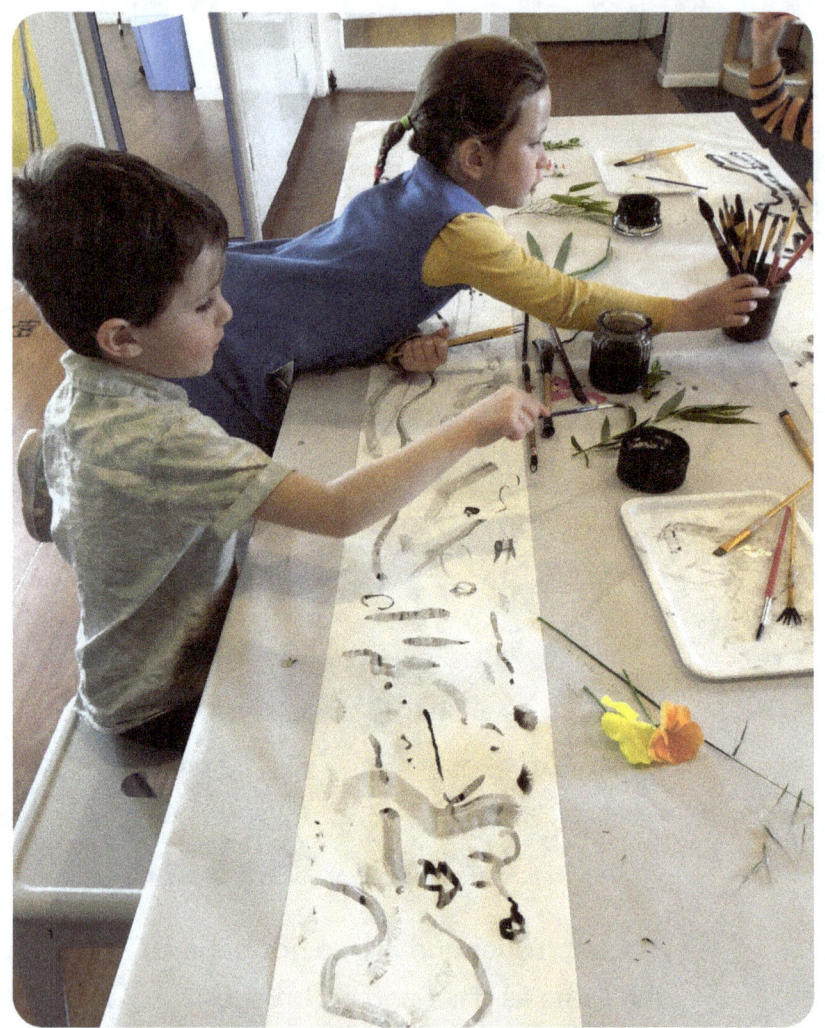

Choosing the right brush is much easier if you have had practice looking at the kinds of marks each one makes.

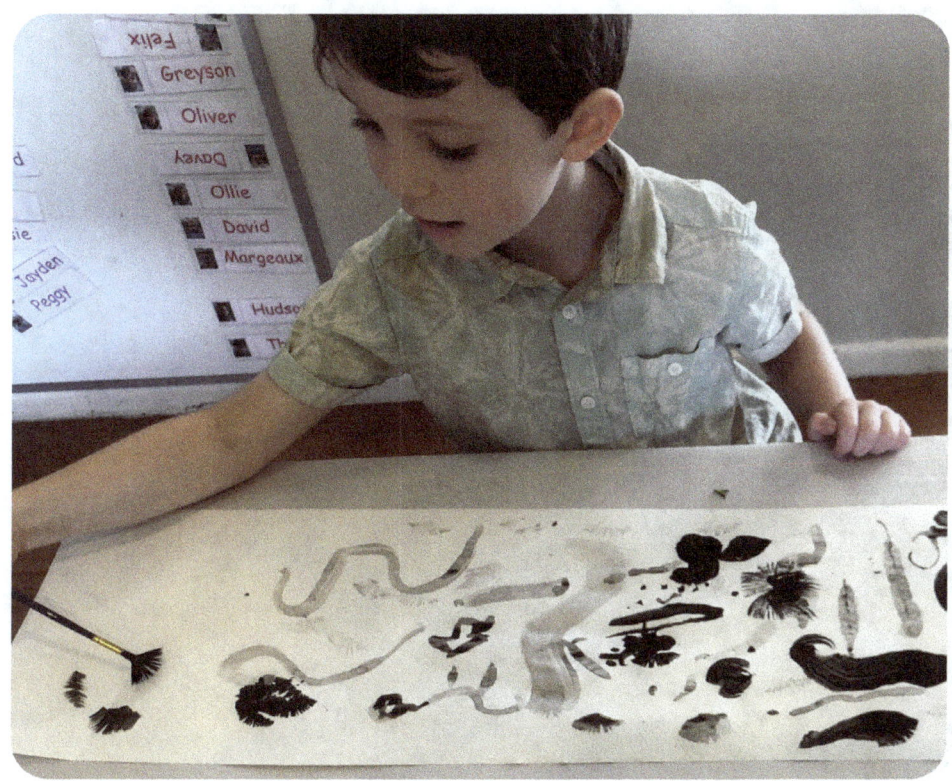

Grayson is getting to know each brush very well.

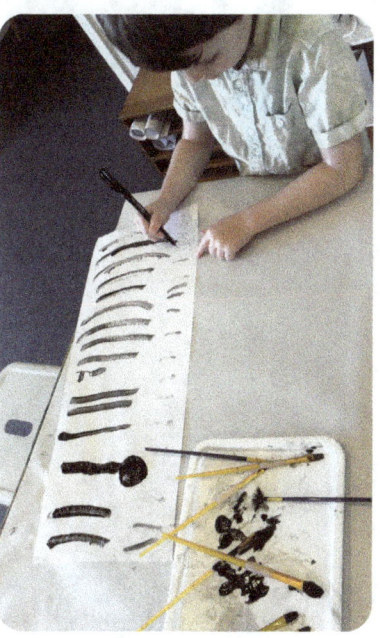

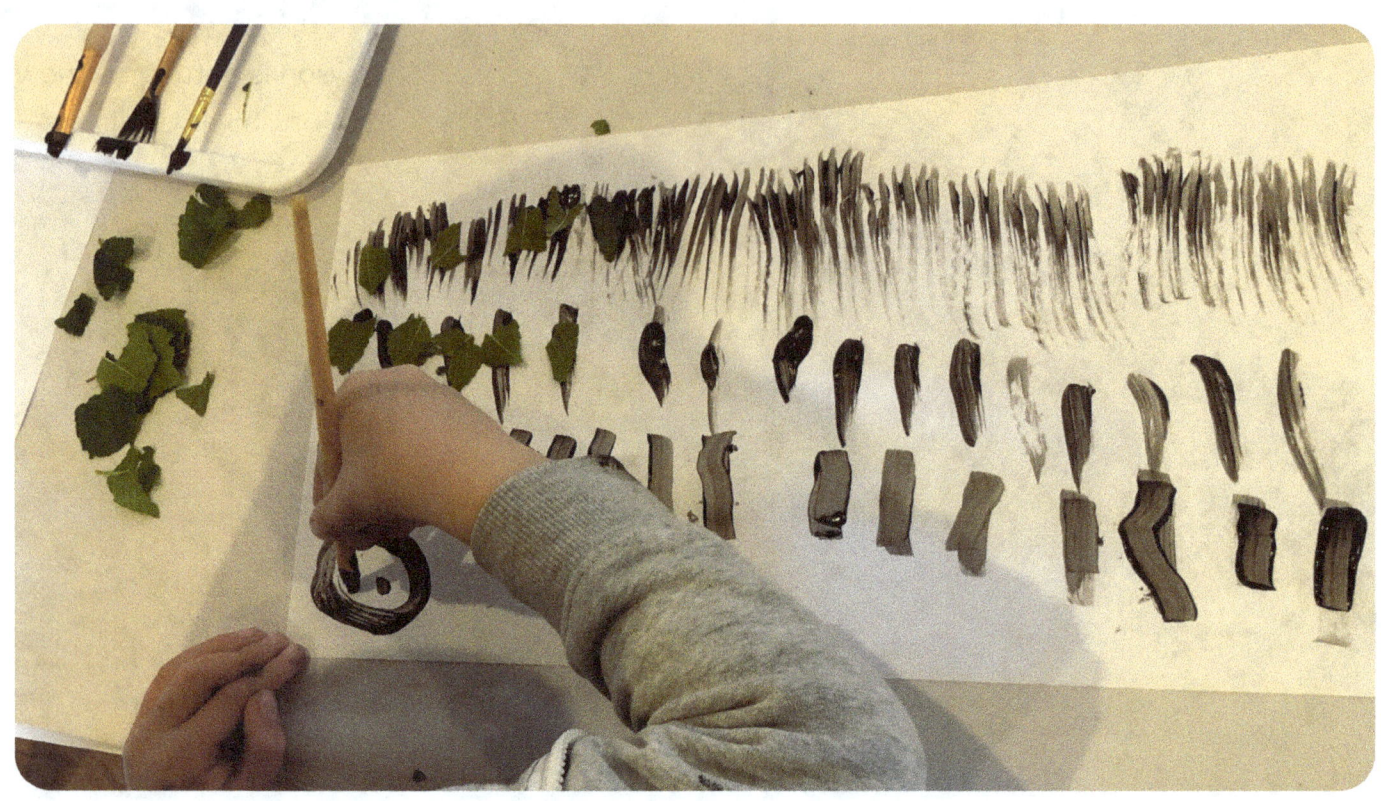

The children created their own experiments. This child was looking at marks repeated by one flat brush load. He was noticing the similarities and differences between brush marks and the way you hold the brush. The top row was the flat brush held sideways. The middle row was a flick of the brush and the bottom row an even and regular pressure.

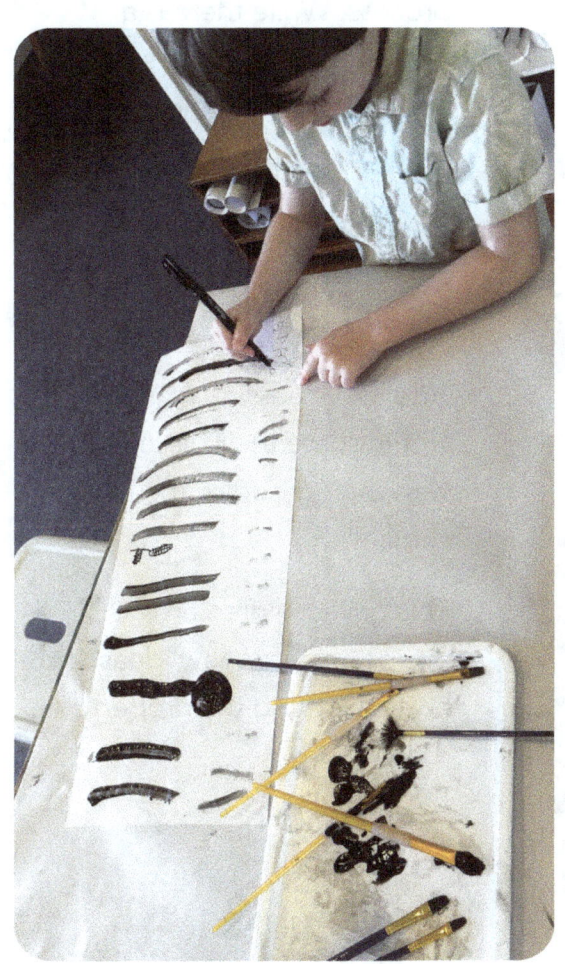

More experimenting with brush marks

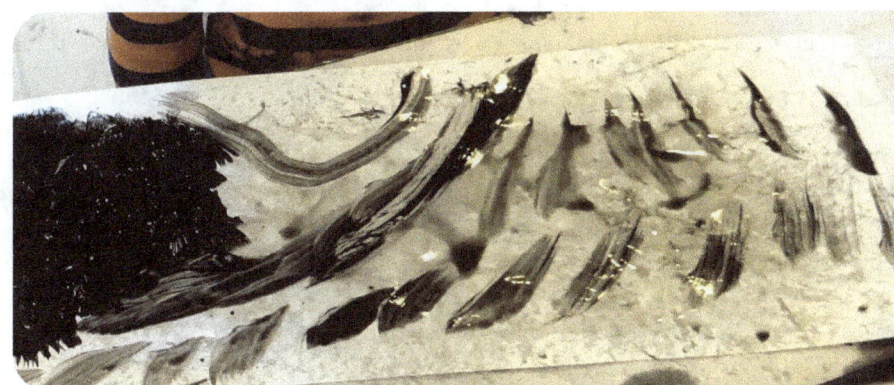

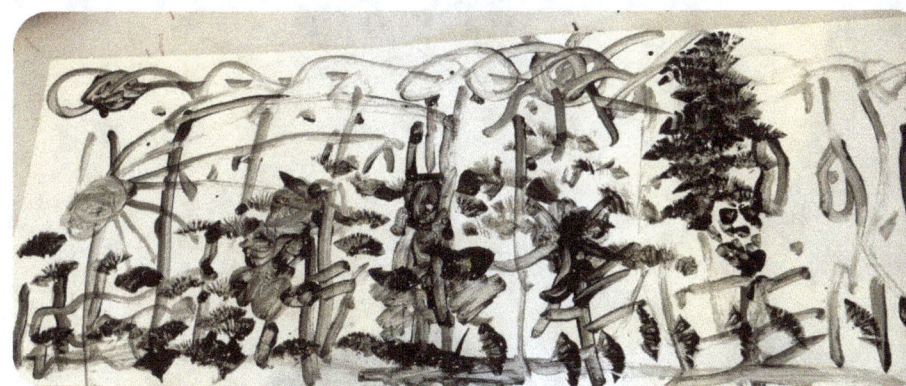

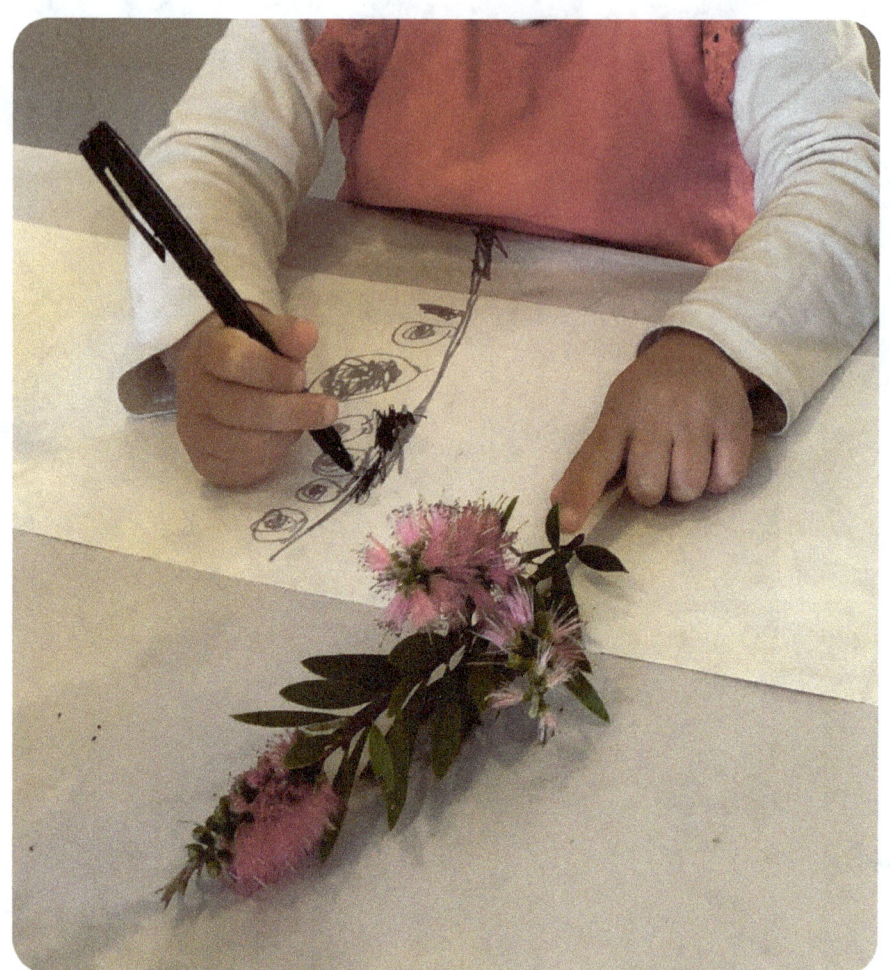

Observational drawing is a strong component of the process. While there is a likeness between the subject and the painting, the focus is more about the details noticed.

Fine tipped black markers were introduced in response to the need to make very thin lines.

After each session, children would share their discoveries with their group or the whole class.

This gave children an opportunity for new ideas and how to extend their repertoire.

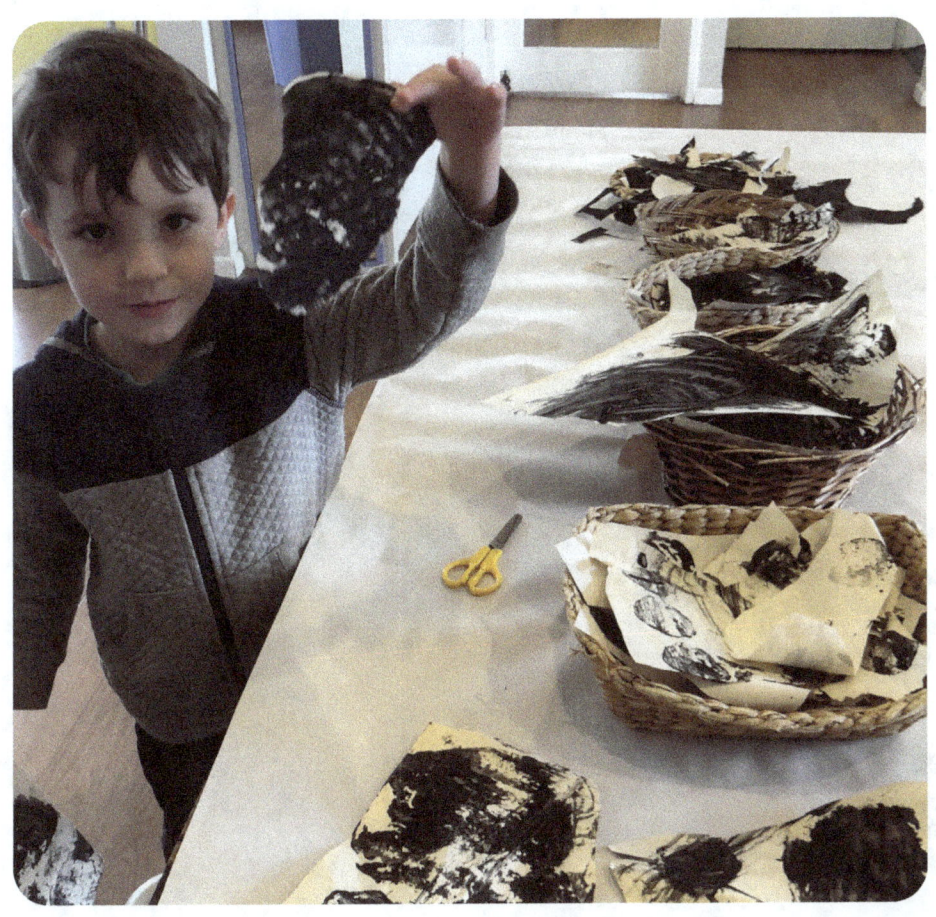

Making marks on a shared roll out of paper meant that we were left with a lot of mark making experiments that could not easily go into the children's portfolios.

We cut the experiments up into chunks of different kinds of marks and sorted them in baskets according to their overall texture.

For example, those pieces with thick black marks, like the child is holding, were put in one basket while those pieces with fine marks were put in another.

This sorting was yet another way to have the children pay attention the qualities of marks.

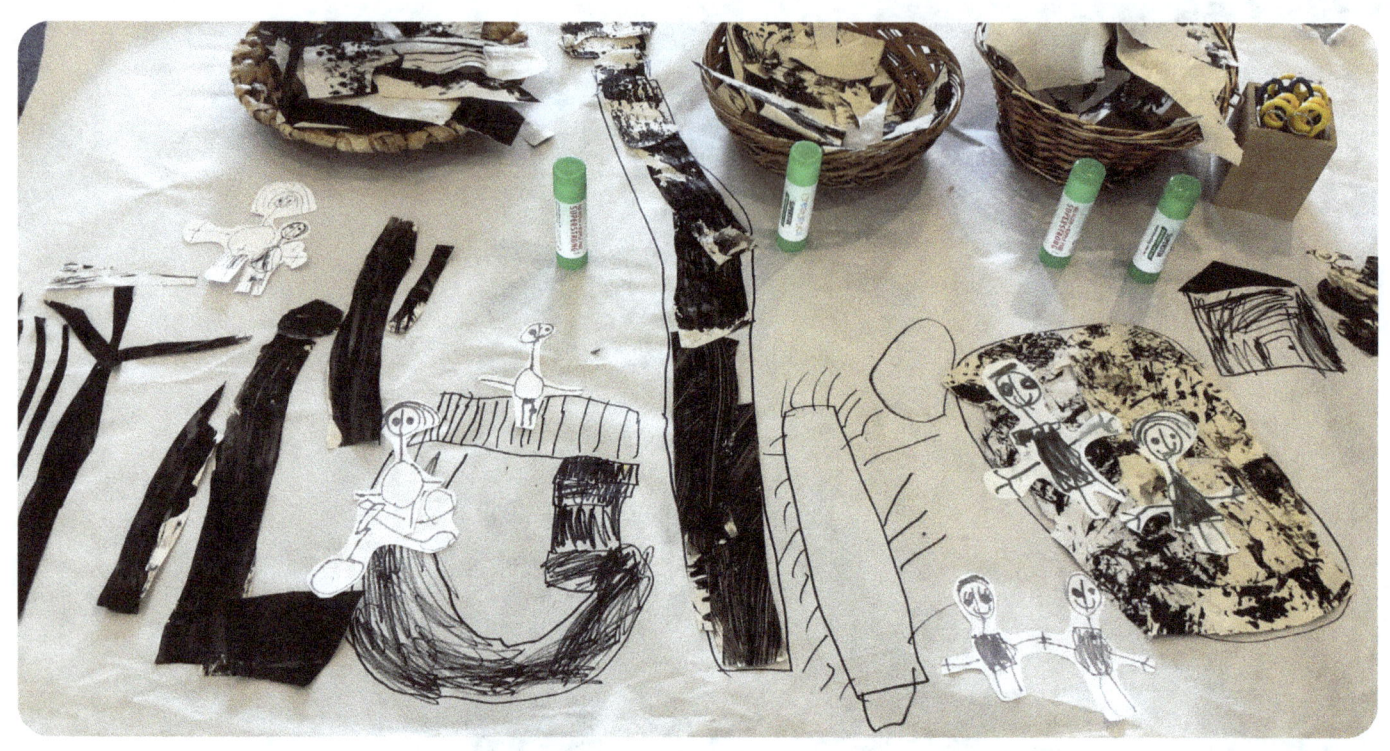

Our next collaborative project was to make a collage picture of their playground using the recycled mark experiments. Children were encouraged to match the marks in the basket with things in their playground.

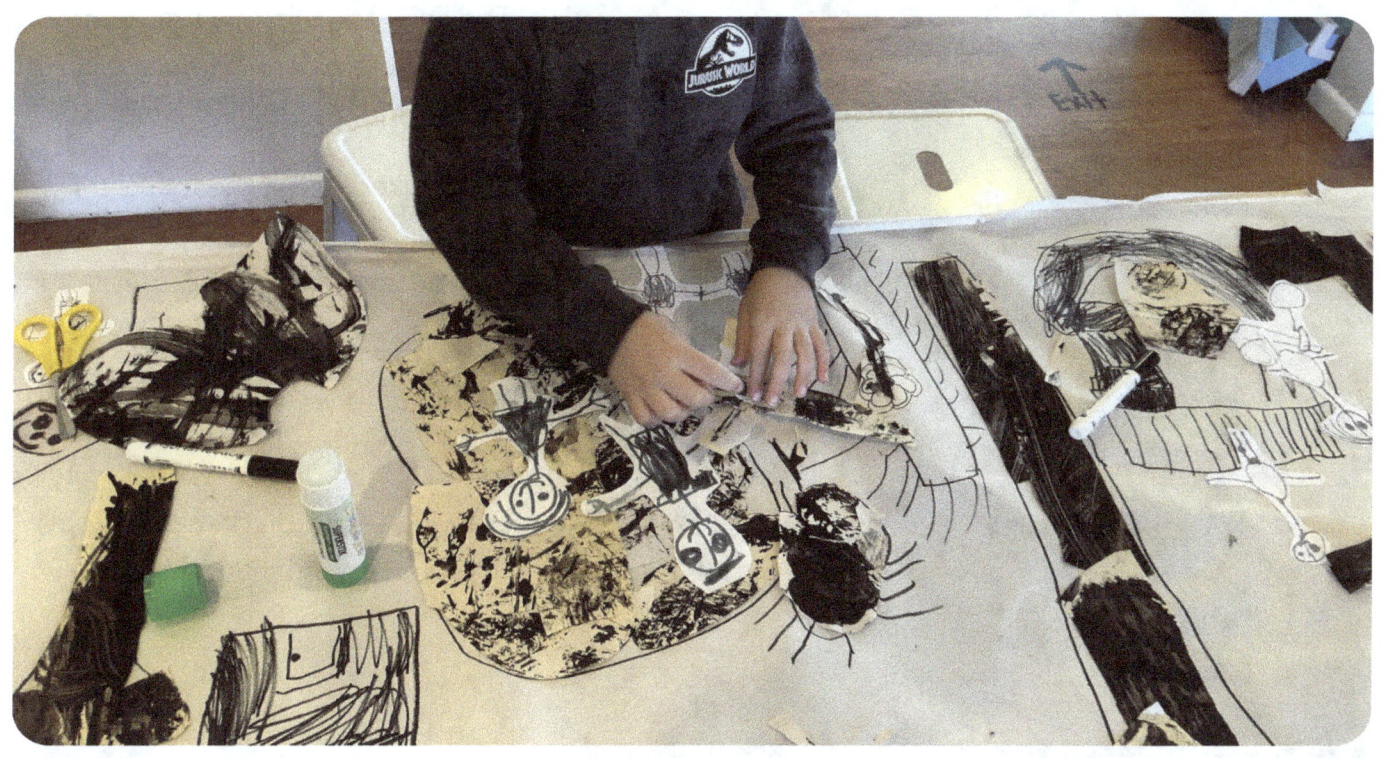

Children also drew pictures of themselves to place in their favorite part of the playground.

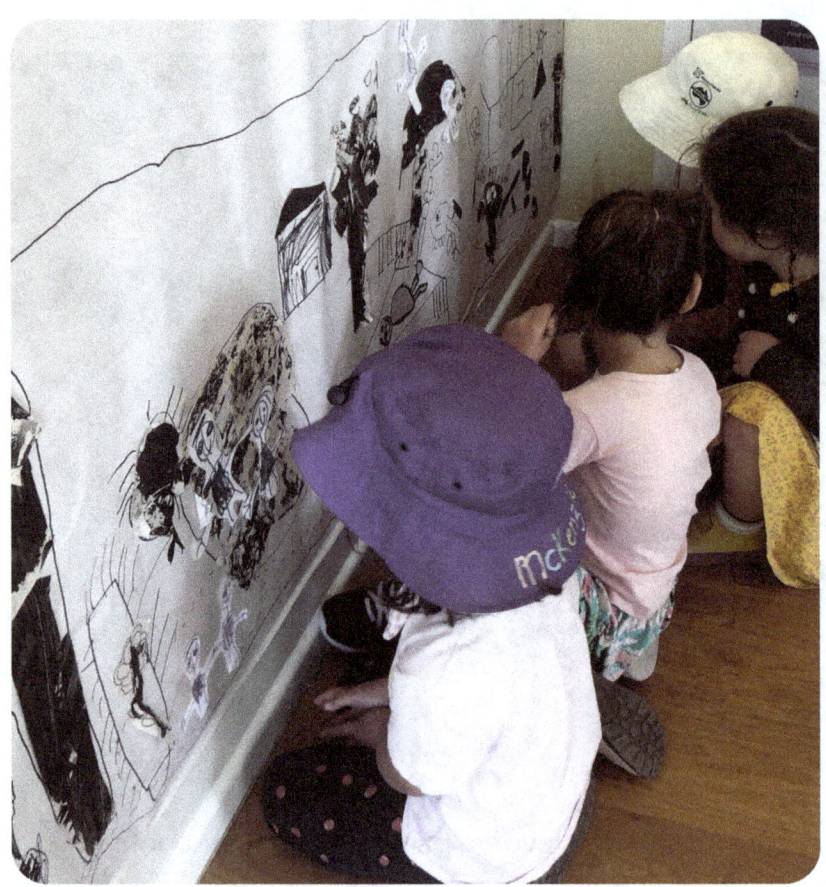

The finished collage mural created great interest. Small groups would gather and discuss and critique.

They talked about the marks they had made and how they were used to represent many things.

Drawing was added to those places where there were no recycled pieces that matched.

Drawing with a black marker kept the focus on the marks made.

More About brushes

Here are some of the most commonly used artist brushes and their unique characteristics (from the left).

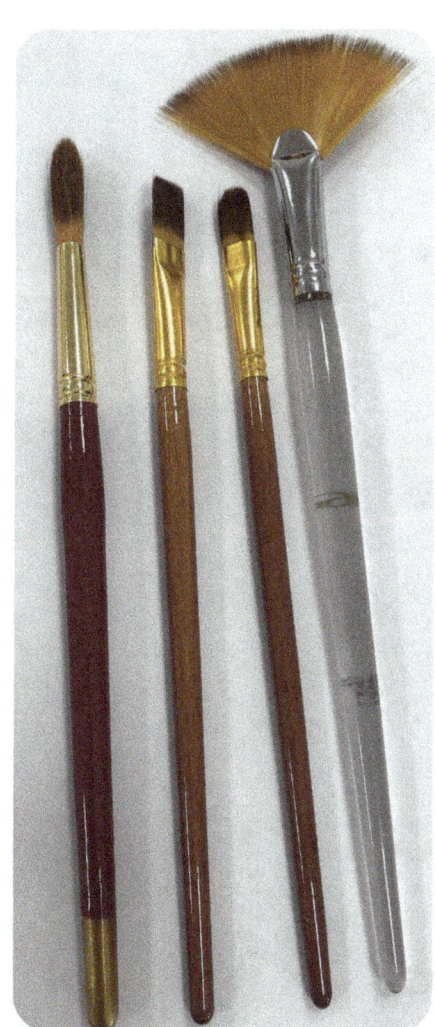

1. Round Brushes: Round brushes are versatile and suitable for a wide range of techniques, from detailed work to creating broad strokes. Their pointed tip enables precise control, making them ideal for intricate details and fine lines.

2. Flat Brushes: Flat brushes have a rectangular shape with straight, even bristles. They are excellent for creating broad strokes, covering large areas, and achieving smooth, even washes of colour. Flat brushes are particularly useful for painting backgrounds or applying base layers.

3. Filbert Brushes: Filbert brushes have an oval-shaped, flat tip with rounded edges. They combine the versatility of flat and round brushes, allowing artists to create both broad strokes and more controlled details. Their shape is ideal for blending and creating soft edges.

4. Fan Brushes: Fan brushes have bristles spread out in the shape of a fan. They are primarily used for creating texture, blending, and adding special effects like foliage, grass, or fur. Fan brushes are also great for dry brushing techniques.

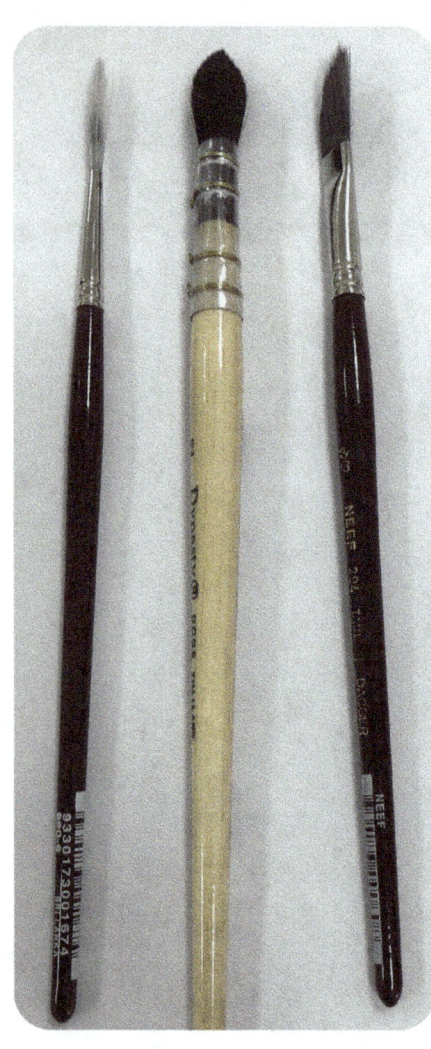

(from the left)

5. Liner Brushes: Liner brushes have long, thin bristles that come to a fine point. They are perfect for creating precise lines, intricate detail work, and adding fine highlights. Liner brushes are commonly used in illustration, calligraphy, and portrait painting.

6. Mop Brushes: Mop brushes have soft, full bristles that come to a rounded shape. They are excellent for creating broad washes, blending colours, and applying glazes. Mop brushes are commonly used in watercolour painting.

7. Dagger Brushes: Dagger brushes have a flat, angled edge that comes to a sharp point. They are great for creating controlled, expressive strokes, achieving crisp lines and adding calligraphic effects. Dagger brushes are particularly useful for creating foliage, petals or architectural details.

Understanding the different types of artist brushes allows the child to choose the right tool for each artistic technique and achieve the desired effects in your artwork. Experimenting with various brushes will help them develop their own unique style and enhance the visual impact of the creations. Remember, brushes are not just tools; they are extensions of creativity and imagination. Embracing the diversity of artist brushes unleashes artistic potential.

Artist brushes are expensive so it is important to look after them well.

Effective brush cleaning:

1. Rinse with water: After completing painting sessions, rinse the brushes under lukewarm water. Gently massage the bristles with your fingers to remove any excess paint. Be cautious not to bend or crush the bristles during this process.

2. Use mild soap: For a more thorough cleaning, use a mild soap specifically designed for cleaning artist brushes. Apply a small amount of soap to the bristles and gently massage it in. Rinse the brush under water until the water runs clear, ensuring all soap residue is removed.

3. Avoid harsh chemicals: Harsh chemicals, such as solvents or turpentine, should be avoided when cleaning your brushes. These substances can degrade the bristles and compromise their quality over time. Stick to gentle soap and water for routine cleaning.

4. Shape the brush: After rinsing, gently reshape the bristles with your fingers. Use a paper towel to blot excess water and reshape the brush to its original form. Avoid leaving brushes to dry with their bristles facing upwards, as this can cause water to seep into the ferrule, loosening the bristles.

5. Air-dry properly: Once you have cleaned your brushes, lay them flat or hang them upside down to air-dry. This ensures that water drains away from the ferrule, preventing damage to the brush handle or bristle adhesion.

Chapter 5

~

Putting It All Together

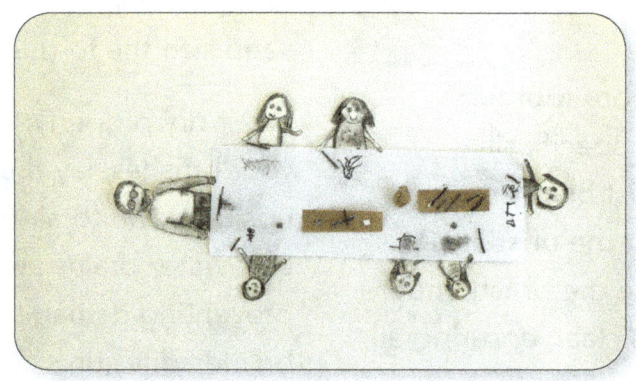

We have experienced being an artist and read about socio-cultural theory, we can now put everything together. This chapter documents young children working with a new media—charcoal. It demonstrates how Vygotsky's theories, artist studio practices, along with curriculum documents, come together to support children's drawing.

Charcoal with young children

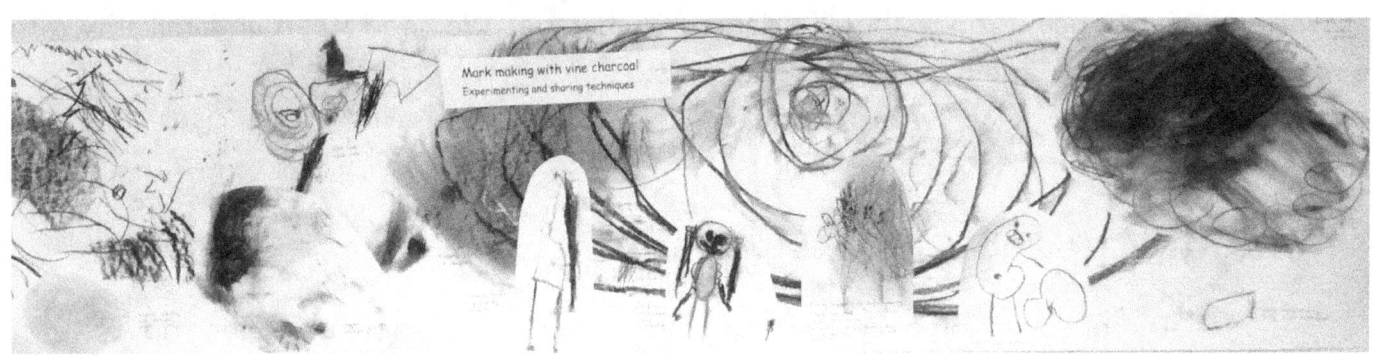

Mark making with vine charcoal
Experimenting and sharing techniques

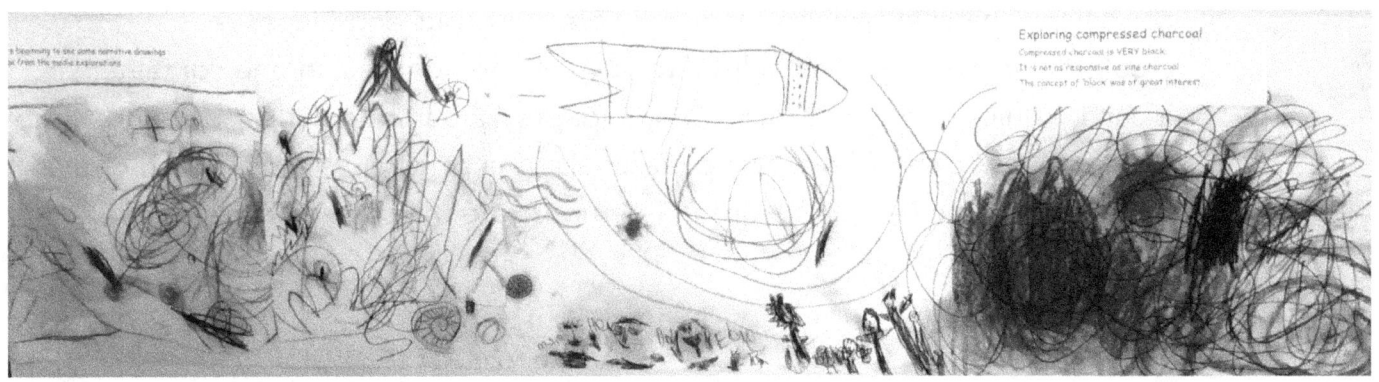

Exploring compressed charcoal
Compressed charcoal is VERY black
It is not as responsive as vine charcoal
The concept of 'black' was of great interest

I consider charcoal one of the essential authentic media for drawing. Charcoal was one of the first drawing tools used in history. We can see examples of this in the cave paintings around the world. Charcoal is easily available and easily made. You might like to do some research about it.

It is worth taking time to explore the media at your own level before working with children. The educator needs to be familiar with the properties of charcoal so they can work beside the children with confidence. I offer some practical advice for working with charcoal with children as well as for introducing you to the affordances of charcoal. We need a certain familiarity with a media before we can use it to express ourselves.

Managing the tools and environment

The presentation of art tools and media needs to be both aesthetic and practical. The materials need to be easy to access, well organized, and in good condition. Charcoal is messy, and there are many bits and pieces required to create different marks. It is helpful to have all the right bits in one container so it can be quickly and easily accessed. I adapted a bamboo cutlery box and filled it with the basic charcoal drawing materials for a small group of children to use. Before giving the box to the group I demonstrate the use and care for each material.

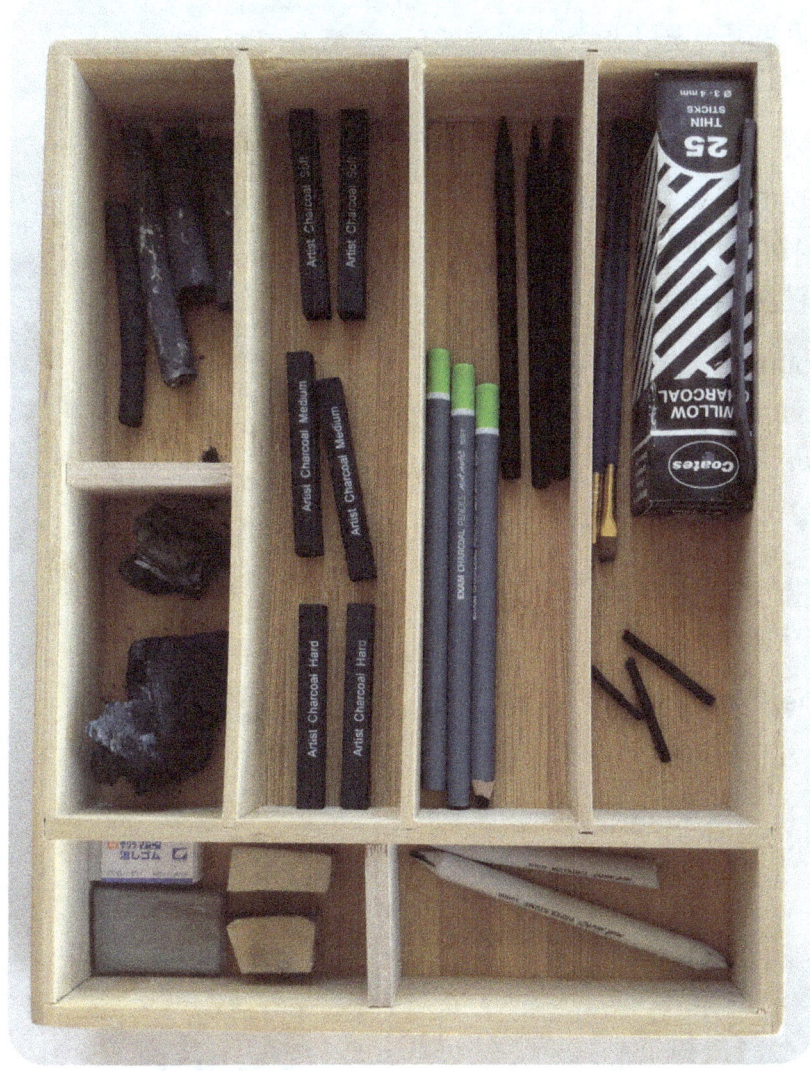

From the top left:

- thick vine charcoal

- compressed charcoal sticks (soft, medium, and hard)

- woodless and wooden charcoal pencils (soft, medium, and hard)

- thin vine charcoal

- brushes

- paper stompers

- gum, putty, and plastic erasers

- fireplace charcoal

The tools:

Thick and thin vine charcoal: these are made from willow branches or grape vines burned to just the right hardness. They are responsive and versatile and leave a soft grey mark. They erase cleanly and are economical to buy. But they can break easily.

Woodless and wooden charcoal pencils (soft, medium, and hard): These are good for more detailed drawing. However, the wooden charcoal pencils are difficult to sharpen.

Compressed charcoal: This is made from ground up charcoal that has been reconstituted and formed into a block with a binding agent. It is much harder and blacker than vine charcoal.

Fireplace charcoal: You can take pieces of charcoal from a fire to draw with. It is often crumbly and scratchy.

Once you have rubbed charcoal on paper there are a range of tools you can use to manipulate the marks:

- brushes: look for firm nylon bristles round and square.

- paper stompers: provide different sizes

- gum, putty, and plastic erasers: each has a different effect

- chamois

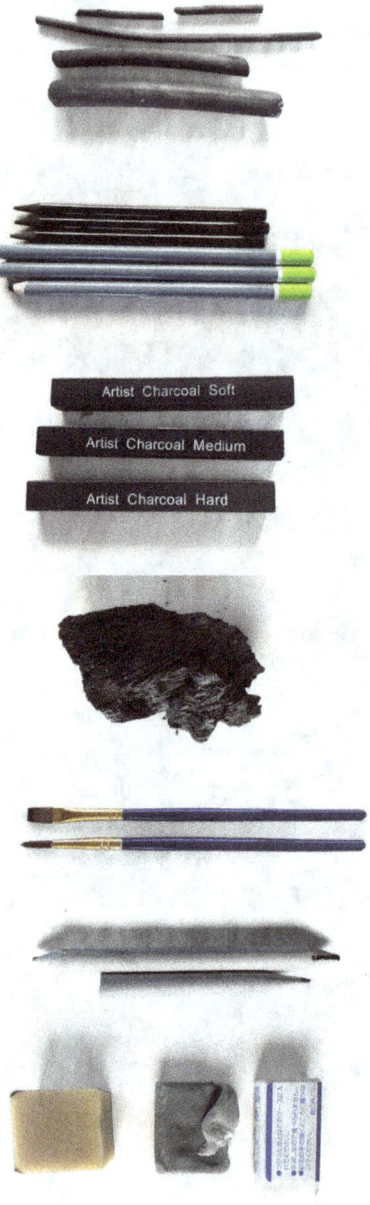

A brush not only blends but also paints with charcoal. Rubbing with a paper stomper embeds the charcoal into the paper. Erasers can be used as drawing tools. Charcoal can be lifted off the paper with a sticky putty eraser (see bottom right). Gum erasers can dig back to the white paper surface and create lighter lines and patches (top right). Fine lines can be drawn with a sharp edged white eraser (bottom left). A chamois can be used much like a paint brush. It softly moves the charcoal around the paper in broad strokes.

Tools to move charcoal around

When you have rubbed charcoal on paper there are a range of tools you can use to make marks.

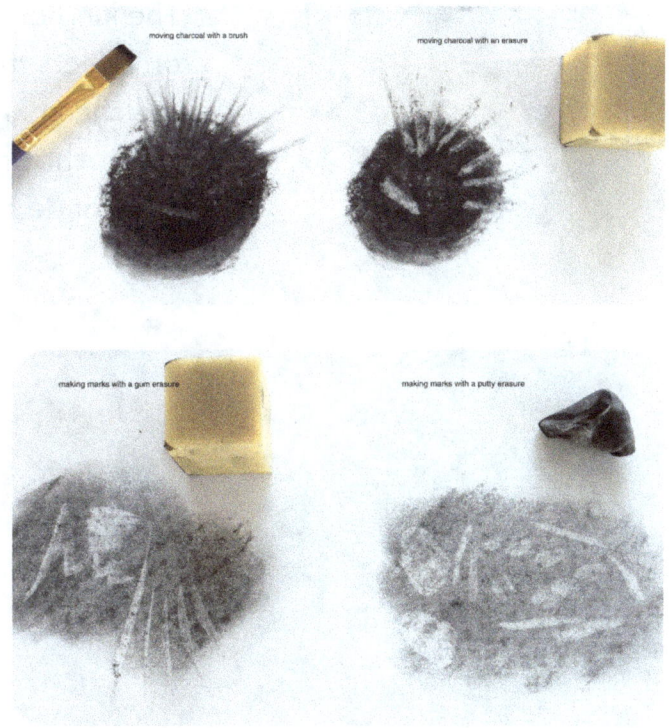

A brush not only blends but also paints with charcoal.

Erasures can be used as drawing tools.

Charcoal can be lifted off the paper with a sticky putty erasure (see bottom right).

Gum erasures can dig back to the white paper surface and create lighter lines and patches (top right).

Fine lines can be drawn with a sharp edged white erasure (bottom left).

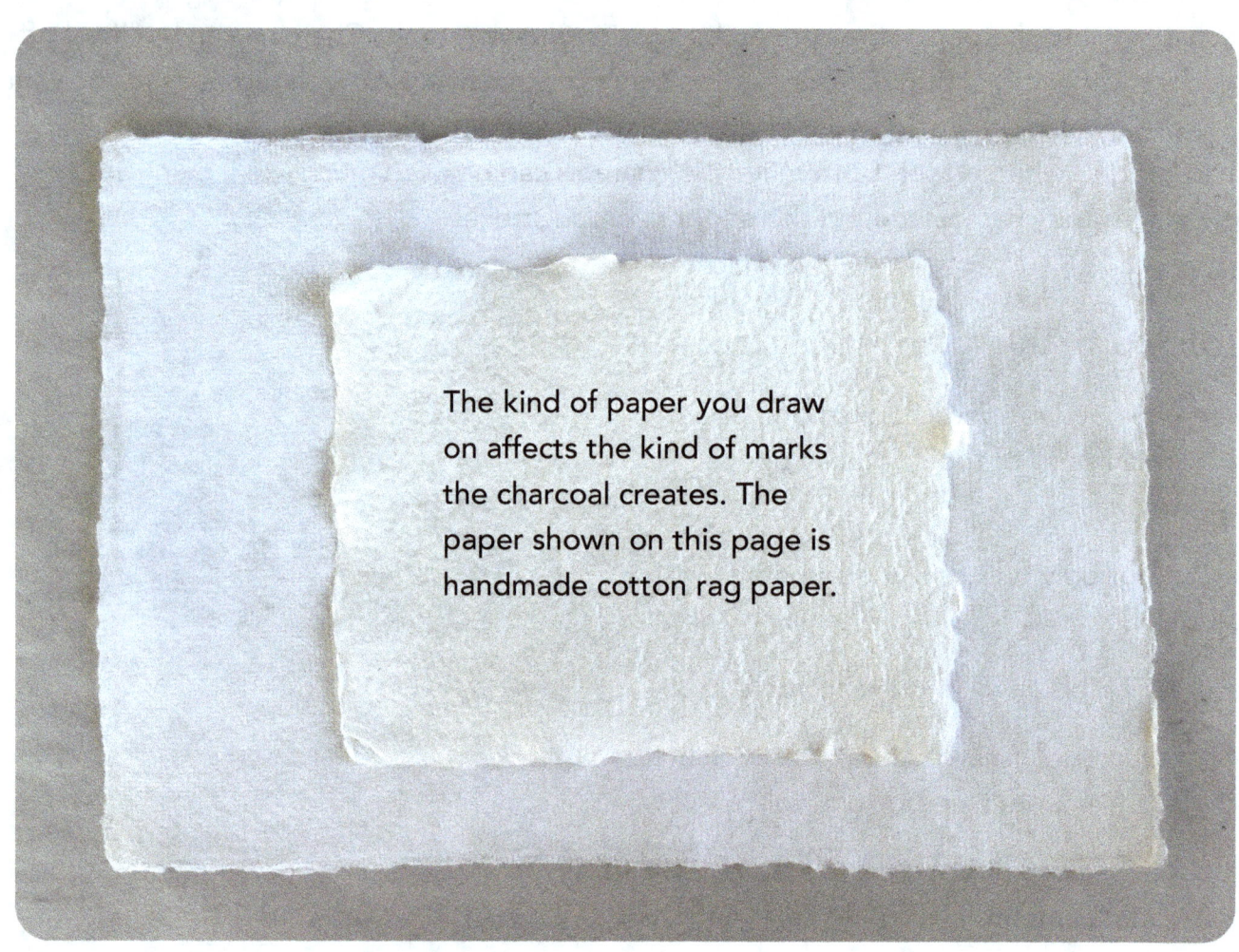

The kind of paper you draw on affects the kind of marks the charcoal creates. The paper shown on this page is handmade cotton rag paper.

Below (from the left) is tracing paper, brown butcher paper, cartridge paper, and heavy Italian art paper.

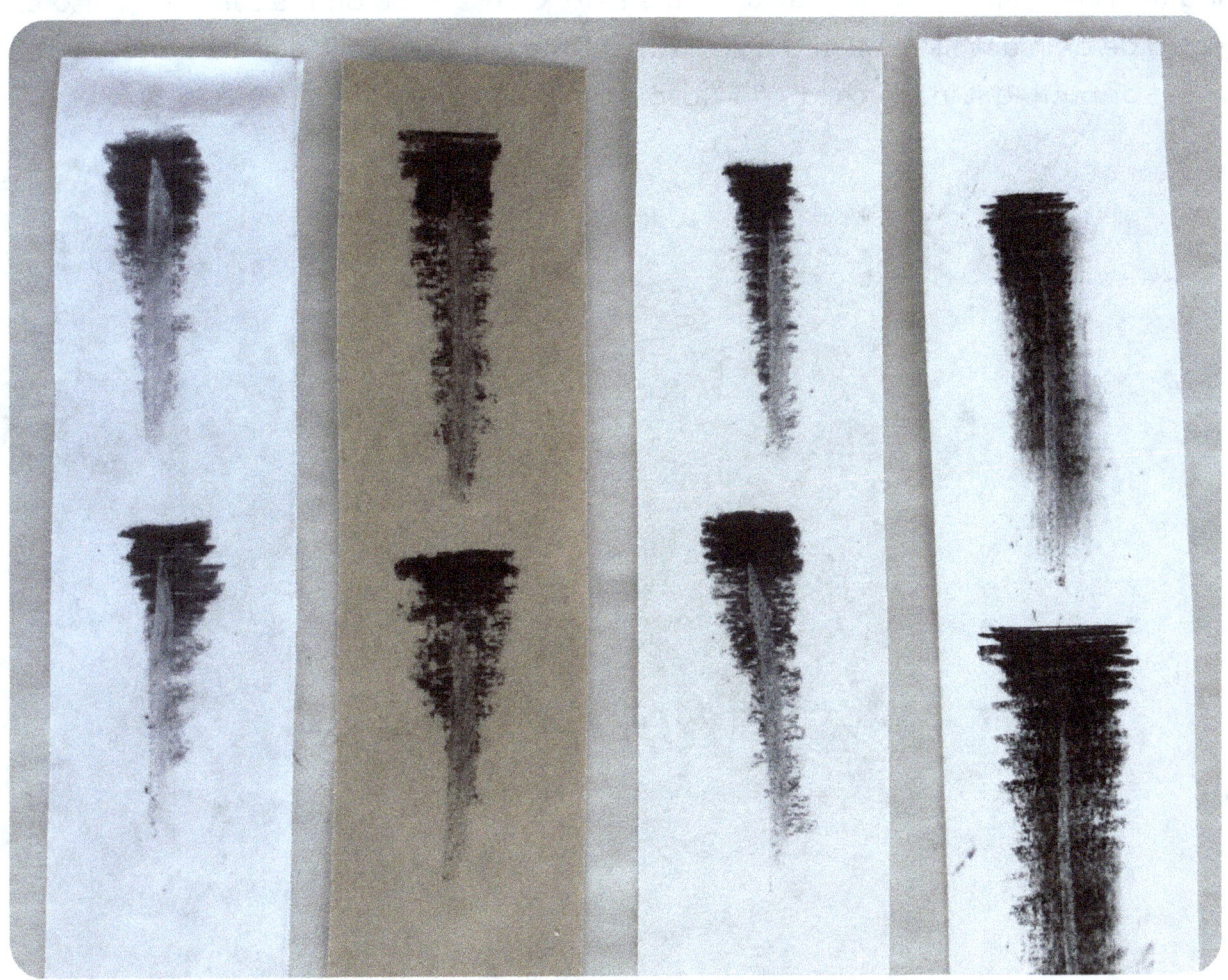

Charcoal smudges and rubs off the paper easily. Artists use a special fixative spray on their finished work to stop it from smudging. However, many of these fixatives are toxic. When working with children I use hairspray to fix their work. Just to be on the safe side I also use the spray outside or in a well-ventilated place without the children. I also let the paper dry before stacking it or putting it in the child's portfolio.

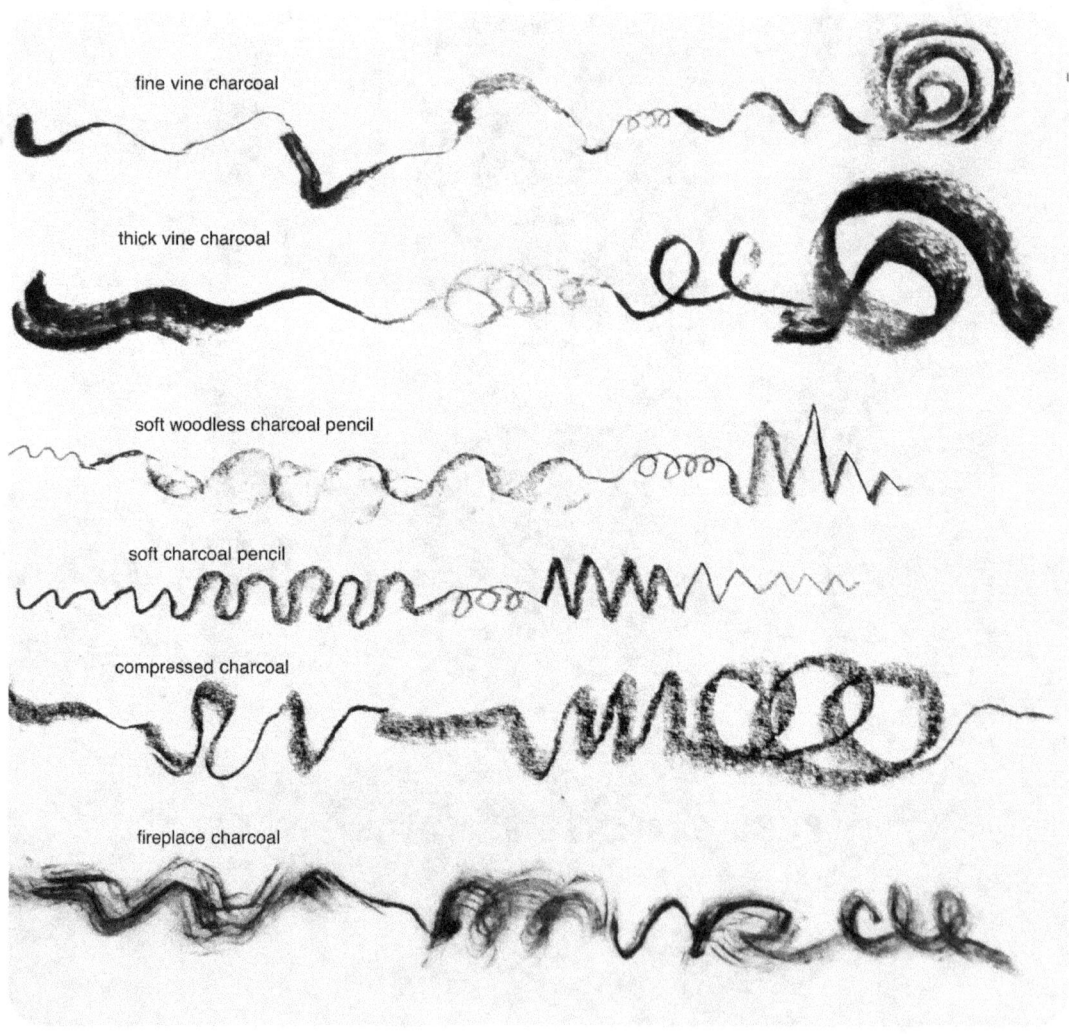

fine vine charcoal

thick vine charcoal

soft woodless charcoal pencil

soft charcoal pencil

compressed charcoal

fireplace charcoal

Suggestions for the adults

Before you rush off to work with the children you need to spend some time experimenting and playing with all the tools and different kinds of charcoal.

Each item has different properties and provides distinctive outcomes. The more techniques you have at your fingertips the better you will be able to express yourself. The wider the range of marks you can make, the better. There is no definitive list of techniques or any set sequence that you need to learn. Marks are created and used differently by each person. The marks emerge in response to a dialogue between the person and the drawing tool.

Think creatively about different ways to hold the tool. Use different parts of the tool to make marks. Use different pressures on the tool and think of different ways of combining marks. Try drawing on different kinds of paper and surfaces. The next few pages have some ideas to get you started.

As a drawing tool, charcoal is very responsive, flexible, and pliable. It creates expressive marks that can easily be adapted and changed with a quick rub of the finger, cloth, or brush. This flexibility allows for quick responses to changes in thinking. Experiment with making adaptations, rubbing back, and redrawing.

Gradations of tone

Tone means how light or dark something appears. Different tones are achieved through the amount of pressure you apply when drawing and the density of your lines. Different media also have different tones. For example, vine charcoal is slightly lighter and more grey than compressed charcoal.

Try shading from dark to light and from light to dark. Try drawing different shapes and filling them in with different grades of tone. Try putting down a base tone and then overlapping other tones on top.

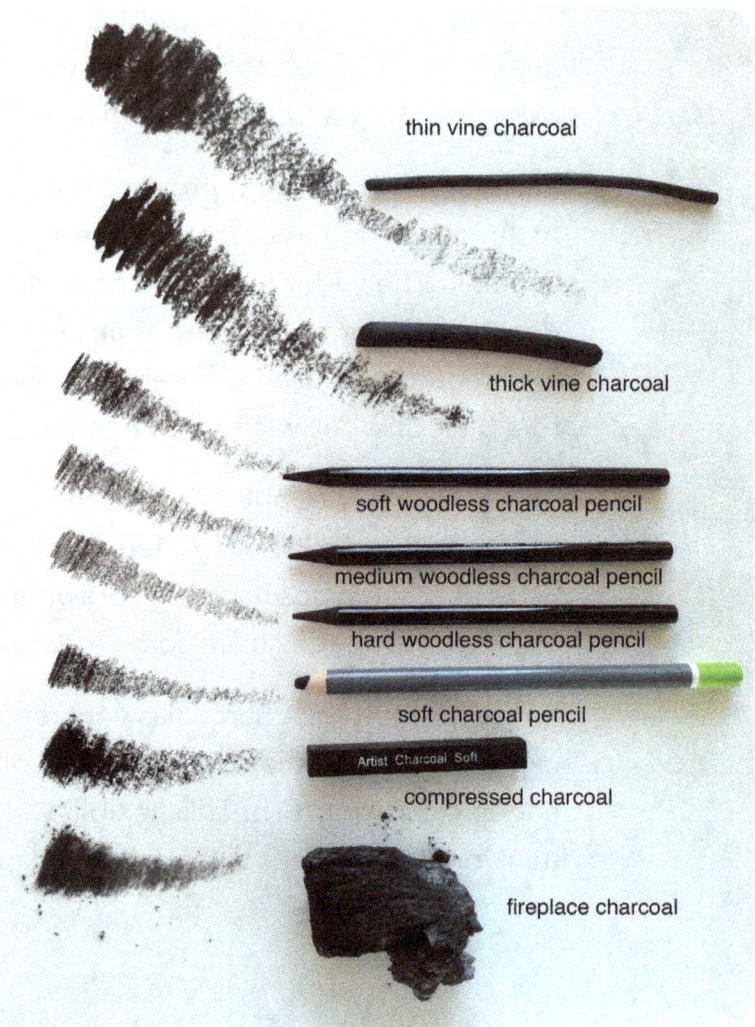

thin vine charcoal

thick vine charcoal

soft woodless charcoal pencil

medium woodless charcoal pencil

hard woodless charcoal pencil

soft charcoal pencil

Artist Charcoal Soft

compressed charcoal

fireplace charcoal

Blending

When you rub your finger or a blending tool over charcoal lines, the lines disappear, and the charcoal moves on the page to create different effects. You need to experiment with each blending tool and become familiar with what it will do.

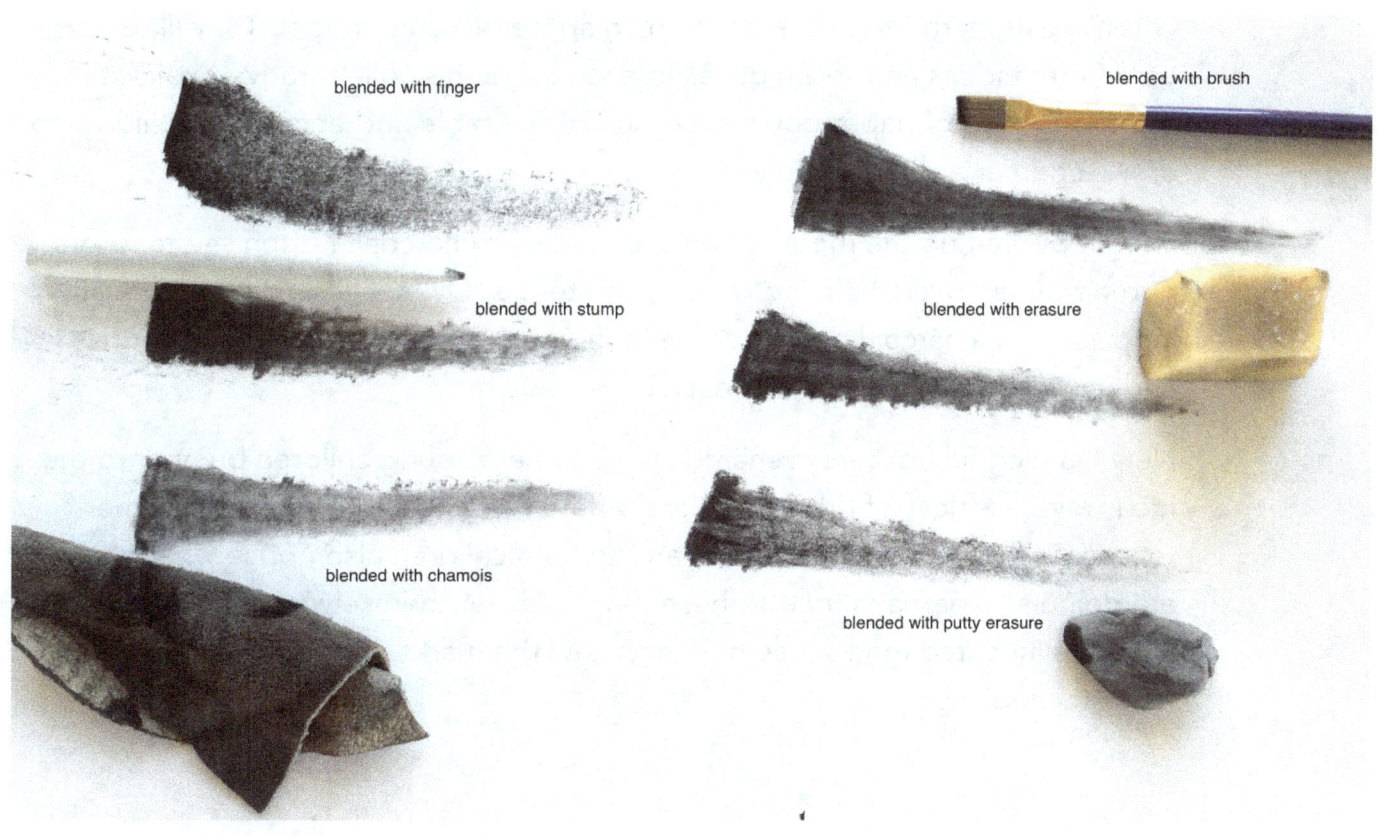

blended with finger

blended with brush

blended with stump

blended with erasure

blended with chamois

blended with putty erasure

Advice for working with children and charcoal

I expect you are thinking "interesting but messy!" We have to think carefully about where and how to introduce charcoal to young children. I have some suggestions from my own experiences. Use a large table with a nice smooth surface that a group of children can work together on. Cover the whole table with blank newsprint to protect it. Art smocks and rolled-up sleeves are essential. Make sure the table has good handwashing facilities near by.

Often artists learn from each other in an apprenticeship model. They like to try on different ideas and techniques. To encourage this collaborative exploration, I run a long strip of paper down each side of the table and encourage children to draw together and in multiple places.

I begin by limiting the media offered to just vine charcoal. I often see teachers putting out an overwhelming range of materials. Over several days I gradually introduce the charcoal pencils and compressed charcoal. I carefully introduce and model the use and care of each new medium.

New learning first occurs in shared spaces where young children bump into the ideas and practices of others that are different to their own. The role of the teacher in this context is to notice and to help children also notice what others are doing and perhaps try out these new ideas for themselves. Discussions about what the invented marks resemble and how the marks might be used helps focus the looking.

Braiding Theories, Studio Practices, and Curriculum

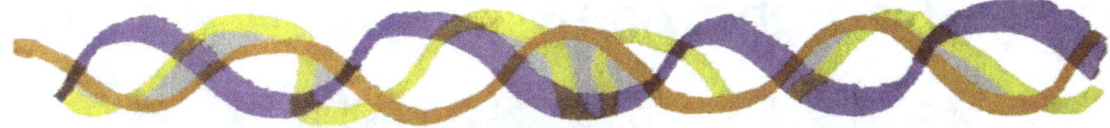

A display board near the working area can show parents, staff, and visitors the importance of art in the classroom, as well as acting as a point of reference for the children. The learning stories we display gain another layer of meaning when we refer to some of the theories that underpin the practice. One set of theories come from my research around young children's drawing from a socio cultural perspective. The other set of theories I have drawn from everyday practices in an art studio. As an early childhood teacher, one is also required to follow any relevant curriculum. Braiding is a process where I take elements from different theoretical frameworks, or lenses, and braid them together into one cohesive position statement. Combined, they form robust statements highlighting the ways visual arts supports and extends young children's thinking, meaning making, imagination, emotions, and skills. I will use the documentation of a charcoal project done with young children to demonstrate how braiding can advocate for the visual arts.

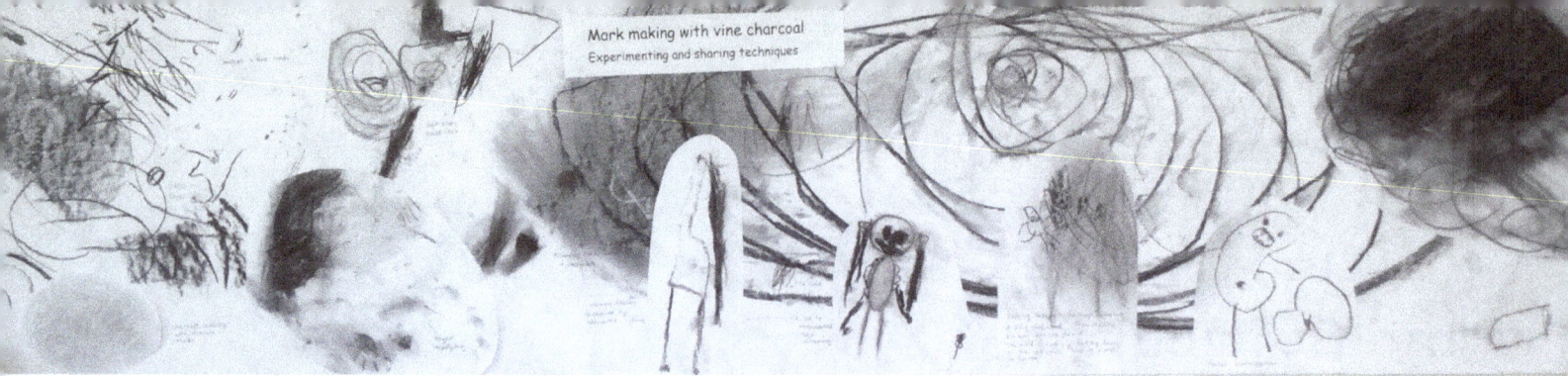

Using Vine Charcoal

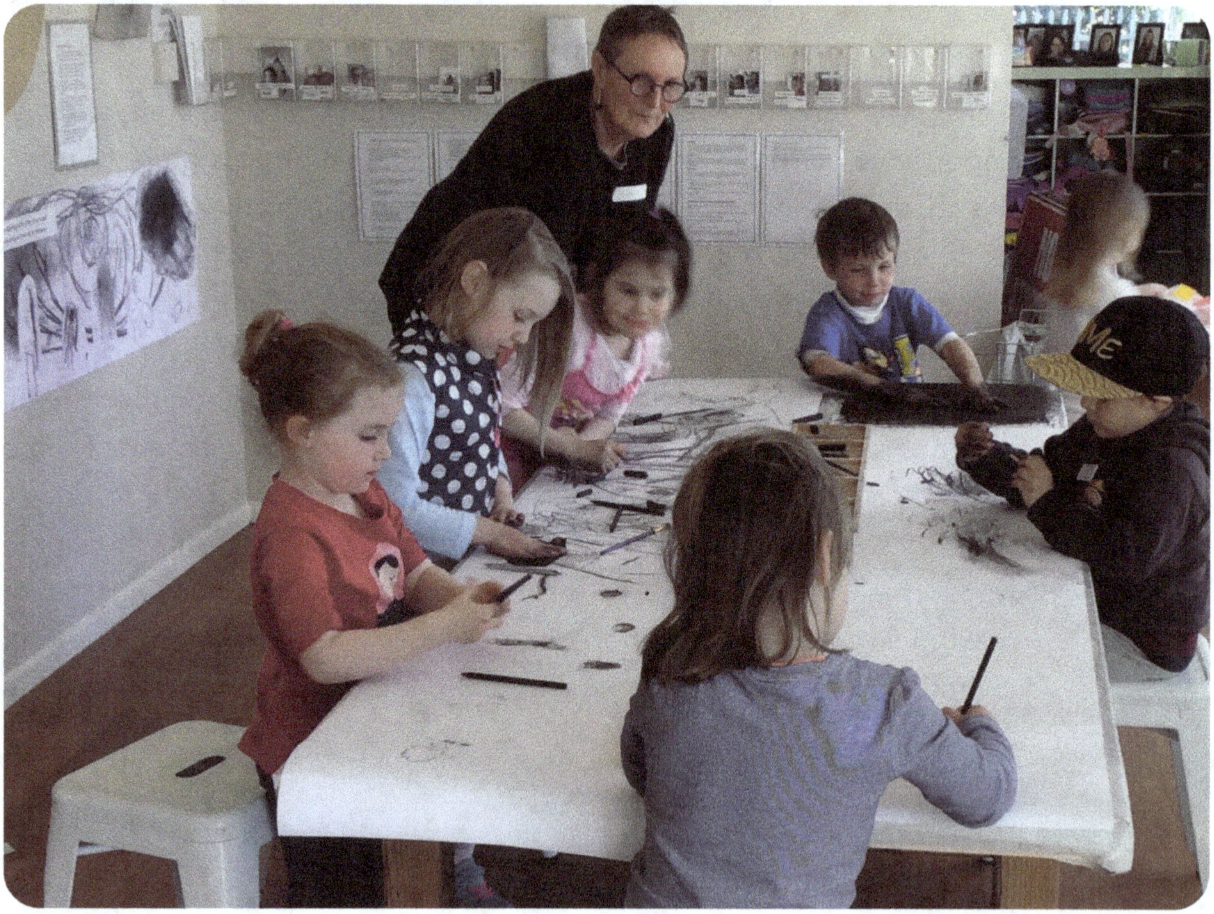

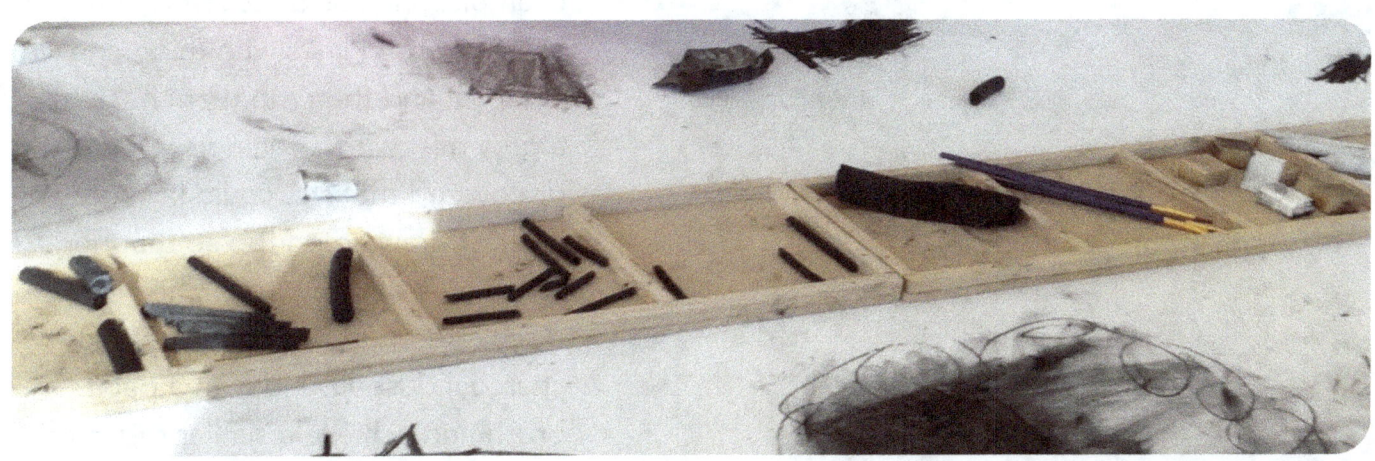

I encouraged children to draw together and in multiple places throughout the day. I facilitated this collaborative exploration by running a long strip of paper down each side of the table. This shared space encourages discussion and sharing of ideas and techniques.

I demonstrated the use and care of materials before the children begin. Children become responsible for managing the space and materials.

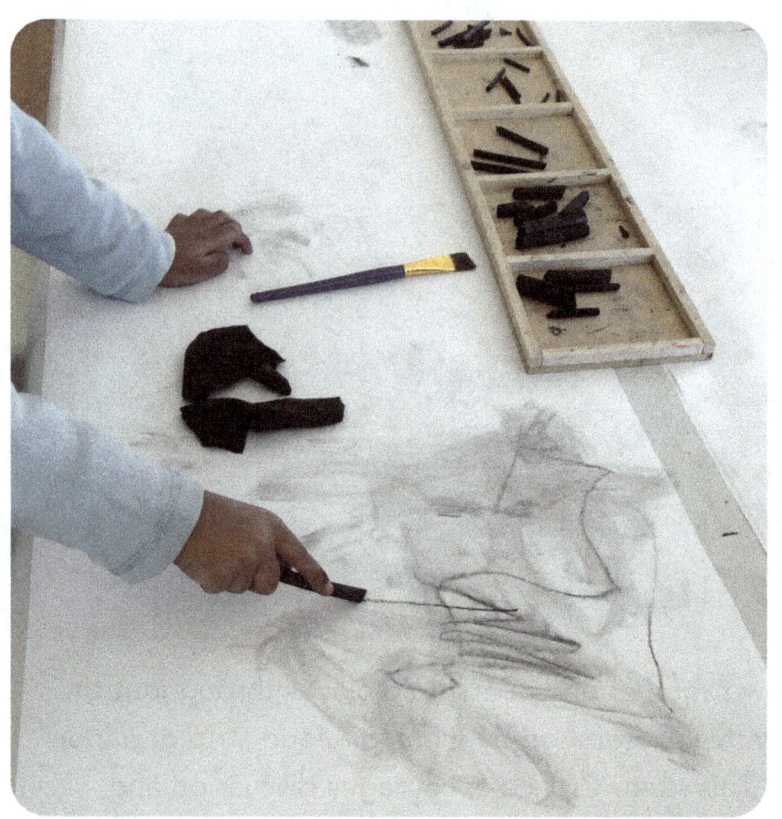

This four-year-old is working independently. She is exploring thick vine charcoal with the brush and the chamois. She has discovered that you can draw bold lines with thick vine charcoal and then rub them back to a grey mist with a chamois. Then she discovered that she could lay another layer of drawing on top so that her first marks show though. She also discovered that she could move the charcoal dust around with a paint brush and achieve a similar result.

When I use the three lenses to analyse what is happening, I can make position statements that demonstrate how learning is happening, explain the important role of the adult, and advocate for the visual arts. See the example below:

Position statements:

- When children are encouraged to experiment and explore the possibilities of art media they gain competency and confidence with the media.

- A certain fluency with media is needed before it can be used expressively and with purpose.

- Having time to repeat and practice techniques builds fluency.

- Children need authentic arts media. Authentic arts media are responsive, expressive, and satisfying to work with.

- Social contexts generate more art experiences.

- When young children are encouraged to share their art making experiences they build a wider repertoire of competencies.

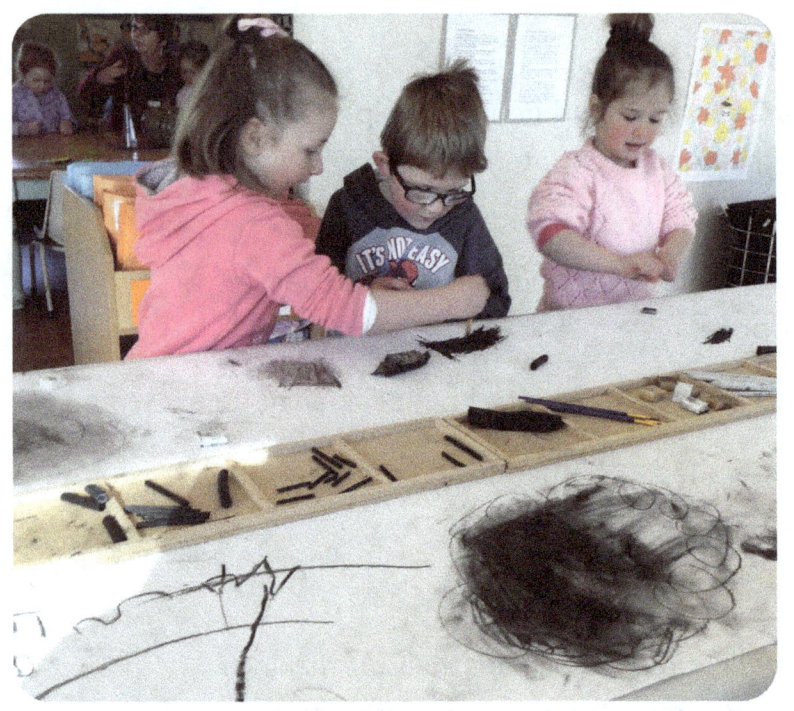

Here Bella is demonstrating to Thomas how to use a brush to move the charcoal around. On the other side of Thomas, Charlotte is listening carefully and later finds a brush to experiment with. They are discovering the flexibility and responsiveness and the wide range of tone available with charcoal. In this context children learn from each other. They are each building a repertoire of skills. Peer support is building a community of learners.

Position statements:

- When children are encouraged to share techniques it builds a supportive community of learners.

- Children acquire their own repertoire of skills and techniques as they are needed.

- A learning community is full of provocations and possibilities that help extend children's understanding and knowledge of the world.

- Learning and development is a dynamic process.

- What a child can do today with the help of a more experienced other, they can do on their own tomorrow.

The educator's role

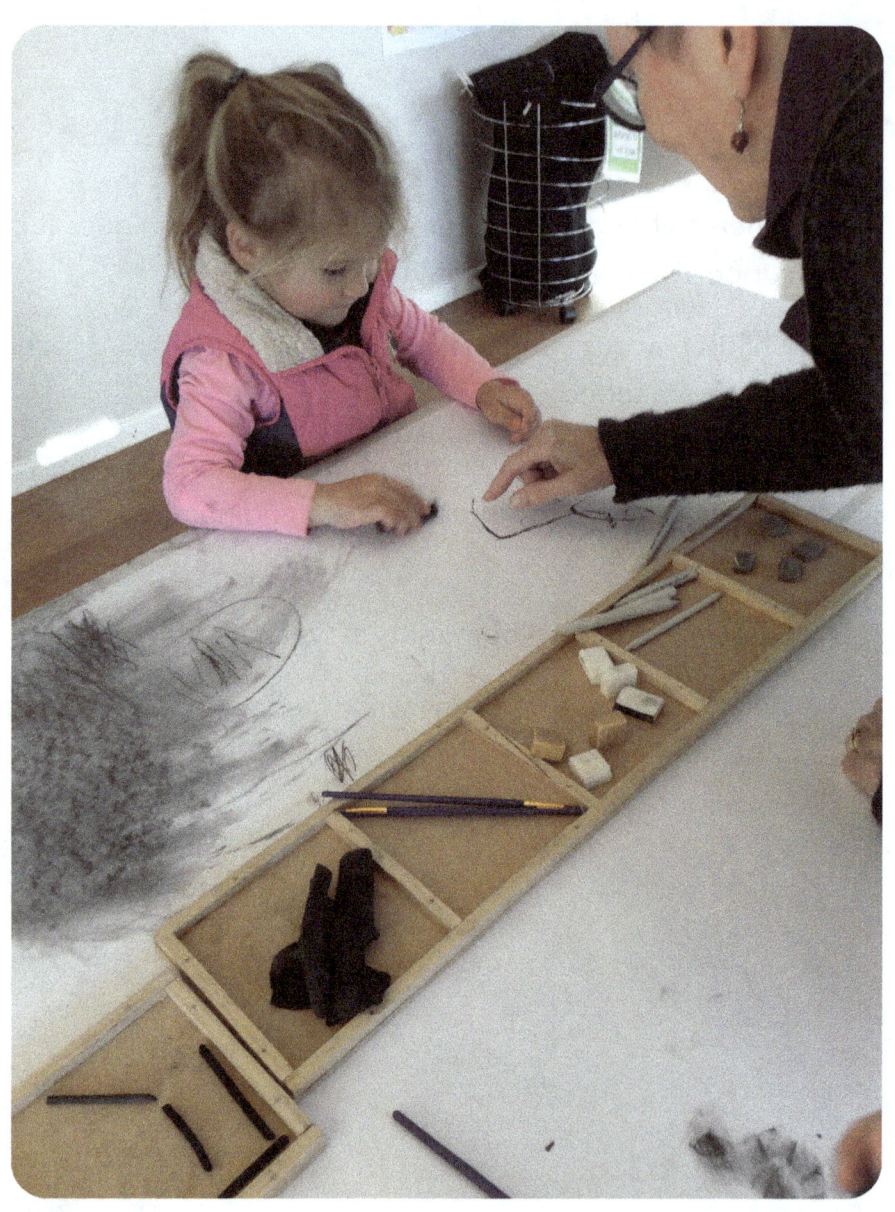

Socio cultural theories advocate that educators and adults play a significant role in supporting young children's mark making. We can provide this support by:

- Showing real interest

- Engaging in a dialogue about the media

- Gentle noticing ("I can see you are pressing softer and harder.")

- Gentle wondering ("I wonder if you have tried holding the charcoal on its side?")

- Active listening

A gentle "noticing" and "wondering" helps children also notice what others are doing and perhaps try out these new ideas for themselves.

In this image I am saying to Scout, "I notice that your line is getting lighter and thinner here. I wonder how this happened?" The interest you take in what they are doing lends importance to the child's task.

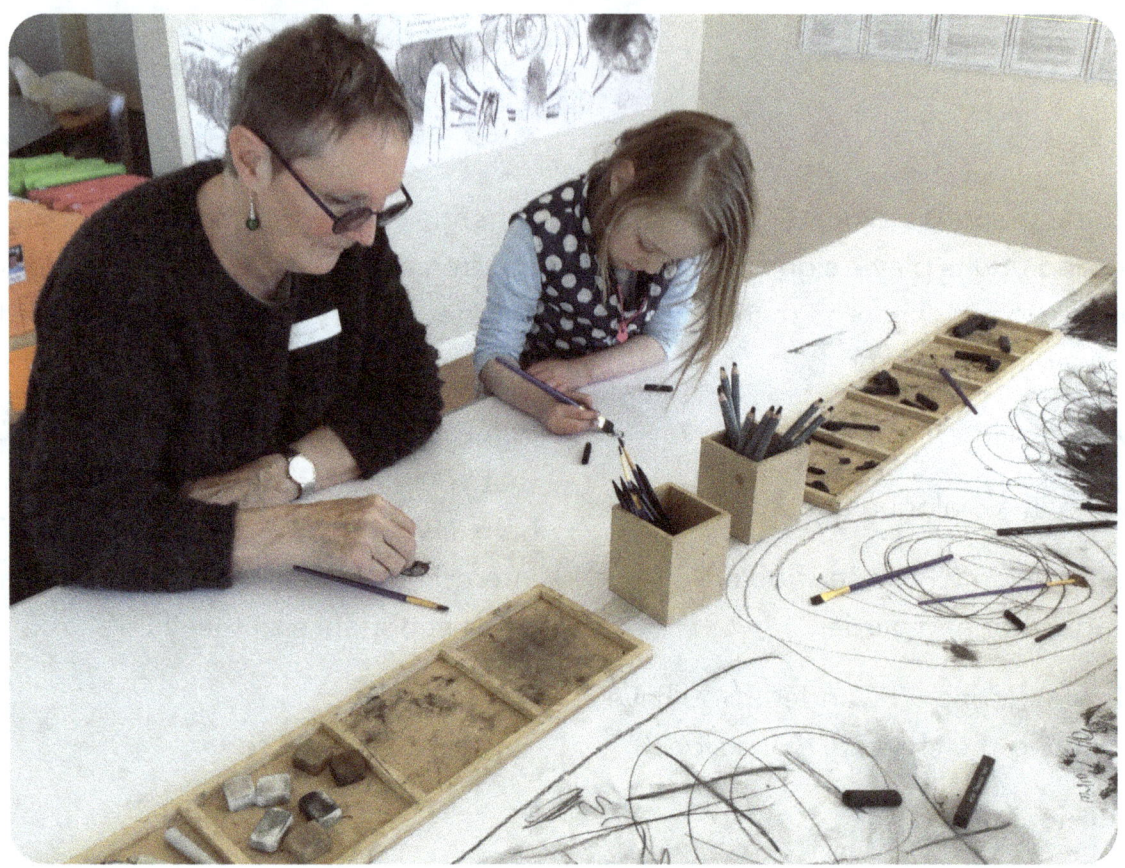

When I draw next to children it lets them know I value drawing enough to do it myself. I talk about my drawing and it lets them know there are many things to consider when drawing, and that I am in a process of trial, error and evaluation.

The children watch with interest and often appropriate thing they see me do and offer suggestions.

Position statements:

- The visual arts encourages problem finding and problem solving.

- Careful observation of the marks made makes visible the results of certain actions.

- The visual arts supports reflection on action.

- There is an important role for the educator

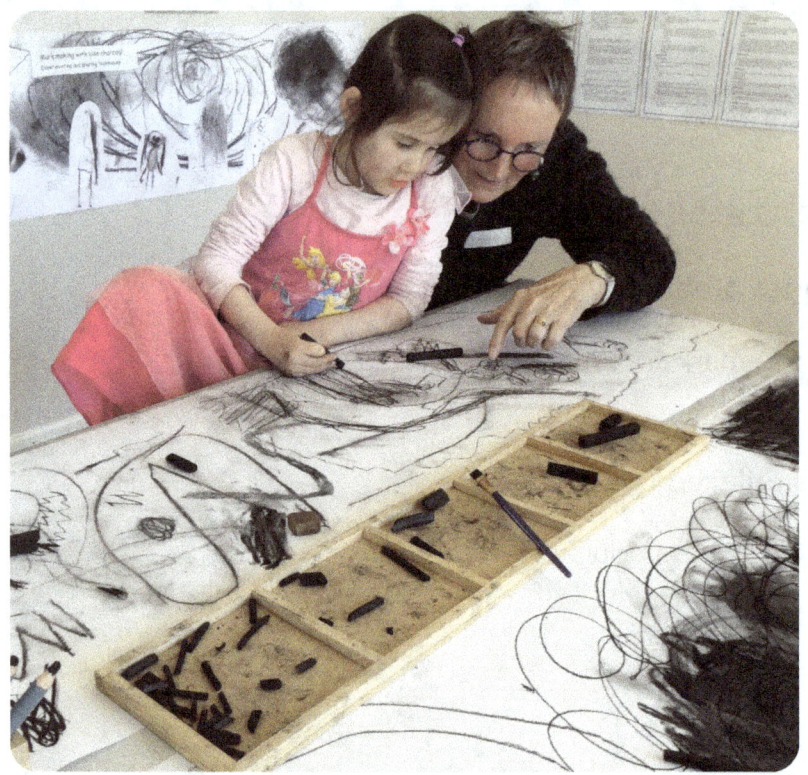

Young children usually enjoy talking to you about their artwork. Here we are discussing the details of what she has drawn. It was a story about three mermaids swimming under the ocean. One of them was getting tangled in the seaweed. They have very long hair and special flippers so they can swim fast. Talking with me reminded her that she had not yet drawn the hair on one of the mermaids. She confidentially told me that their hair was just like seaweed and they used this attribute to disguise themselves and hide.

Position statements:

- Educators need to be pedagogically active.

- Through a gentle "noticing" and "wondering" educators can support experimentation and artistic dialogues.

- Providing children adequate time for experimentation supports their competencies with new media.

- When engaging in sustained shared thinking, first unpack the narrative and then the technique.

- Young children usually enjoy talking to you about their artwork.

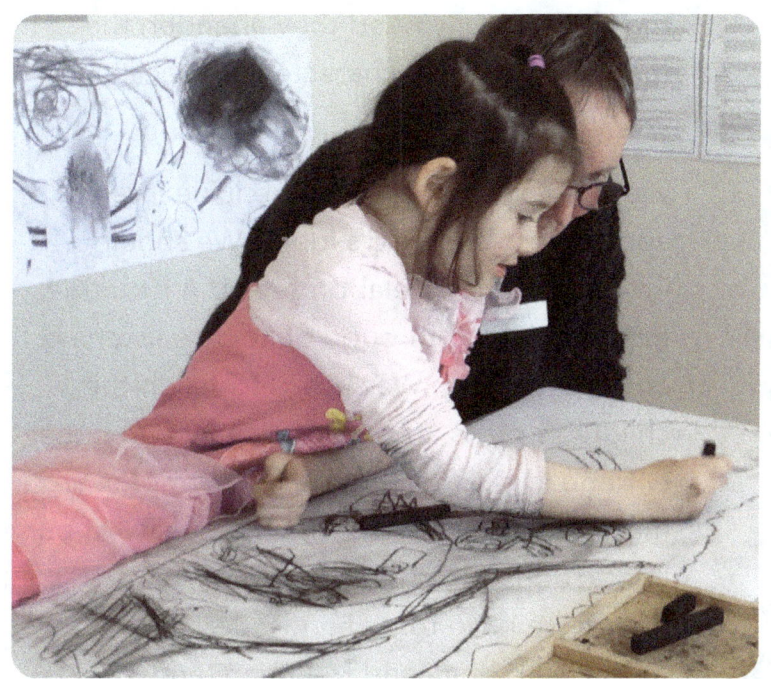 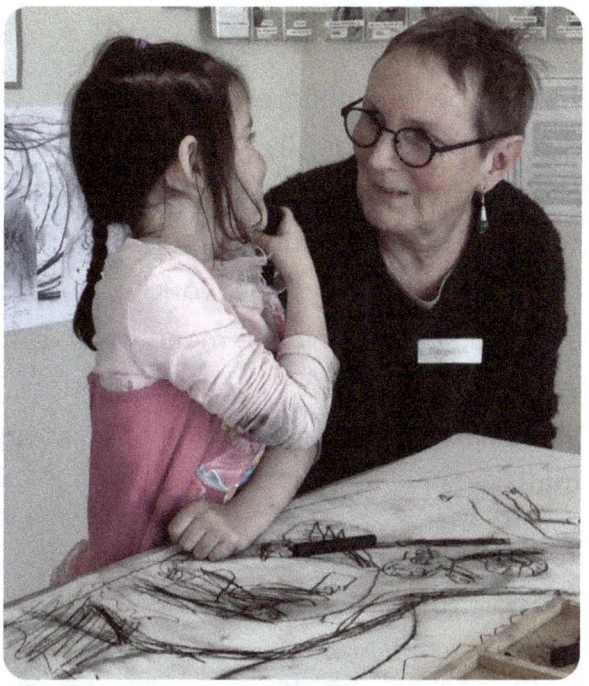

They were hiding from a big octopus and did I know that octopus are super clever. But mermaids have a little bit of magic. She discussed just how she had used the marks she had discovered yesterday to create the hair. I wondered what kind of marks she might use for the octopus and she thought carefully about maybe using the little cloth to make the smooth head of the octopus.

What does it mean to be pedagogically active?

To engage with children and their art is to be pedagogically active. To be pedagogically active requires one's whole being to be attentatively attuned to the child's experience of the world. By being pedagogically active we mean that we are engaged with the art and investigations in mindful ways that aim to extend children's thinking.

Young children require a high level of support to engage in the arts meaningfully. However, teachers often are reluctant to be actively involved with children's art making. Many hold onto the mistaken belief that we should not interfere. If we had the same hands-off approach to literacy and math, there would be a national uproar. How can children be expected to learn the basic vocabulary of art if we don't help them? How can they create if they don't know how

to use the tools? When children do not find the support they need they abandon the task, and we see a characteristic decline in engagement with art.

We need to tune in, show genuine interest, and respect the child's ideas. We should invite the child to elaborate and encourage further thinking through our active listening and speculating. We should focus on the children's plans and support them when they engage in more elaborate and complex art making. We are aware that the quality of our interactions with children is important. This means we have to pay undivided attention, to listen, to hear, and to understand. It means we are mindful that our talking with children is not just managerial talk but rather talk that elevates their ideas and articulates their thinking. We should always be on the lookout for opportunities to engage in rich discussions with children about their big ideas. Big ideas often become visible through their art.

Position statements:

- The visual arts is an important way of sharing your knowledge about the world.

- The visual arts is a powerful tool for communication.

- The visual arts allow children to make connections between their experience, their memory, and their imagination.

Teaching observational drawing

Observational drawing supports many important skills, dispositions and concepts. The ability to draw involves the ability to see and lots of practice. Observational drawing focuses attention and requires intense observational viewing of the subject. When children draw, they demonstrate concentration and thoughtfulness. When studying a topic of interest, drawing elements of the topic is crucial for building a deeper understanding of the topic. Drawing engages the child in active exploration of the topic much more than just talking about it. Observational drawing slows and intensifies their looking and holds their attention. The child notices details and drawings become more thoughtful and richer. Children's thinking is extended beyond the immediate first encounter to a more complex, scientific level that supports higher orders of thinking.

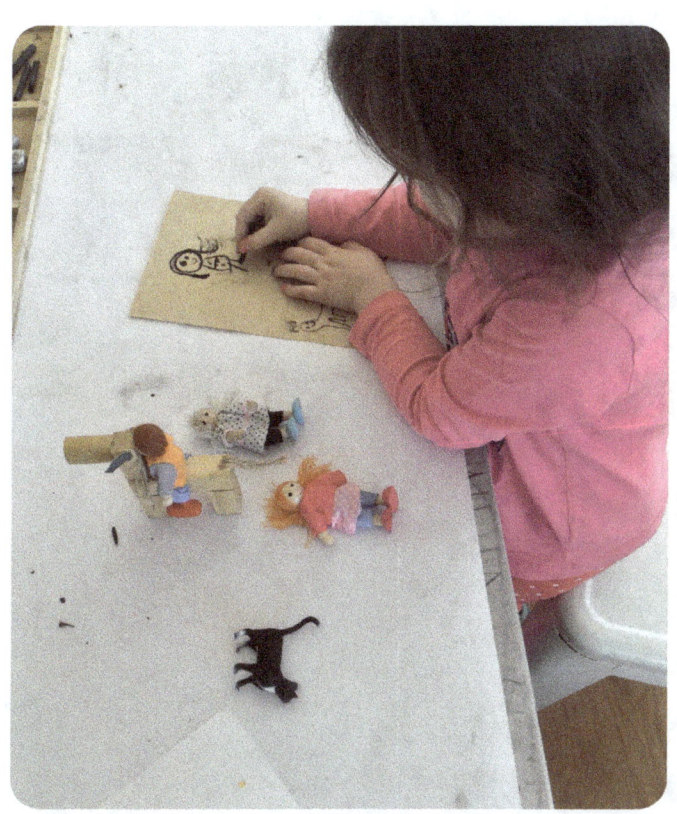

Amy set herself the task of drawing each figure, saying "Each one is different and I want to know why."

Drawing from observation

- engages the mind

- brings something more clearly into consciousness

- focuses attention

- assists with the formation of ideas

- mediates between a child's spontaneous and scientific concepts

- supports higher mental functions

- is a powerful metacognitive tool

- assists with consequential progression

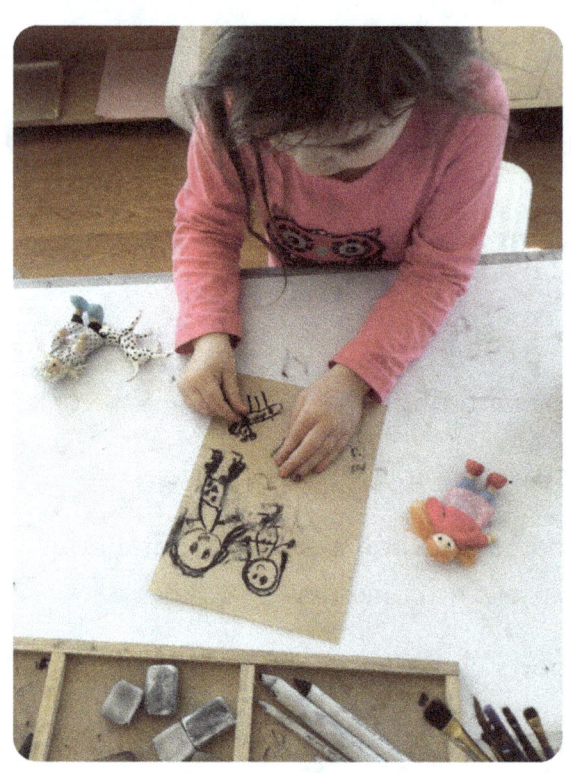

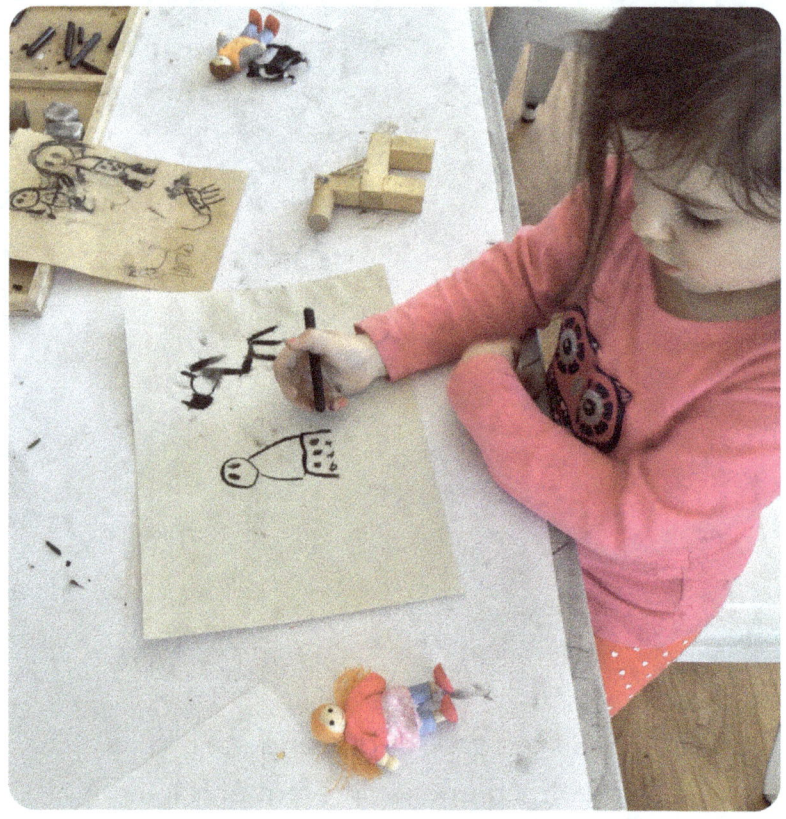

To talk a child through an observational drawing,

- acknowledge the complexity

- discuss where to begin

- ook for shapes

- do preliminary air drawing

- look for more details

- squint with half-closed eyes

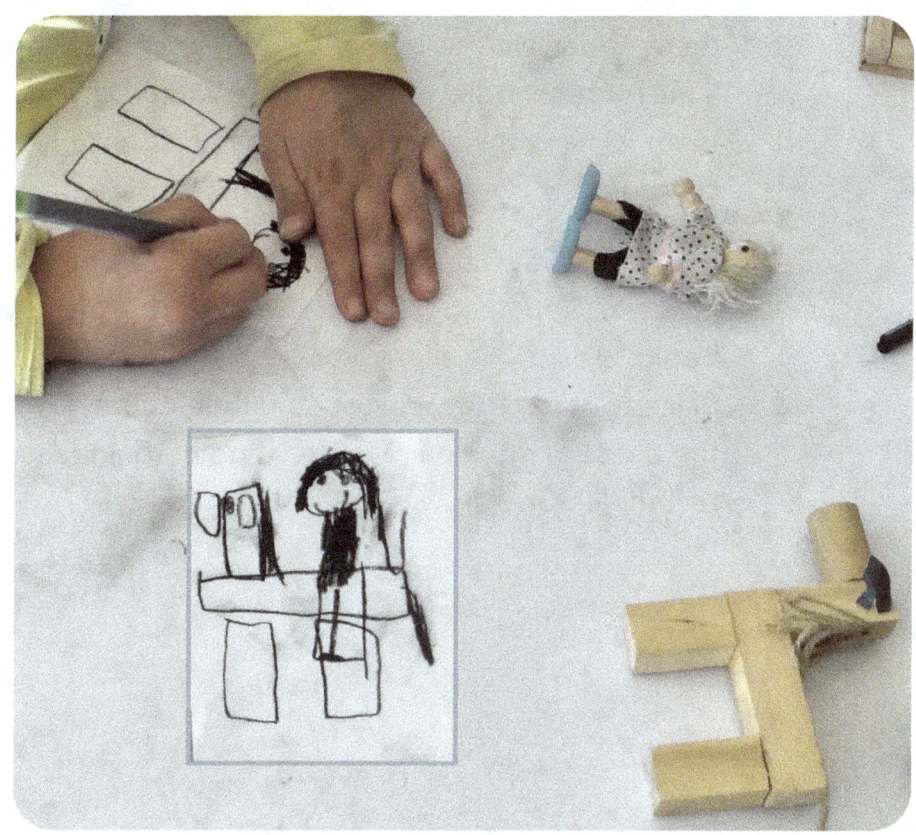

Helping children who think they can't draw

Where do children get the notion that they cannot draw? I believe it is partly learned from the attitudes of those around them. When we decline to draw for or with children we send a message that drawing may be too difficult and not for them. When others have a negative response to the art, it is contagious.

In one case my help was in the form of talking through the process. "You need to decide what to draw first, where to begin," I said. "The legs," she replied. "OK, the legs are a good place to start. They are just rectangles. Draw two rectangles at the bottom of the page, here." I pointed and "air drew" two rectangles. She drew these with confidence.

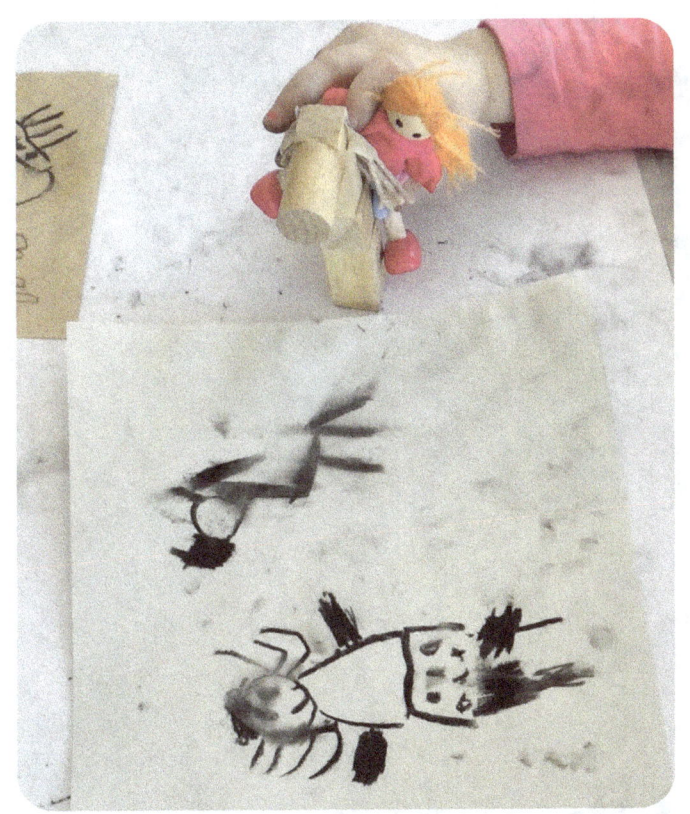

"Now the body is another rectangle, here." I pointed and "air drew" again. Slowly a very satisfactory drawing of the wooden horse appeared. She smiled and said, "I did it!"

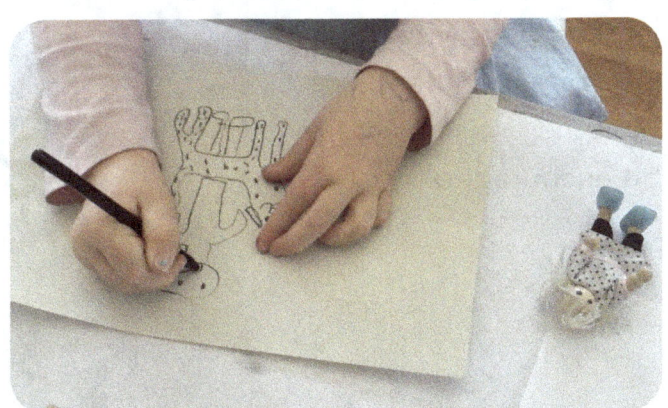

Bella drew three versions of Lisa under the tree. Each time she adjusted the drawing slightly to bring it closer to her aspirations. The large paper invited this kind of experiment. Multiple drawings are to be encouraged.

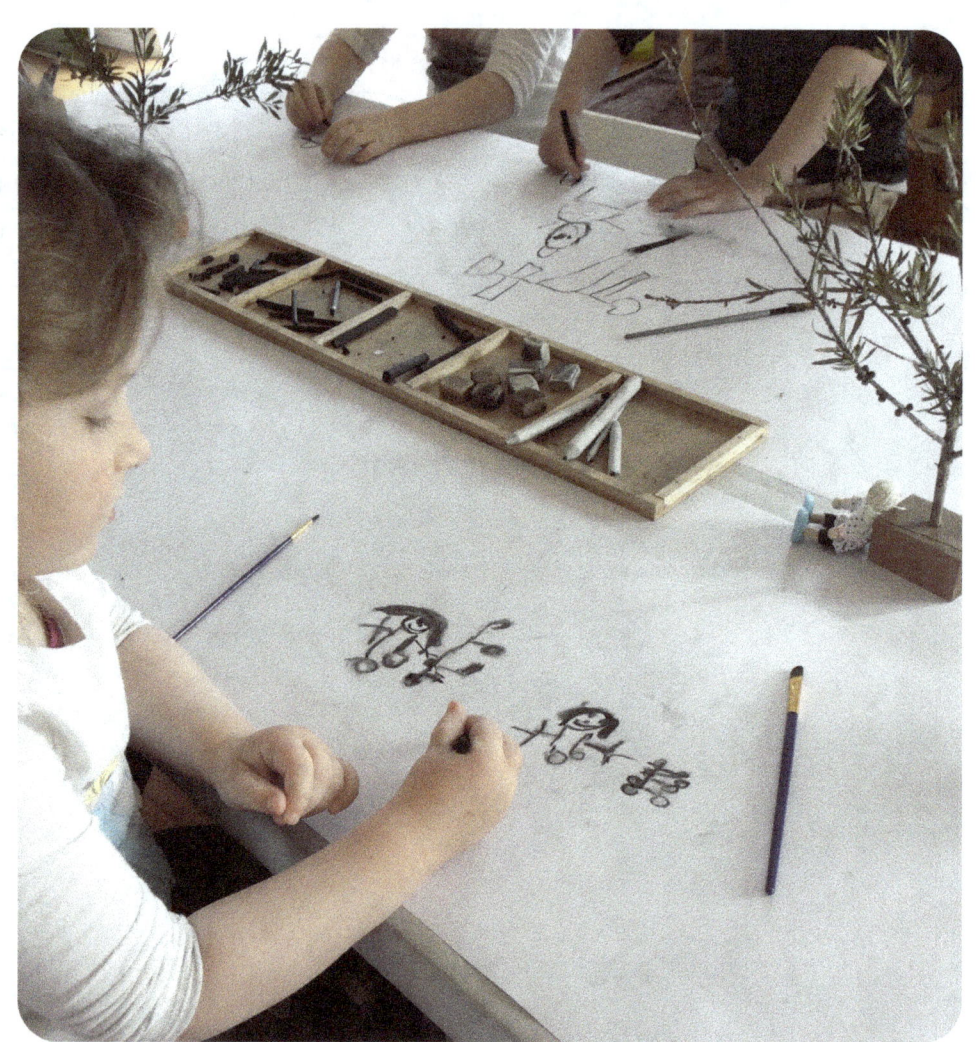

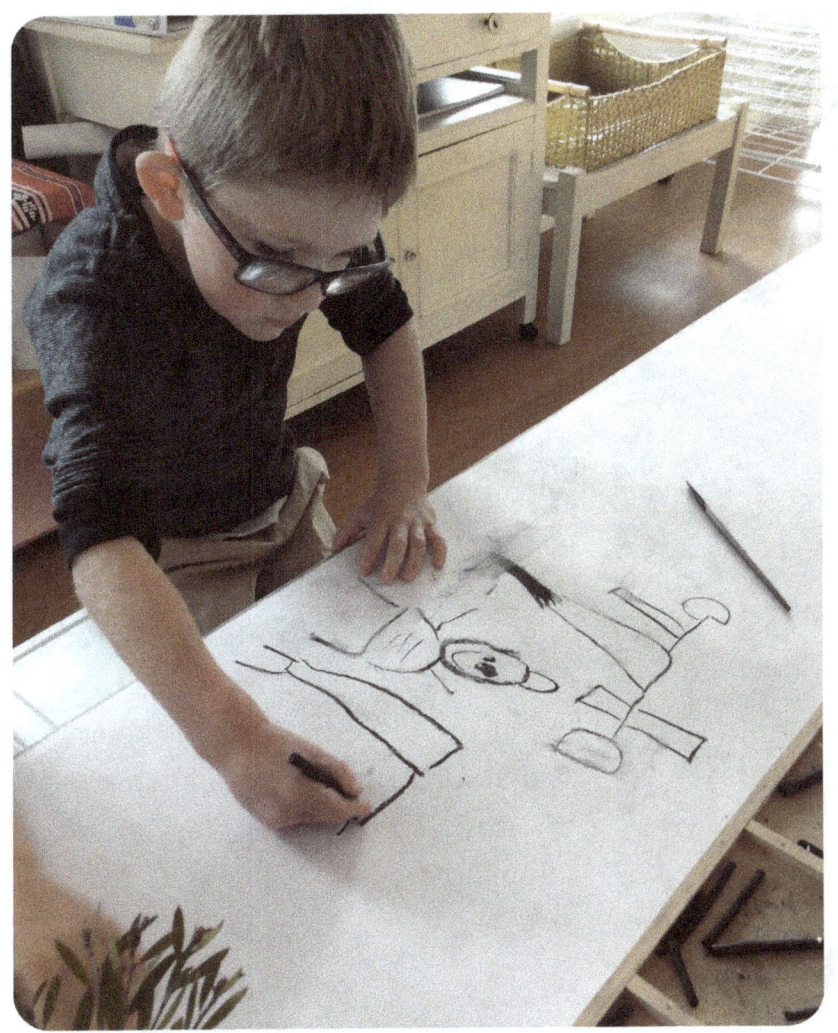

Thomas often draws at the same time as Bella. They seem to like sharing ideas and techniques. Thomas drew the boy doll, John, complete with striped t-shirt and cap. Then he decided John needed something to play with and added a swing and monkey bars. Bella looked over at his drawing and reminded him to draw the tree too. Narrative often accompanies children's drawings. Through narrative they bring elements of their lives to the drawing.

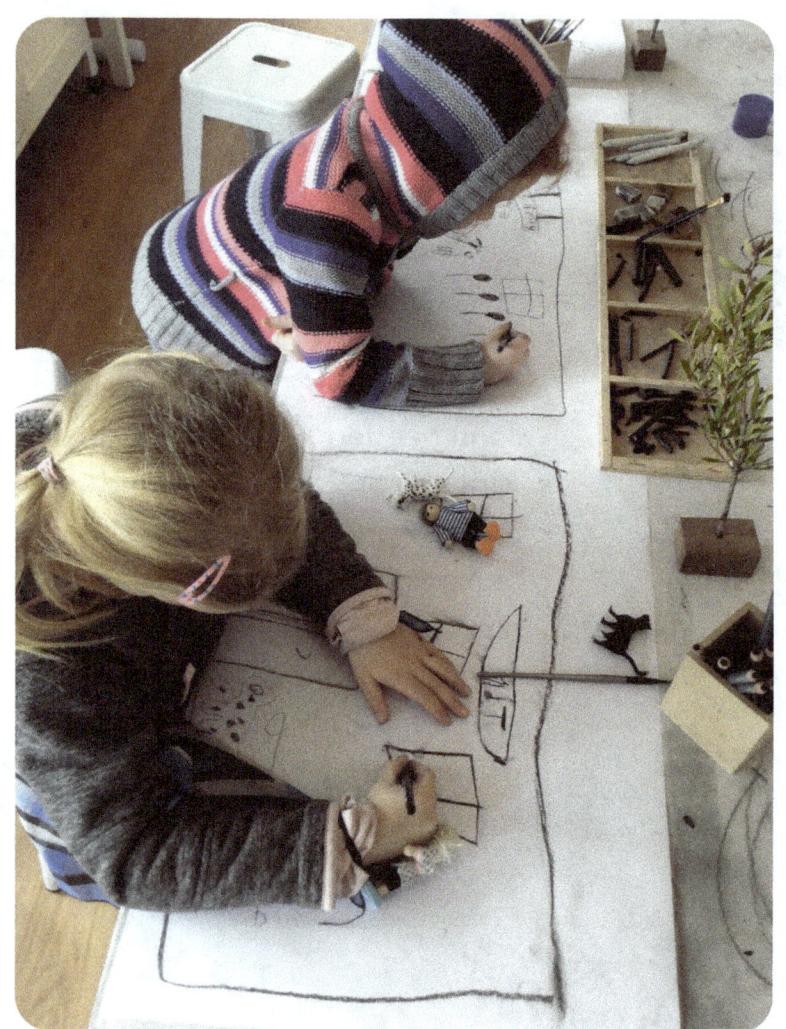

Representations are often accompanied by role play. These two girls are playing shop. One has a sweet shop and the other a pet shop. The making of the image is driven by the play and interactions between the two friends. Common elements between the two drawings come from the sharing of ideas and techniques. The dolls and animals are an integral part of the play, so the two girls also draw items to meet their needs. The girls keep up a dialogue between the image and the toys, so the toys "play" in the drawing.

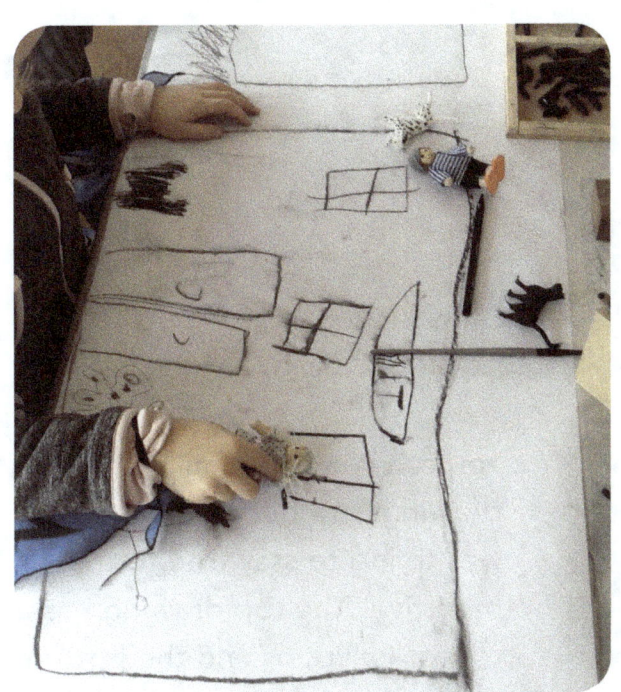 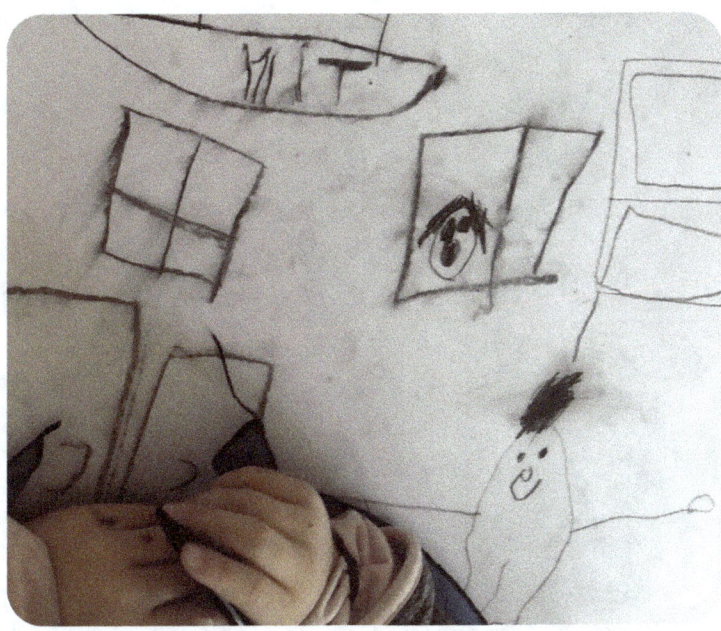

Tilley pretends the girl doll is looking for a new puppy. She can't see in the window of the pet shop so Tilley has to lift her up to see. This prompts Tilley to draw the face of the doll in the window.

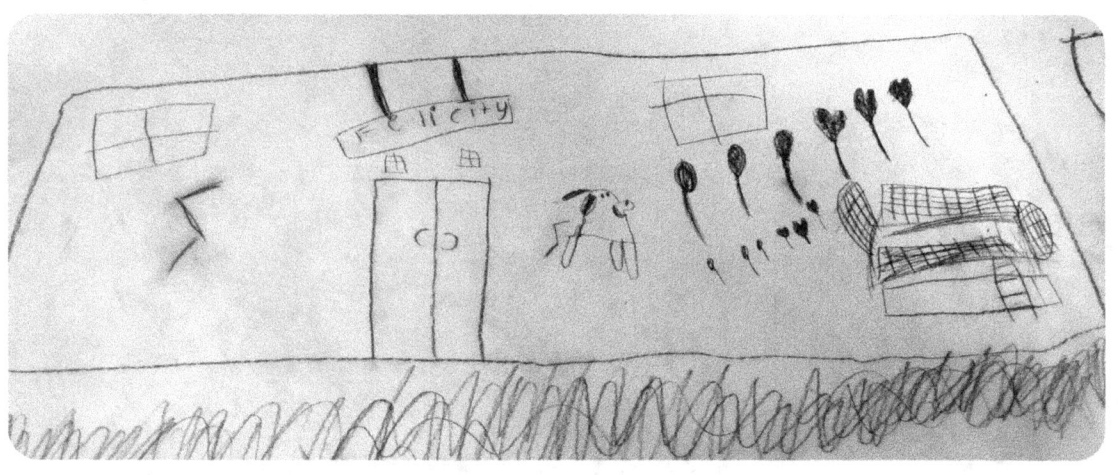

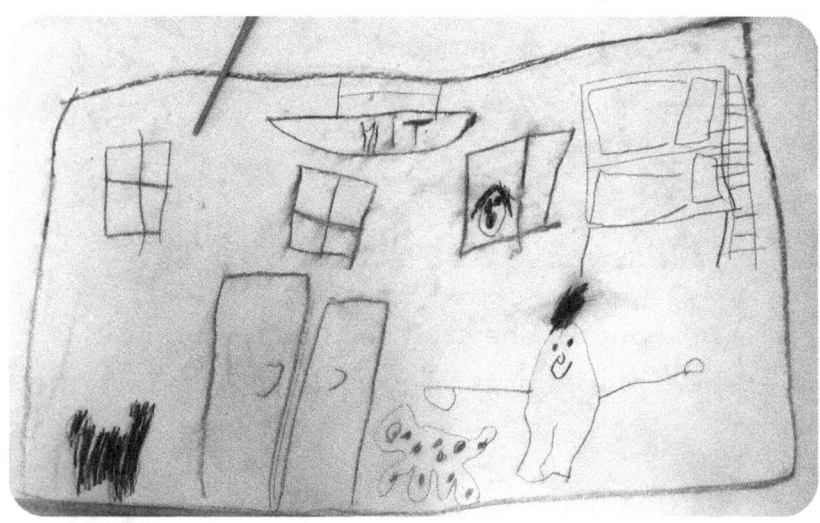

You can see how similar the drawings are because each was trying to stay true to the narrative. The top drawing has a row of lollypops and the bottom drawing has some pets. Both have bunk beds.

Position statements:

- Listen carefully to children as they draw to gain insights to the big ideas behind the drawing.

- Encourage multiple drawings to explore the different ideas and perspectives that re-presenting can illuminate.

- Peer-to-peer discussion and sharing extends children's awareness of different approaches and styles.

- Encourage in-depth exploration. You will be surprised at the complex thinking taking place while the child is creating.

- It is important that children see differences in drawings as part of another's thinking or style rather than being wrong.

- Learning and development is a dynamic process. Learning leads development.

- The visual arts is the leading activity driving developmental accomplishments.

Building on the children's interest in drawing houses, shops, and their bed and playrooms, I introduced a similar context for the dolls I had provided for them to draw. I created a simple house interior with a few bits of basic furniture. I wanted the shape and space to be the focus of attention so I left everything plain cardboard brown. The children were invited to set up the rooms as they liked. Representing three-dimensional objects and spaces is challenging even for adults. I was not sure how the children would respond to this. I limited the media to vine charcoal to simplify choices so they could focus on the model.

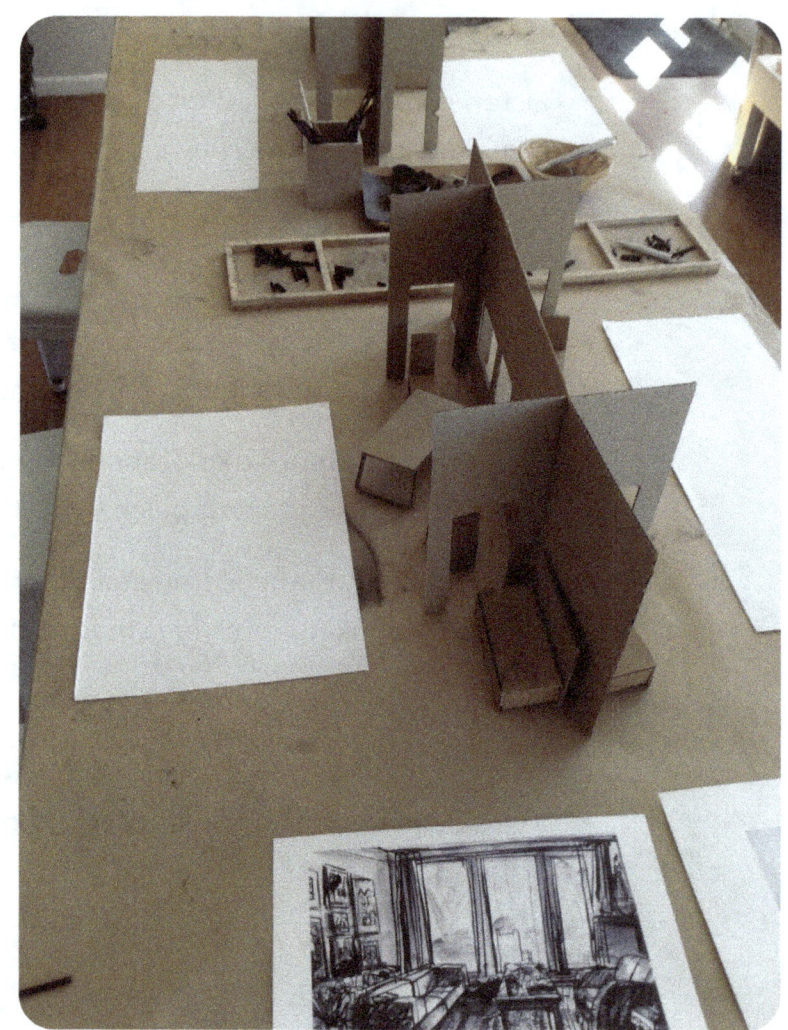

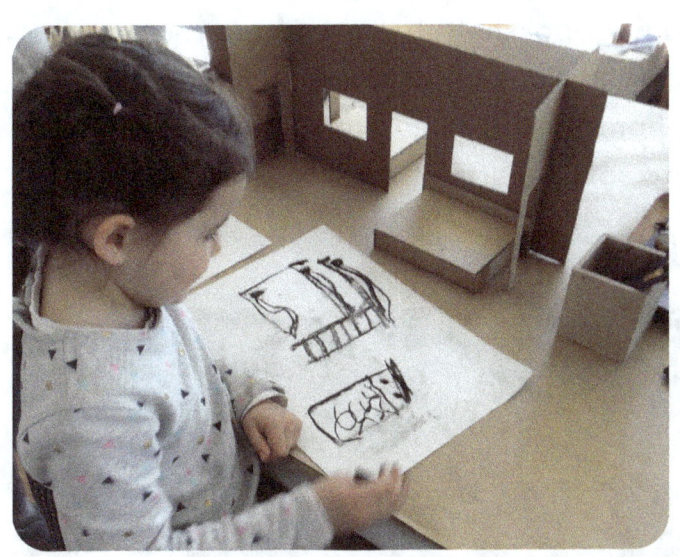 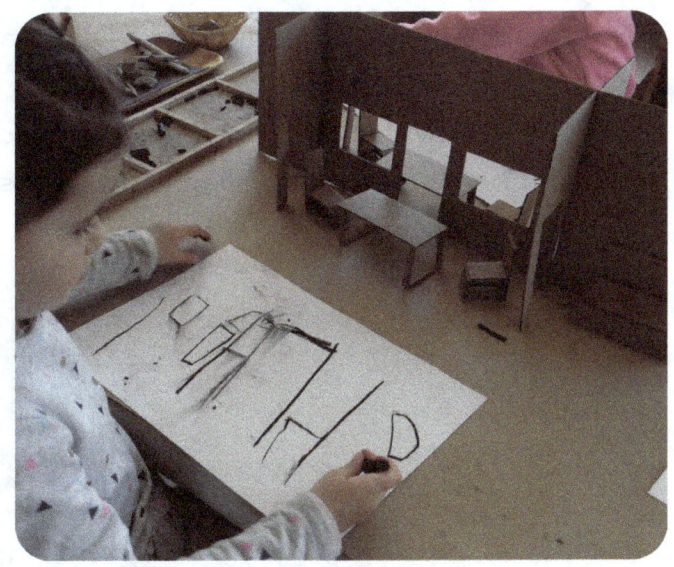

Eidie was keen to draw. Her first drawing took in the whole scene. But she said it was really difficult to draw everything. So she decided to focus on the furniture. She drew bunk beds with three children in them and a double bed with mum and dad in it. The double bed was drawn in "plan" perspective—that is, as if seen from above—while the bunk beds were drawn in regular view. Eidie said she needed to practice more but first she wanted to play in the house with the dolls. Playing gave the drawings a narrative, and the handling of the figures and furniture helped the children better understand how they might be drawn.

Ellen had been watching Eidie draw the beds and decided to do her own drawing. She carefully placed the cardboard bunk beds nearby so she could reference them. She also drew children in the beds, telling me that she had bunk beds at home and she too slept in the top one. She also added her toy box and her bookshelf that was in her room. Bringing elements from home into drawings is very gratifying for children, and for the educators it provides a window into the child's home life so that connections can be made between home and school. Ellen used a brush to soften parts of the drawing and move the charcoal to where she wanted it.

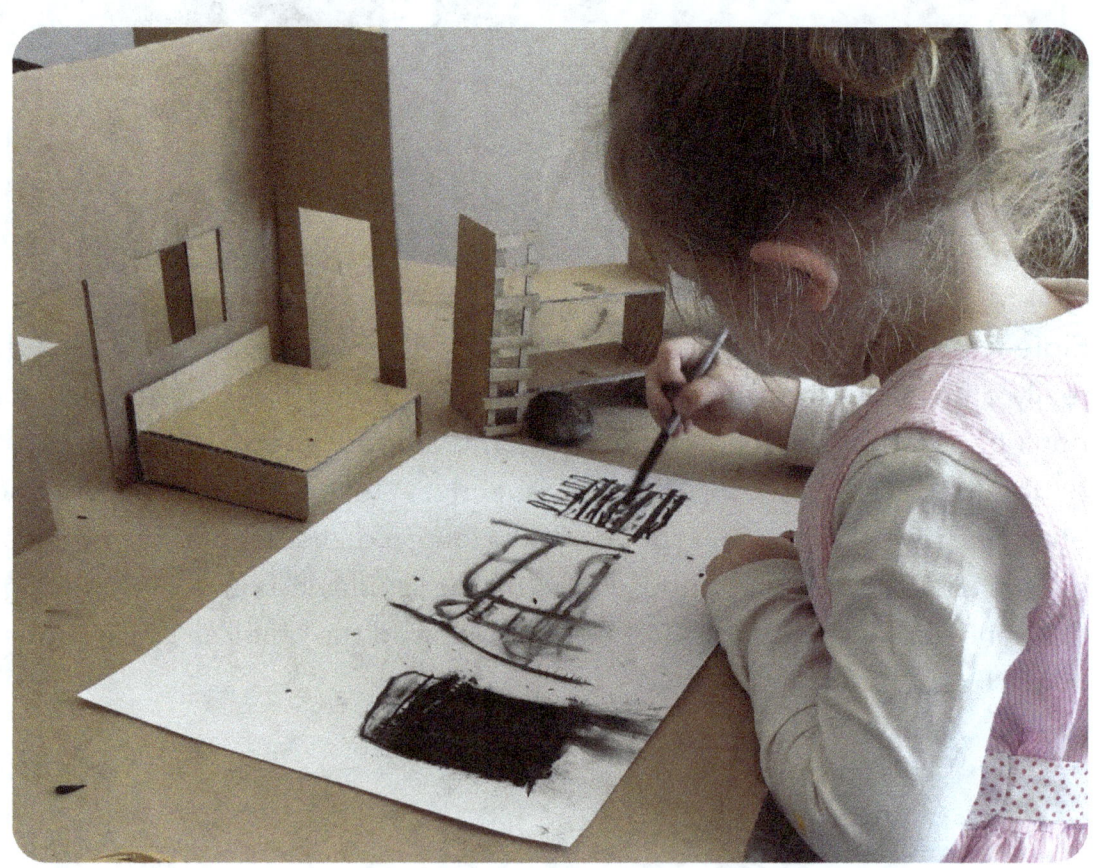

The children in this project continued to play and draw many different setups of the house and furniture. Some days they played and some days they made more furniture and paper people. Some days they just drew.

From the braiding that has been demonstrated in this section I have compiled the position statements and developed a manifesto that can stand on its own as a guide for practitioners.

My manifesto of pedagogical practices for the visual arts in early childhood education

This list is not in any order, so begin anywhere, hop around, and pick and choose

Be pedagogically active. There is an important role for the educator in children's art making. This involves more than just providing materials and space and stepping back. Engage with children's big ideas. Practice shared sustained thinking.

Notice and wonder. Educators can support experimentation and risk taking through artistic dialogues that honour the intent of the child.

Draw. Draw. Draw. Everyone draw, every day.

Provide opportunities to draw in all contexts of the program. When children draw they make connections between their experience, their memory, and their imagination, bringing together three important modes for learning, understanding, and remembering.

Encourage multiple drawings. Explore the different ideas and perspectives that re-presenting can illuminate. More drawings encourage more thinking.

Revisit drawings. Keep a selective portfolio and revisit it often. They can be full of wonderful surprises while also helping children build on ideas.

Provide authentic art media and tools. When children are given authentic arts media like clay, charcoal, and watercolors and quality tools they will better produce quality art.

Allow time to explore, repeat, and practice techniques. This builds fluency with media. Fluency with media is needed before it can be used expressively and with purpose.

Do it again.and again and again – be prolific and expansive.

Draw from observation. This focuses attention, aids concentration, and moves the child to operate at higher cognitive levels. Observational drawing requires organizing information on a page, planning ahead, and paying attention to proportion and positioning.

Look and look again. The intense looking required for observational drawing aids and gives access to a greater level of detail and later ease of recall.

Provide a safe context for sharing art making experiences. Give voice to the first tentative beginnings of an idea. Help children talk about their art.

Let art making be a social process. Make spaces and provisions for group work. Children and artists learn from each other. Share, share, share.

Share ideas and techniques. When children are encouraged to share ideas and techniques a supportive community of learners is built. A learning community is full of provocations and possibilities that help extend children's understanding and knowledge of the world.

Make the most of teachable moments. Help children acquire their own repertoire of skills and techniques as they are needed.

Encourage reflective practice. Careful observation of the marks made makes visible the results of certain actions. Take time to consider them.

Encourage meaning making and expression. Encourage children to move beyond the first encounter and experimentation with media and encourage them to use it to express themselves, explore concepts, and make meaning.

Performance comes before competence. Children understand by doing. Don't underestimate what children can do. Aim high and children will rise to the challenge.

Don't be afraid to help. What a child can do today with the help of a more experienced other she can do on her own tomorrow.

Don't be shy. Model techniques and use of materials and tools. Draw and paint with children. Model persistence, trial and error, resilience, and pleasure.

Listen. Listen carefully to children as they draw and you will gain insights to the big ideas behind the drawing.

Representation is an essential activity for young children. Representation requires skill, planning, and organizing information. When we represent something, we have to transform our current understanding into a form that not only carries the essence of this understanding but that also makes sense to others.

Go deeper. Representation is a way of getting to know more about something at a deeper level. When children are engaged in representing they are able to focus their attention and notice much more than by just looking.

Problem solve and problem find. Differentiate between a drawing problem and a cognitive or social problem. Use drawing to solve problems. Encourage many solutions.

Art is generative. Utilize peer interactions. Go with the flow. Toss ideas around. Make lists.

Provide studio spaces full of inspiration and ease of access. Teach the children how to use the space and materials.

Make collections. Collections of all sorts help children see order and patterns in the environment.

Display and discuss. Children need to hear the many interpretations an audience brings to their work. Children need to see the many different styles and ways of representing the same thing.

Practice. Like many other things practice makes perfect. Use it or lose it.

[Inspired by Bruce Mau (http://www. manifestoproject.it/bruce-mau/) I created a manifesto that aims to transform our pedagogy and visual arts practices with young children.]

Conclusion

I have unpacked, discussed some of Vygotsky's theories, provided examples of contemporary uses and systematically applied his theories to the visual arts for young children. While the thinking required to understand his theories is challenging, I believe it is worth it. It elevates the visual arts to be more than a leisure activity or a decoration or something you do on a Friday afternoon to pass the time. It puts the arts at the center of the curriculum.

The examples of work done by children and their teachers clearly demonstrate how the visual arts can support children's thinking and meaning making. It is through the arts that children make sense of the world in which they live. In this art making process there is a vital role for teachers. This role should not be unfamiliar because the theoretical framework it comes from now matches that of the rest of the curriculum in the early years.

Vygotsky's theories acknowledge that the visual arts are a young child's primary means of communication. Before children can read and write, drawing and the arts are a natural, and often the main means of communication. Understanding the ways in which the arts can support in-depth investigations, thinking, and learning, predisposes and encourages us to provide for and support art across the curriculum and into primary.

If you have enjoyed this book you might be interested in the companion book *Drawing to Learn*

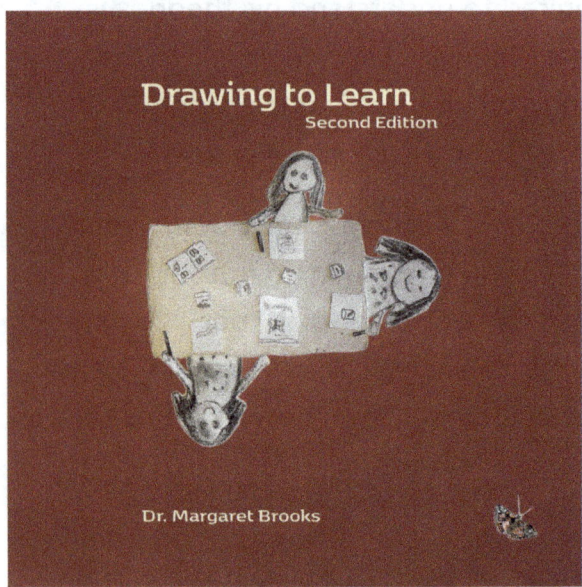

To receive a poster go to
artinearlychildhood.org

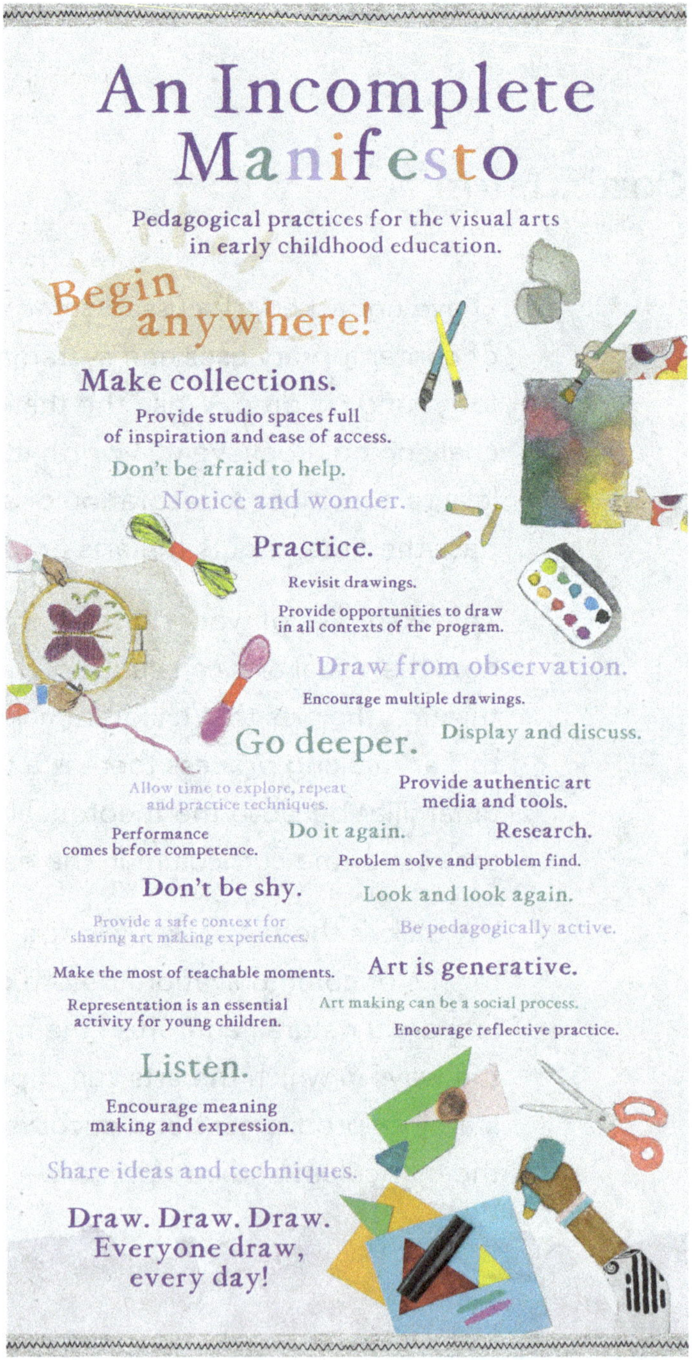

An Incomplete Manifesto

Pedagogical practices for the visual arts
in early childhood education.

Begin anywhere!

Make collections.

Provide studio spaces full
of inspiration and ease of access.

Don't be afraid to help.

Notice and wonder.

Practice.

Revisit drawings.

Provide opportunities to draw
in all contexts of the program.

Draw from observation.

Encourage multiple drawings.

Go deeper.

Display and discuss.

Allow time to explore, repeat
and practice techniques.

Provide authentic art
media and tools.

Performance
comes before competence.

Do it again.

Research.

Problem solve and problem find.

Don't be shy.

Look and look again.

Provide a safe context for
sharing art making experiences.

Be pedagogically active.

Make the most of teachable moments.

Art is generative.

Representation is an essential
activity for young children.

Art making can be a social process.

Encourage reflective practice.

Listen.

Encourage meaning
making and expression.

Share ideas and techniques.

Draw. Draw. Draw.
Everyone draw,
every day!

www.ingramcontent.com/pod-product-compliance
Lightning Source LLC
Chambersburg PA
CBHW080958170526
45158CB00010B/2835